AF361319

BECOMING GOD

BECOMING GOD

The Doctrine of Theosis in Nicholas of Cusa

Nancy J. Hudson

The Catholic University of America Press
Washington, D.C.

LIBRARY OF CONGRESS
CATALOGING-IN-PUBLICATION DATA
Hudson, Nancy J., 1966–
Becoming God : the doctrine of theosis in Nicholas of
Cusa / Nancy J. Hudson.
p. cm.
ISBN-13: 978-0-8132-1472-6 (cloth : alk. paper)
ISBN-10: 0-8132-1472-6 (cloth : alk. paper)
1. Nicholas, of Cusa, Cardinal, 1401–1464.   2. Deification
(Christianity)   I. Title.
BT767.8.H83 2007
234—dc22

2006009903

To Annelise

CONTENTS

In Europe and the United States, Nicholas of Cusa has been the focus of research for many years. Both his medieval mysticism and his foreshadowing of modern philosophical and cosmological notions have made him attractive to generations of scholars. Yet despite this intensive interest in his thought, insufficient attention has been paid to Cusanus's understanding of theosis, a doctrine that can be viewed as the crowning summation of his mysticism. It is my hope that this study will contribute to the broader field of Cusanus studies by examining his doctrine of deification in an organized and detailed manner.

This work would not have been possible without the wisdom and kindness of my mentors at Yale, especially Louis Dupré, Cyril O'Regan, and Rowan Greer. Above all, I would like to thank Louis Dupré, who directed my research for this book and also my education at Yale. My initial introduction to Nicholas of Cusa occurred in one of Professor Dupré's seminars, and his deep enthusiasm for Cusanus constantly fed my own.

I owe the original suggestion of the topic to Wilhelm Dupré of the University at Nijmegen in the Netherlands. Although most of my research was conducted at Yale University, I enjoyed the advice of scholars of many nationalities whom I met through the American Cusanus Society. For the help of Christopher Belitto, H. Lawrence Bond, Elizabeth Brient, Gerald Christiansen, William Collinge, Donald Duclow, Walter Andreas Euler, Lawrence Hundersmark, Thomas Izbicki, Il Kim, Thomas McTighe, Clyde Lee Miller, Thomas Morrisey, and Morimichi Watanabe I am sincerely grateful. I also owe a debt of gratitude to Peter Casarella, whose unflagging support guided me through many revisions. My heartfelt thanks also go to Donald Duclow and Klaus Reinhart for their detailed comments on the manuscript.

I also would like to thank my colleagues and students in the philosophy departments at the University of Toledo and California University of Pennsylvania. Their interest and encouragement in my work has been a great source of inspiration and pleasure. The Center for the Study of Religion at Princeton University provided a delightful year for me in 2003–2004 as a visiting fellow. An article, revisions of this book, and plans for future work were possible thanks to that fellowship. Encouragement from other scholars at Princeton, including Sarah Coakley and Stephen Teiser, was of inestimable value.

My editor at the Catholic University of America Press, Gregory LaNave, has been both patient and encouraging. I am grateful for the initial interest in the manuscript expressed by his colleague David J. McGonagle. Finally, I would like to thank my parents, Craig and Barbara Walker, and my sister, Faith Walker.

ABBREVIATIONS

DC	*De coniecturis*
DDA	*De Deo abscondito*
DDI	*De docta ignorantia*
DFD	*De filiatione Dei*
DG	*De genesi*
DPF	*De pace fidei*
DNA	*Directio speculantis seu de Non Aliud*
DP	*Trialogus de possest*
DPL	*De dato Patris luminum*
DQD	*De quaerendo Deum*
IDM	*Idiota de mente*
IDS	*Idiota de sapientia*
DVD	*De visione Dei*
LM	*The Life of Moses*
MM	*On the Making of Man*

BECOMING GOD

INTRODUCTION

Although it is an integral part of his theology, Nicholas of Cusa's doctrine of salvation has received little scrutiny. The absence of a thorough understanding of theosis has contributed to frequent misunderstandings of his work. He has been interpreted as both a Scholastic and a fideist, a medieval and an early modern, a monist and a pantheist. He has also been suspected of Platonizing the Christian faith and hailed as one of the first theologians who stressed God's immanence in creation. An examination of theosis, or becoming God, will help in the effort to correctly place Nicholas of Cusa and his understanding of the creation-creature relationship.

The variety of opinions about his thought echo Cusanus's (his Latinized name) multifaceted career. Conciliarist, canon lawyer, bishop, cardinal, and scholar, this perplexing figure was born in 1401 in Kues, a small town on the Mosel River near Trier. Though early chronicles of his life allege that he studied with the Brothers of the Common Life in Deventer, uncertainty remains about the truth of these claims. It is known, however, that he attended the University of Heidelberg before entering the University of Padua a year later. There he obtained a doctorate in canon law in 1423 and was a fellow student of mathematics and science with Paolo Toscanelli. At the University of Cologne, where he studied philosophy and theology, he was introduced to the works of

Pseudo-Dionysius and Raymond Lull, who were to have such a great effect on his own thought.[1]

In the 1430s he was ordained to the priesthood and participated in the Council of Basel. His work *De concordantia catholica* reflects his advocacy of conciliarism, the movement that argued for the authority of a general council over the papacy. Later his loyalties shifted toward the papacy and he became a papal delegate. His duties included accompanying a group of Orthodox patriarchs from Constantinople to Italy for the projected Council of Florence. It was on this mission, returning from Greece by ship, that Nicholas received "what I believe was a supreme gift of the Father of Lights from Whom is every perfect gift,"[2] the gift of learned ignorance. His treatise *De docta ignorantia (On Learned Ignorance)* is a development of this, his unique version of negative theology.

This early work (1440) was followed by a significant number of later texts, ranging from epistemological treatises (*De coniecturis,* for example) to mystical works *(De visione Dei).*[3] The final collection of his work also included philosophical dialogues *(De Deo abscondito* and *Idiota),* a defense against misinterpretation *(Apologia docta ignorantiae),* and one of the earliest Renaissance texts about universal religion *(De pace fidei).*[4] One of his treatises from 1445, *De filiatione Dei,* explores *theosis,* or deification,

1. For a more detailed biography see Donald Duclow, "Nicholas of Cusa," in *Dictionary of Literary Biography,* vol. 115: *Medieval Philosophers,* ed. Jeremiah Hackett (Detroit: Bruccoli Clark Layman, 1992), 289–305.

2. From the dedicatory page of *De docta ignorantia,* addressed to Cardinal Julian Cesarini. The reference is to James 1:17. This is also the first line of Pseudo-Dionysius's *The Celestial Hierarchy,* a work with which Cusanus was familiar.

3. *De coniecturis, On Surmises,* 1443, hereafter abbreviated as *DC; De visione Dei, The Vision of God,* 1453, hereafter abbreviated as *DVD.*

4. *De Deo abscondito, The Hidden God,* 1444, hereafter abbreviated as *DDA; Idiota, The Layman,* 1450, hereafter abbreviated as either *IDM (Idiota de mente)* or *IDS (Idiote de sapientia); De pace fidei, On The Peace of Faith,* 1453, hereafter abbreviated as *DPF,* trans. H. Lawrence Bond, *Nicholas of Cusa on Interreligious Harmony: Text, Concordance, and Translation* of De Pace Fidei, Texts and Studies in Religion (Lewiston, N.Y.: Edwin Mellen Press, 2000). An earlier translation was done by Jasper Hopkins, *"Nicholas of Cusa's De Pace Fidei*

a concept that figures prominently in Cusanus's philosophy and theology.[5]

The origins of theosis, variously defined as becoming divine, identity with God, and similitude or being closely united with the divine, can be traced to Neoplatonic philosophy. By the time of Nicholas of Cusa, however, it was not unprecedented in the Christian tradition. The Greek fathers had employed the concept, and it has enjoyed a long history in the Eastern Church ever since. From whom Cusanus himself acquired the notion is unknown.

Controversy envelops the direct influence of the Greek fathers on Cusanus. At one time it was thought that he studied their works on his trip to Constantinople and conversed at length with the Greek patriarchs during the voyage from Greece by ship. Yet it has become clear that the duration of his stay in Constantinople was far too short (two months) for extensive study and that he most likely adhered to tradition and traveled on a different ship from the patriarchs.[6] Even his command of the Greek language has been called into question by scholars,[7] who cite the paucity of marginal notations in the Greek manuscripts of his collection.

During Nicholas's studies in Cologne, however, he almost certainly read Berthold of Moosburg's *Commentary on Proclus' Elements of Theology,* a text that was widely available at that time. From this treatise and

---

and *Cribratio Alkorani: Translation and Analysis,* 2nd ed., in *Complete Philosophical and Theological Treatises of Nicholas of Cusa,* vol. 1 (Minneapolis: Arthur J. Banning Press, 2001).

5. *De filiatione Dei, On Being a Son of God,* trans. H. Lawrence Bond, "On Divine Filiation" (2000) online; available from http://www.appstate.edu/~bondhl/defil.htm [accessed 12 December 2005]; hereafter abbreviated as *DFD.*

An earlier translation by Jasper Hopkins, *"On Being a Son of God,"* in *A Miscellany on Nicholas of Cusa* (Minneapolis: Arthur J. Banning Press, 1994), is available.

6. Nicholas of Cusa was in Constantinople from September 24 to November 27, 1437.

7. Notably Peter Casarella. For more on the debate concerning the significance of Cusanus's trip to Constantinople and his return voyage, see Marjorie O'Rourke Boyle, "Cusanus at Sea: The Topicality of Illuminative Discourse," *Journal of Religion* 71 (April 1991).

other secondary sources, including the works of Meister Eckhart and John Scotus Eriugena, Cusanus may well have become acquainted with the thought of Gregory Nazianzus, Gregory of Nyssa, Maximus the Confessor, and Origen.

In the treatise *De filiatione Dei (On Being a Son of God),* Cusanus frequently employs the term "theosis." Here he declares, "Moreover, in summary, I consider filiation of God to be reckoned as nothing else than deification, which, in Greek, is also called *theosis.*"[8] Cusanus uses the metaphor of a mirror to demonstrate that theosis or sonship is fundamentally Christological and intellectual in nature. He writes:

> However, I would like to provide a likeness to guide you. I know that you are not in the least unaware that forms of equal size in straight mirrors appear less equal in curved mirrors. Therefore, imagine that there were a highest reflection of our Beginning, of glorious God, in which God were to appear, that the reflection were a mirror of truth, without blemish, absolutely straight, boundless, and most perfect, that all creatures were mirrors that were more or less contracted and differently curved, and that among them the intellectual natures were mirrors that were living and clearer, and straighter. Since such mirrors were living, intellectual, and free, conceive them to be able to curve, to straighten, and to cleanse themselves.[9]

8. *DFD* I h 52, Bond; "h" refers to the number of the paragraph in the critical edition, the Heidelberg Academy of Letters edition. *Nicolai de Cusa opera omnia iussu et auctoritate Academiae litteratum heidelbergensis ad codicum fiden edita* (Leipzig/Hamburg: F. Meiner, 1932–present).

Ego autem, ut in summa dicam, non aliud filiationem dei quam deificationem, quae et theosis graece dicitur, aestimandum iudico.

9. Ibid., III h 65, 67.

Sit igitur altissima resplendentia principii nostri dei gloriosi, in qua appareat deus ipse, quae sit veritatis speculum sine macula rectissimum atque interminum perfectissimumque, sintque omnes creaturae specula contractiora et differenter curva, intra quae intellectuals naturae sint viva, clariora atque rectiora specula, ac talia, cum sint viva et intellectualia atque libera, concipito, quod possint se ipsa incurvare, rectificare et mundare . . . In speculo igitur illo primo veritatis, quod et verbum, logos seu filius dei dici potest, adipiscitur intellectuale speculum filiationem, ut sit omnia in omnibus et omnia in ipso, et regnum eius sit possessio dei et omnium in vita gloriosa.

The Logos, in which God appears, is the medium for sonship. Divine sonship means that the intellectual nature is united to and possesses not only God, but all things. Nicholas argues that sonship is unity with Infinite Reason[10] and that theosis includes the realization that there is no *otherness,* or difference, between God and the intellectual spirit. Insofar as the created order traces its origins to the unfolding of the divine Being itself, it can be asserted that deification is an *original* condition for all things.

Furthermore, to the extent that even in creation God is present, theosis can be viewed as an *already realized* destiny. The latter thesis is supported by passages such as the following:

> Therefore, this is the pathway of pursuit of those who strive toward
> *theosis:* to perceive the one in the diversity of any modes whatsoever.
> For when any pursuer, by a subtle consideration, observes how the one,
> which is the cause of all things, is unable not to be expressed in every
> expression, just as a word is unable not to be spoken with everyone who
> is speaking, whether he says that he is speaking or whether he says that
> he is not, then it is manifest to the pursuer that the power of the ineffa-
> ble embraces every sayable thing and that nothing can be said in which
> in its mode the cause of every saying and of everything said does not
> shine forth.[11]

Here Nicholas of Cusa does not appear to be urging us toward deification, but laying out an already existing condition. Theosis is the intellectual process of perceiving that the One, or God, is the *immanent* Cause of all things in the same way that a person who speaks shines forth in his own words.

---

10. Infinite Reason or Wisdom is another word for God the Son. See *Idiota de sapientia,* as well as chapter 4 of this book.

11. *DFD* VI h 84, Bond.

Haec est igitur via studii eorum, qui ad theosim tendunt, in modorum quorumcumque diversitate ad unum ipsum advertere. Quando enim quicumque stuiosus subtiliter considerando attendit quomodo ipsum unum omnium causa non potest non exprimi in omni loquente, sive se dicat loqui sive se dicat non loqui, tunc sibi manifestum est virtutem ineffabilis omne dicibile ambire et nihil dici posse, in quo modo suo causa omnis dicentis et dicti non replendeat.

This does not mean, however, that theosis is identical with theophany, or divine self-manifestation. Cusanus makes it clear, especially in the third book of *De docta ignorantia,* that Christ is the goal and fulfillment of all creation. Theosis is in no way a monist or static condition; it comprises both the autonomous existence of the created order and its return movement toward God. Christ is the Exemplar of all things, drawing them into union with himself and, through himself, into union with God the Father.

Cusanus's notion of deification includes themes of ontology, epistemology, revelation, and soteriology. The question then arises whether theosis is a philosophical or a theological concept. Insofar as the term involves human intellectual ascent to God, it has definite philosophical elements. Its incarnational aspect, however, is undeniably theological. This leads to the broader question of whether Nicholas of Cusa is a philosopher or a theologian. The relationship between his largely Neoplatonic philosophy and his Christian theology is instructive in uncovering his orthodoxy. Perhaps it is not quite fair for the modern world, where the split between philosophy and theology is a historical fact, to ask this of a thinker from an age when the two disciplines were not adversaries. Nevertheless, recognizing that he has both philosophical and theological concerns is useful in uncovering his own presuppositions as well as his relationship to other thinkers.

As on other issues, Cusanus has been accused of opposite and mutually exclusive tendencies. His doctrine of theophany, or divine self-manifestation, might be seen as a justification for a philosophical approach to God, while his development of negative theology would argue for a theological approach dependent on revelation. On the one hand, his penchant for mathematical metaphors and his focus on divine immanence have led to assertions that he is primarily a natural theologian. On the other hand, his negative theology, including his denial of traditional analogical relations between God and creation, has led scholars to take one of two approaches. One alternative is that of

Klaus Jakobi, who argues that Cusanus has embarked on an epochally new theological project that blends theology and the approach of natural reason.[12] An opposing view is held by Rudolf Haubst, who sees this interpretation of radical innovation as the equivalent of fideism.[13] In defense of his own position, Haubst interprets Cusanus more as a medieval thinker, in line with the Scholastic tradition of the *analogia entis,* than as a modern one.

But this itself is the subject of controversy. In many ways Nicholas of Cusa stands at the dawn of Renaissance humanism. He speculates, for instance, on what has been called "intensive and extensive infinity." That is, the soul is viewed as having infinite value and the universe as being unbounded in space.[14] Both positions are, of course, thoroughly modern. In addition, Nicholas's epistemological orientation, with its suspicion of human powers of reasoning, can be viewed as a break with the traditional medieval confidence in the mind's ability to speculate about God and the universe. Others, such as Rudolf Haubst and Jasper Hopkins, point out that he is firmly rooted in the Middle Ages. Whatever one concludes, Nicholas is clearly a key figure, anticipating modernity but still standing in the shadow of medieval theology.

The importance of resolving the various debates escalates with the realization that it is through the mind that theosis occurs. The pairing of intellect and mysticism is unusual only to those familiar only with the ecstatic, emotional love mysticism of thinkers such as Bernard of Clairvaux or Teresa of Avila. But, as Donald Duclow notes in his essay on mystical theology and the intellect in Nicholas of Cusa, Cusanus "places intellect at the center of his mystical theology, as he

12. Klaus Jakobi, *Die Methode der Cusanischen Philosophie:* Symposion 31 (Freiburg-Muenchen: Alber, 1969).

13. Rudolf Haubst, "Theologie in der Philosophie—Philosophie in der Theologie des Nikolaus von Kues," in *Streifzuege in die Cusanische Theologie* (Muenster: Aschendorff, 1991).

14. For more on this see Karsten Harries, "The Infinite Sphere: Comments on the History of a Metaphor," *Journal of the History of Philosophy* 13 (Jan. 1975): 5–15.

links learned ignorance with mystical vision and *filiatio* or sonship."[15] Furthermore, ascertaining whether deification is reached by the natural powers of the intellect or through divine revelation touches the question of Nicholas's orthodoxy. That is, these controversies reflect the definitive Christian issue of nature and grace. The influence of Neoplatonism on Cusanus's thought and the resulting sapiential salvation, including the notion of the *mens* (mind) as the locus of the *imago Dei,* raises the issue of the Platonization of Nicholas's Christianity. If unity with the divine is accomplished by philosophical reflection, Cusanus has lost the essential Christian notion of grace and abandoned the theology of the cross. If, however, there is a transformation of the human person that is traced to the agency of the divine and communicated via revelation, a transformation that has repercussions for the human sinful condition, Nicholas has not strayed from the tradition, though he may have a unique emphasis.

Is Cusanus a modern philosopher who has adopted the Neoplatonic natural theology? Or is he a fideist who has jettisoned the approach of reason altogether, including both the Neoplatonic and the Scholastic traditions? Or can he be brought back into the fold by interpreting him as accepting the medieval confidence in analogy between God and humanity? Perhaps he is a Neoplatonist mystic who merely employs the cloak of Christian terminology. How can the monism implied by his strong view of divine immanence and the return of all things to God in theosis be resolved with the dualism implied by his understanding of transcendence?

Clearly, a host of issues emerge upon even a brief overview of Nicholas of Cusa's concept of theosis. Only an organized excursus into his thought can untangle these and other questions raised by the ideas of this enigmatic figure. Therefore, this book will begin with a historical introduction of the term "theosis" as it was developed in the thought

15. Donald F. Duclow, "Mystical Theology and Intellect in Nicholas of Cusa," *American Catholic Philosophical Quarterly* 44 (1990): 111–29.

of Gregory of Nyssa, Maximus the Confessor, and Pseudo-Dionysius. Only after this background will it move on to Cusanus's own doctrine.

Just as theosis is a transformative movement returning the created order to God, it is matched by an outward movement of divine self-manifestation. This movement, known as theophany, is foundational to theosis because of the original unitive relationship between the two orders that it establishes. Nicholas's understanding of the divine immanence in creation, directly attributable to theophany, can itself be understood as an already realized deification. Thus, a look at the theme of theophany is a prerequisite for understanding theosis and is the subject of chapter 2.

Balancing God's immanence is, however, divine transcendence and the consequent prominence of negative theology in Cusanus's thought. An examination of the distance between God and the world and the human attempt to bridge that distance will follow in chapter 3. Only after these issues of theophany and Nicholas's epistemology have been explored will the topic of theosis itself be broached in the fourth chapter. Because of its significance for the location of Nicholas of Cusa in the history of Christian thought, chapter 5 will be devoted to the question of intellectual salvation and the influence of Neoplatonism on his soteriology.

It is necessary to note that, although the focus of this project is deification, the coherence of Nicholas's theology impels the scholar to consider many disparate aspects of his rich corpus. This essay is not, therefore, an exhaustive account of the architecture of Cusanus's thought. Rather, it is an attempt to follow a single theme through the structure of his theology and philosophy, taking into account the major debates and Cusan scholars, but forced by constraints of space to ignore or only briefly acknowledge others.

This treatise will conclude that Cusanus is unparalleled in his ability to hold together a variety of tensions, including those between immanence and transcendence, monism and dualism, anticipation of modernity and medieval tradition, and Eastern and Western Christianity. His theology stresses immanence enough to provide a foundation for theosis, but not enough to make him a metaphysical monist. He neither capitulates to Greek philosophy, nor becomes an early nominalist, nor loses his medievalism. His doctrine of the relationship between the divine and human orders, a relationship centering in the human intellect and culminating in theosis, is unique, but not unprecedented in the Christian tradition. In sum, Nicholas's doctrine of theosis can be used as a lens through which many of his other positions, philosophical and theological, can be brought into focus. An analysis of the role of theosis in his thought will demonstrate that it is paradigmatic for the relationship between the divine and created orders. It is, indeed, the origin, goal, and realized destiny of creation.

I

THEOSIS IN THE GREEK FATHERS AND PSEUDO-DIONYSIUS

The notion of theosis refers to an original and essential relationship between the divine and created orders: the finite returns to the Infinite from which it is derived. It describes a soteriology in which the individual not only is saved from death and eternal punishment, but is deified. Instead of merely living in eternal relationship with God, the individual reclaims the union with God that was lost or weakened by his earthly, finite, and sinful life. Some theologians conceive theosis as the destiny not just of the human being, but of the entire created order. God, who poured himself out into his creation, returns it to himself, where it exists in eternal union with him.

Nicholas of Cusa's own understanding of deification is multifaceted. When expounding on the term "theosis" itself, he argues for its Christological character and links it to divine filiation (being a son of God).[1] Divine sonship means that human intellectual nature is united

1. *DFD* I h 52, Bond.

with Infinite Reason and through Infinite Reason with all things.[2] The larger picture of his thought reveals that he saw theophany and divine immanence as aspects of theosis as well. For Cusanus, theosis pervades the entirety of the dynamic relationship between Creator and creation. It infuses at once creation's origin, its existence as itself, and its ultimate return to God.

When discussing theosis, Nicholas himself remarks that it is a Greek term.[3] Moreover, his doctrine of theosis seems to bear great similarity to the tradition developed in the Greek Christian church. Although the extent of this tradition's direct influence on Cusanus has yet to be determined, a look at the doctrine of theosis that had developed by the time of his writing is relevant as background for his own thought.

Due to Nicholas of Cusa's incontrovertible familiarity with the Dionysian corpus, much of modern scholarship restricts itself to the influence of Pseudo-Dionysius's Neoplatonism on Nicholas's thought. Although it is customary to refer to the "Neoplatonic elements" of his mystical metaphysics and to see a Dionysian influence in his doctrine of theosis, a study that neglected the Patristic tradition of theosis would be incomplete. Likewise, an inquiry that returned to the Greek fathers only *after* examining the Neoplatonism of Nicholas of Cusa would render the former merely an interesting postscript. It is essential to review the Patristic tradition of theosis because it contributed to the theological background against which Nicholas of Cusa worked.

This is not to say with certainty, however, that Cusanus read the important treatises of Eastern Christianity. Nicholas's direct exposure to Byzantine theology has been a matter of historical contention. Though his library contains Byzantine manuscripts, both his knowledge of Greek and his opportunity for extended contact with Eastern patriarchs have been called into question. At a minimum, evidence for Cusanus's fa-

---

2. Infinite Reason or Wisdom is another word for God the Son. See *Idiota de sapientia,* as well as chapter 4 of this book.

3. *DFD* I h 52, Bond.

miliarity with Maximus the Confessor is found in *Apologia doctae ignorantiae* where he mentions "Maximus the Monk" in company with Hugh of St. Victor, Robert of Lincoln, John the Scot, and the Abbot of Vercelli.[4] Moreover, Peter Casarella in his article "Wer Schrieb Die Ex Greco-Notizen im Codex Cusanus 44?" finds marginal notations in a Dionysian manuscript that are quotes from Maximus the Confessor to be indicative of Nicholas of Cusa's familiarity with Greek Christian thought.[5] However, a complete study needs to be done in this area. It must be noted, however, that the importance of critical editions to modern philosophical analysis was unknown to medieval thinkers. Because it was the idea and not the footnote that mattered, unreferenced sources may have influenced Cusanus. And even if the primary Patristic texts eluded him, he did have secondary sources available. Berthold of Moosburg's *Commentary on Proclus' Elements of Theology* and the works of Meister Eckhart and John Scotus Eriugena were repositories of the thought of Gregory Nazianzus, Gregory of Nyssa, Maximus the Confessor, and Origen, among others.

Although Pseudo-Dionysius is himself sometimes characterized as Byzantine and some Greek fathers can hardly be separated from him, in this study he will be considered apart from two representative Greek fathers. Nicholas of Cusa's acknowledged dependence on his theology and the clear references to his treatises warrant a discrete treatment of Pseudo-Dionysius.

Leaving aside for the moment the explicit Dionysian influence, it is equally instructive to consider Patristic sources of theosis. Such an approach will give a background for the foregoing interpretation of Cusanus by sketching the then contemporary notion of theosis—the ideas, if not the texts, with which he must have been familiar. It will

---

4. *Apologia doctae ignorantiae discipuli ad discipulum*, h 21. Trans. Jasper Hopkins, *Nicholas of Cusa's Debate with John Wenck* (Minneapolis: Arthur J. Banning Press, 1988), 56.

5. Peter Casarella, "Wer Schrieb Die Ex Greco-Notizen im Codex Cusanus 44?" *Mitteilungen und Forschungsbeitraege der Cusanus Gesellschaft* 22 (1995): 123–32.

also help resolve the issue of Nicholas of Cusa's modernity versus his medievalism by aligning him with the Eastern Church in which such a rupture never occurred. Additionally, it will avoid fracturing the Cusan corpus into Neoplatonic/Dionysian and Patristic components by treating the Dionysian influence as a specific instance of an already established tradition. Above all, it will counter the tendency to treat Neoplatonism as an importation into an otherwise Christian system, as though it were something hostile if not diametrically opposed to Christianity, and the consequent view of Christian Neoplatonists as somewhat less than orthodox.

The case for the Cusan corpus's location in a solid but not fully recognized Neoplatonic Christian tradition is buttressed by a recent monograph by Elizabeth Brient. In *The Immanence of the Infinite: Hans Blumenberg and the Threshold to Modernity* she considers both Meister Eckhart and Nicholas of Cusa in arguing for a more mainstream presence of Neoplatonism in the late Middle Ages than had previously been acknowledged.[6] Since the specifics and significance of this comparison are well documented in the above-mentioned work, I focus here on the precise differences between the two thinkers in an effort to uncover the uniqueness of Nicholas of Cusa's doctrine of theosis.

Insofar as he sees humanity, and ultimately the universe as a whole, as possessing an ontology that is dynamically oriented to God and "open," rather than static and closed, Cusanus is indebted to several early Greek Christian thinkers. An examination of two representative church fathers will show that their genuine Christian synthesis of Neoplatonism and Christianity provides the anchor for the later doctrine of Nicholas of Cusa.[7] The following chapter is an attempt to explore

6. Elizabeth Brient, *The Immanence of the Infinite: Hans Blumenberg and the Threshold to Modernity* (Washington D.C.: Catholic University of America Press, 2002).

7. For an examination of Neoplatonic themes in other church fathers, including Philo, Clement of Alexandria, Origen, Eunomius, and Evagrius of Pontus, see Alexander Golitzin, *Et Introibo ad Altare Dei: The Mystagogy of Dionysius Areopagita, with Special Reference to its Predecessors in the Eastern Christian Tradition* (Thessaloniki: George Dedousis, 1994).

the philosophical theology of Gregory of Nyssa, Maximus the Confessor, and Pseudo-Dionysius as a background for the thought of Nicholas of Cusa.

While Gregory of Nyssa will help put Cusanus's thought in context along the creation axis, Maximus will do the same along the redemptive and Christological axis. Pseudo-Dionysius, the theologian so frequently cited by Cusanus himself, is important because of his overt use of Neoplatonist philosophy and his direct influence on Cusanus. Whether it is an issue of divine theophany in creation or a question of Christological redemption, the notion of theosis is deeply embedded within these topics and is also the crowning summation of them.

THEOSIS IN GREGORY OF NYSSA

One of Gregory of Nyssa's contributions to the developing doctrine of theosis is his positive understanding of the created, material world. A similar notion would later appear in the Cusan corpus. The ultimate destiny of humanity is *theosis,* rather than merely *redemption,* because it is directed by an original divine intentionality instead of the retrieval of a fallen spiritual universe. Humankind is not just restored to an original condition but is exalted to the point of deification. Because the material world in its present state is a good thing, indeed a place where the divine makes itself present, both Gregory of Nyssa and Nicholas of Cusa are able to interpret salvation as theosis. Moreover, it is precisely this opposition between Creator and creation, and not between God and nothingness, that distinguishes their thought as Neoplatonic Christianity rather than as Christian Platonism.

After expounding on the creation of the world, Gregory begins *On the Making of Man* by describing the "royalty" of humanity.[8] Man is "great and precious," a "king" who was created last only because his

8. *The Nicene and Post-Nicene Fathers of the Christian Church: Second Series,* ed. Philip Schaff and Henry Wace, vol. 5: *Gregory of Nyssa: Dogmatic Treatises, Select Writings, and*

dominion had to be prepared for him.[9] Man's royalty and the wonder of his making is rooted in the fact that he is made in God's image:

> For as, in men's ordinary use, those who make images of princes both mould the figure of their form, and represent along with this the royal rank by the vesture of purple, and even the likeness is commonly spoken of as "a king," so the human nature also, as it was made to rule the rest, was, by its likeness to the King of all, made as it were a living image.[10]

Gregory does not focus on a purely spiritual or intellectual definition of humanity, but formulates a sort of theological physiology of man. The physical details of man's daily existence have theological significance for Gregory, and only after discussing them does he move on to questions of the soul and its resurrection. For instance, "man is destitute of natural weapons and covering," without "prominent horns or sharp claws, nor with hoofs nor with teeth, nor possessing by nature any deadly venom in a sting,"[11] in order to encourage his dominion over other species. The royal nature of mankind, bestowed by the *imago Dei,* is fostered by the physical vulnerability that forces man to use the labor of the ox to plow and the skin of the animal for covering. Moreover, man's form is upright as a mark of his sovereignty, and his hands are dexterous in order that they might record the products of his rational nature.

Though he does distinguish between mind and body, spiritual and material, Gregory of Nyssa consciously anchors mankind to the material. Even his analysis of sleep, yawning, and dreams illustrates his aver-

---

Letters (Grand Rapids, Mich.: W. B. Eerdmans, 1994). *On the Making of Man* I–XXX, at pp. 386–427, hereafter abbreviated as *MM.*

9. *MM* II, 390.

10. The passage continues, ". . . partaking with the archetype both in rank and in name . . . but instead of the purple robe, clothed in virtue . . . and in place of the scepter, leaning on the bliss of immortality, and instead of the royal diadem, decked with the crown of righteousness." *MM* IV, 1, 391.

11. *MM* VII, 1, 392.

sion to making the incorporeal aspect of the human being something detachable from physical existence and the sole locus of human identity.[12]

The dreamer finds himself "in absurd and impossible situations" because though the more excellent faculties of the soul are at rest, they are "accidentally moulded in the less rational part of the soul."[13] Just as various parts of a limb act in concert with one another, "similarly in the case of the soul, even if one part is at rest and another in motion, the whole is affected in sympathy with the part; for it is not possible that the natural unity should be in any way severed, though one of the faculties included in it is in turn supreme in virtue of its active operation."[14]

Gregory's view of the body is relevant to theosis because it distinguishes him from the more Platonic thought of Origen and because it is one of his similarities with Nicholas of Cusa. Body and soul are inseparable because the creation of the material world is a result of divine purpose. In *Idiota de mente,* Nicholas speaks of body and mind as "concreated" and made for one another.[15]

12. "Hence the mind of man clearly proves its claim to connection with his nature, itself also cooperating and moving with the nature in its sound and waking state, but remaining unmoved when it is abandoned to sleep." *MM* XIII, 5, 400.

13. Ibid., 400–401.

14. *MM* XIII, 7, 401.

15. *Idiote de mente* 4 h 77. Translated by Jasper Hopkins as "The Layman on Mind" in *Nicholas of Cusa on Wisdom and Knowledge* (Minneapolis: Arthur J. Banning Press, 1996), 197, 199. Hereafter abbreviated as *IDM.*

Idiota: Indubie mens nostra in hoc corpus a deo posita est ad sui profectum. Oportet igitur ipsam a deo habere omne id sine quo profectum acquirere nequitg. Non est igitur credendum animae fuisse notions concreatas quas in corpore perdidit, sed quia opus habet corpore ut vis concreata ad actum pergat. Sicuti vis visiva animae non potest in operationem suam, ut actu videat, nisi excitetur ab obiecto; et non potest excitari nisi per obstaculum specierummultiplicatarum per medium organi; et sic opus habet oculo; sic vis mentis, quae est vis comprehensiva rerum et notionalis, non potest in suas operations, nisi excitetur a sensibilibus; et non potest excitari nisi mediantibus phantasmatibus sensibilibus.

Also *IDM* 5 h 80–81, Hopkins, 201, 203.

Philosophus: Visne mentem, quam et animam fateris intellectivam, ante corpus fuisse, prout Pythagorus et Platonici, et postea incorporam?

The two thinkers also share a common view of the positive status of the physical world. Nowhere in Gregory's work is this clearer than in his meditation on the beauty of the earth. The genesis of the world was a joyful occasion that saw all things "adorned with their appropriate beauty."[16] The wonderful variety of plants, fish, birds, and animals were born of the earth by the power of Divine will. Indeed, the created order is so beautiful that humanity was made to witness it.[17]

The physical beauty of the world is tied to the purpose of man's life. He is to share it with God, to behold and enjoy it, and to know its Maker through it. Mankind was created to be ruler and beholder of the divine manifestation in the universe. There is something of God in creation so valuable that God created man to witness it. Mankind did not "fall" into the world, but he was created for it (indirectly) and it for him.

Certainly, Gregory does see some aspects of physical existence as results of the fall. Human sexuality is the most obvious example, having been instituted so that humanity would not disappear once it had fallen from "that mode by which the angels were increased and multiplied."[18] We now need marriage to multiply, whereas previously "whatever the mode of increase in the angelic nature is (unspeakable and inconceivable by human conjectures, except that it assuredly exists), it would have operated also in the case of men."[19] But this view is far from the

---

Idiota: Natura, non tempore. Nam, ut audisti, eam visui in tenebris comparavi. Visus autem nequaquam actu fuit ante oculum nisi natura tantum. Unde quia mens est quoddam divinum se- mesn sua vi complicans omnium rerum exemplaria notionaliter, tunc a deo, a quo hanc vim habet eo ipso quod esse recepit, est simul et in convenienti terra locatum, ubi fructum facere posit et ex se rerum universitatem notionaliter explicare. Alioquin naec vis seminalis frustra data sibi foret, si non fuisset sibi addita opportunitas in actum prorumpendi.

16. *MM* I, 5, 389.

17. Gregory writes, "and the gentle motion of the waves vied in beauty with the meadows, rippling delicately with light and harmless breezes that skimmed the surface; and all the wealth of creation by land and sea was ready and none was there to share it." *MM* I 5, 389–91.

18. *MM* XVII 4, 407.

19. *MM* XVII 2, 407.

idea that all of physical existence results from the fall and that only the mind is worthy of theosis.

Throughout his main anthropological treatise, Gregory is clearly arguing with an Origenistic idealism that would fragment the creative act into spiritual and material aspects and thus would split the redemptive act as well. He repeatedly insists not only on the goodness of the earth, but also on the unity and goodness of the body. The mind is not enclosed by the body as casks or other things are placed inside one another, "but the union of the mental with the bodily presents a connection unspeakable and inconceivable."[20]

Gregory's unique employment of the tripartite model of the soul also distinguishes him from more Platonic philosophers.[21] He stresses that the three parts, vegetative, sensitive, and intellectual, support and nurture one another. Indeed, for man's defining attribute, the reason, to function, the lower parts of the soul are necessary. Just as a musician depends on the form of his instrument for the production of his music, man needs his voice, hands, and other bodily parts to be a *rational* animal.

There is no suggestion of shedding the body or returning to a purely intellectual state. Certainly, the physical passions must be ruled by the soul, but it is the free choice to allow them to run rampant that is evil, not their material aspect. Body and soul were created together out of nothing by the divine will; they neither emanated from a divine nature nor descended in such a way that the soul is destined for theosis. The careful analysis that Gregory gives of the mind's self-expression through the body is evidence of an understanding of the unity of the mind and the body, intellectual and physical existence that anticipates the philosophy and psychology of a later age.

20. *MM* XV 3, 404.
21. "For this rational animal, man, is blended of every form of soul; he is nourished by the vegetative kind of soul, and to the faculty of growth was added that of sense . . . then takes place a certain alliance and comixture of the intellectual essence with the subtle and enlightened element of the sensitive nature." *MM* VII 5, 394.

While he found Origen's notion of human free will an important corrective to Neoplatonism, he perceived that in seeing the physical world as a result of evil, Origen failed to grasp the coherent nature of divine theophany. Because he would unite the preexisting soul to God before the (regrettable) making of the material world, Origen would have the soul return alone to God in static unity. He did not allow for the harmony between creation and redemption brought about by theosis and expressed in cosmic redemption.

For Gregory, created being is opposed to uncreated being rather than to the world of pure intelligibility. That is, the essential distinction is between what is generated (heaven and earth) and what generates (God), not between spiritual and material being, nor between God and nothingness. He stresses that even if heaven and earth *are* taken to be opposites, they themselves are mixtures of flux and immutability and therefore not pure. Immediately, then, Gregory has distinguished himself from more Platonic and Neoplatonic systems.

It is the relationship between Creator and created that is instructive, not the dichotomy of being and nonbeing, nor intelligibility and unintelligibility. Creation can itself be divinized, rather than either negated or seen as having only formal reality. Granted, the universe is only *created,* but it is not a fall from true ideal being into something approaching nothingness, nor must its true ontological status be found in abstraction from it. For the individual, this means that Gregory is thinking of a nondegenerative dynamism that defines the self as self. The movement of God in the creation of the whole person is totally productive, and the point of departure for theology is the God-creation distinction, with the latter including a material element.

Gregory underscores the above with a discussion of creation *ex nihilo,* a doctrine that allows for theosis by protecting the created order from ultimately being either resolved into Oneness or shed in favor of purely spiritual existence.[22] The world is not an emanation from the

---

22. Though Scripture tells us that creation has its beginning from God, those who argue for its coeternality ask, "For if these things are believed to have their existence

One but has been given metaphysical autonomy. Likewise its materiality does not cloak its reality but is an integral part of it. The movement of the soul toward God in theosis is the outcome of the real ontological status granted to the world by its intentional creation out of nothing.

We saw above that Gregory's positive view of the material world is suggestive of a totally cosmic theosis. However, he is more explicit about universal salvation, the reconciliation of all *people* with God, than he is about cosmic redemption. In his *Life of Moses,* for instance, Gregory sees the outstretched hands of Moses as indicative of the salvation of all people. Even those who have been punished in hell will ultimately be restored to God.

The subtitle of the key passage emphasizes universal and infinite resurrection as part of "the very necessity of things."[23] In other words, Gregory's understanding of creation leads him to postulate epectasis as demanded by the natural order, rather than as a consequence of biblical declaration. It is as when a celestial body throws a shadow upon another, and the shadow is limited by the light of the sun.[24] Eventually, all things, no matter the direction in which they are moving, will emerge from the shadow of evil into the endless light of divine goodness.

In contrast to Origen, the human soul cannot be isolated from the body, and the created cosmos is not something to be transcended in redemption. The fact that the world cannot be sundered into an

---

from that source, they clearly come into existence after being in Him in some mysterious way; but if material existence was in Him, how can He be immaterial while including matter in Himself?" *MM* XXIII 3, 413. But neither can we conclude that God is material, nor that he imported something external to himself when he created the world. The former would admit a Manichaean definition of God, and the latter would suppose "two eternal and unbegotten existences." Gregory concludes his argument for not only the beginning of the world in God, but also its end, with the following words: "Consequently, as we suppose the power of the Divine will to be a sufficient cause to the things that are, for their coming into existence out of nothing, so too we shall not repose our belief on anything beyond probability in referring the World-Reformation to the same power." *MM* XXIII 5, 414.

23. *MM* XXI, 410.

24. If one were to pass "beyond the measure to which the shadow extends, he would certainly find himself in light unbroken by darkness." *MM* XXI 3, 411.

original lost perfection and a later evil materiality means that theosis is something integral to it. For Gregory, it is only creation's limitation and disorder that must be conquered. God is no less universally active in redemption than he is in creation, and theosis is a fulfillment of the cosmos rather than an abstraction from it. Universal salvation is more than the salvation of the spirits of all persons, and personhood is more than being a disembodied spirit. It is Gregory's anthropology that protects him from a Neoplatonist intellectualism that would deify the soul without the body, and thus the spiritual world alone. Man internally reflects his external position between heaven and earth. All of creation is returned to God insofar as man, through Christ, brings his soul *and body,* into divine renewal.

Moreover, humanity is oriented toward God from the very beginning. Gregory's *Life of Moses* is an entire treatise devoted to the progress of the spiritual life, as the human will is endlessly called to transform passion into virtue. Human contingency—indeed, all contingent being—is authenticated by its openness to the divine. It is created by God in order to infinitely realize its own identity in its Creator. Because it is *created for theosis,* its goal is not to be reabsorbed into a Neoplatonic Oneness nor to escape its contingency and materiality into an ideal world of spirits or forms. Its created being itself makes a true theosis possible. If the world were merely an emergence from a higher substance, the eschaton would lack the tension and promise that it holds in Christian theology, and its existence in time would be evacuated of significance. Creation has reality apart from God (albeit a lesser reality) to be divinized, and it has purpose in its actual, material, time-bound character.

Gregory develops a doctrine of creation and an anthropology that are the foundation for a soteriology of deification. His positive view of the material world excludes an intellectual salvation that would deify the mind alone. Yet, the individual spiritual journey toward God is described in the *Life of Moses.*[25] Using Moses as a type for the perfection

---

25. Sometimes titled *On Perfection* or *On the Life of Moses the Lawgiver: A Treatise on Perfection,* this is one of his latest works and is dated between AD 390 and 395.

of the believer, Gregory describes salvation as the purification and illumination of the mind.

Gregory uses the flame that burnt the "thorny bush" as a lesson in both Christology and soteriology:

> For if truth is God and truth is light—the Gospel testifies by these sublime and divine names to the God who made himself visible to us in the flesh—such guidance of virtue leads us to know that light which has reached down even to human nature. Lest one think that the radiance did not come from a material substance, this light did not shine from some luminary among the stars but came from an earthly bush and surpassed the heavenly luminaries in brilliance.[26]

The light of God manifested itself in the human person of Christ, and there it is to be experienced and known as truth. Moses' removal of his sandals before this light teaches us that purification is a prerequisite to illumination.

In addition to a life unenslaved to the material pleasures offered by the evil one and trained in the pursuit of purity, the virtuous life is free of ignorance and equipped with the wealth of learning. Only a body that is morally pure can sustain a mind that seeks the intellectual virtue of truth. "Truth is the sure apprehension of real Being,"[27] the real Being that appeared to Moses in the light of the burning bush and in the flesh of the person of Christ. To mistake things that have mutable and dependent being (i.e., are nonbeing) for what is immutable and self-subsisting is to be separated from the light of truth. Like Moses, we are to purify ourselves by divesting our minds of false opinions about what is real Being.

Gregory's self-conscious employment of Platonic terminology raises the same concerns that Nicholas of Cusa will later face. At issue is

---

26. Gregory of Nyssa, *Life of Moses* II 20, trans. Abraham J. Malherbe and Everett Ferguson, Classics of Western Spirituality (New York: Paulist Press, 1978), 59.

27. Ibid., 166, 96. He argues that we should learn from Pharaoh who treasured only the fleshly and material, refusing to listen to or know Yahweh. His irrational values caused him to "... disdain the discussion of Being as so much idle talk." Ibid., 35, 62.

the extent to which, in an attempt to mine Greek thought for its richness and truth, the essential core of Gregory's Christianity has been replaced or "Platonized." Although he is critical of "pagan philosophy," Gregory is not hostile to it. Profane learning is correct in its assertions of the immortality of the soul and the existence of God. But its notions of the transmigration of the soul and of God's materiality are mistaken. The former are the "pious offspring" of pagan philosophy, while the latter are its "absurd additions."

Nicholas of Cusa will later follow in Gregory's footsteps, freely making use of Platonic concepts, yet never surrendering his Christianity. Gregory's apophatic theology is one of the key parallels between the two thinkers. The process of drawing near to God is not an intellectual ascent composed of discriminating between true and false assertions. Gregory develops a negative theology based on Exodus 20:21, "Moses approached the dark cloud where God was." As one draws nearer to God, the truth that illuminates us with rays of light is encountered in darkness.[28] Although Moses was lifted up through such "lofty experiences" as seeing the burning bush, he was "still unsatisfied in his desire for more."[29] The soul's response to the mystery of God is an unquenchable longing to experience the mystery more deeply.[30] Epectasis, the perpetual progress toward God discussed above, is thus fueled by unsatisfied desire.

Gregory of Nyssa originates a concept of theosis that will be developed by later thinkers, including Nicholas of Cusa. Because they are anchored together in the divine purpose, created out of nothing by God's will, creation in general, and the human being in particular, is threatened neither by an inevitable return to static Oneness nor

28. "Moses entered the darkness and then saw God in it." Ibid., 162, 94–95.

29. Ibid., 230, 114.

30. The analogy continues, "He still thirsts for that with which he constantly filled himself to capacity, and he asks to attain as if he had never partaken, beseeching God to appear to him, not according to his capacity to partake, but according to God's true being." Ibid.

by a fragmentation of its very self. The world does not lose itself in its own unreality or in its dual aspect as both intelligible and material. Its integrated existence is rooted in the creative act of God. Its goal is, of course, not yet but infinitely realized. Gregory argues that due to the infinity of God, the journey of personal deification is endless. Although he has been accused of having been overly influenced by Origen and of letting idealism dominate his thought, an analysis of his doctrine of theosis shows that his soteriology directly results from the points at which he stood against Origen and Neoplatonism.

The similarities between the two thinkers' doctrines of theosis are numerous. In addition to the obvious common interest in negative theology, Nicholas of Cusa echoes Gregory's positive view of the created order. He not only reflects on natural beauty of the earth, but underscores the positive ontological status possessed by all created things. He, too, sees the mind and body as an integrated unit and makes it evident that he is aware of the pitfalls of Neoplatonism.[31] He also has an understanding of deification as an infinite process that is fulfilled, but never completed, in the life to come.[32] While emphasizing the intellect in salvation, Cusanus, like Gregory, is not blind to the importance of virtue and, indeed, views virtue and wisdom as a seamless whole.[33] A major point of disparity, however, between the two thinkers is the notable ab-

31. *IDM* 7, especially h 102, Hopkins, 231.

Unde cum mens has faciat assimilations ut notiones habeat sensibilium, et sic est immerse spiritui corporali, tunc agit ut anima animans corpus.

32. *Idiote de sapientia* I h 18.

Semper enim guadiosissimo desiderio movetur, ut attingat quod numquam de delectabilitate attactus fastiditur. Est enim sapientia cibus saporosissimus, qui satiando desiderium sumendi non minuit, ut in aeterna cibatione numquam cesset delectari.

Translated as "The Layman on Wisdom" by Jasper Hopkins in *Nicholas of Cusa on Wisdom and Knowledge* (Minneapolis: Arthur J. Banning Press, 1996): "For the intellectual spirit is always moved by most joyous desire, so that it will attain unto never becoming satiated with the delightfulness of its contact with Wisdom. For Wisdom is a most delicious food—one which, in satisfying, does not diminish the desire of the consuming intellect, so that the consuming intellect will never cease to take delight in its eternal repast." See also *DFD* IV h 72.

33. See chapter 5.

sence of the Christological element in Gregory of Nyssa.[34] It is Maximus the Confessor, our next topic, whose rich Christology offers the greatest similarity to Cusanus's own thought in this area.

MAXIMUS THE CONFESSOR

If Nicholas of Cusa's doctrine of creation echoes that of Gregory of Nyssa, the Christological element within Cusanus's thought is reminiscent of the thought of Maximus the Confessor. In developing the mystical theology of Gregory of Nyssa along Christological lines, this father of the Eastern Church begins with the tension between God's presence in and separation from the created world. Instead of using the human spiritual and physical constitution as a lens through which to view the whole of creation, he employs a theological anthropology that is *theandric* at its root.[35]

Theandric unity is based upon the divine-human unity in Christ as defined at the Council of Chalcedon. Theandricity is precipitated by the tension between the divine immanence in creation and the divine transcendence above it and is expressed in cataphatic and apophatic theology. The theandric aspect of the divine-human relation is fulfilled through the link established between these two movements by theosis.

Influenced by the works of Origen, Evagrius, the Cappadocians (including Gregory of Nyssa), and Pseudo-Dionysius, Maximus has

34. For more on this see Hans Urs von Baltasar, *Presence and Thought: Essay on the Religious Philosophy of Gregory of Nyssa*, trans. Mark Sebanc (San Francisco: Ignatius Press, 1995).

35. The word "theandric" was first used by Pseudo-Dionysius in his *Letter* 4 to Gaius. Here he refers to "the new theandric energy." Maximus the Confessor used the term throughout his work. An excellent definition of "theandric" is found in Lars Thunberg, *Man and the Cosmos: The Vision of Maximus the Confessor* (Crestwood, N.Y.: St. Vladimir's Seminary Press, 1985), ch. 4, 71: "'Theandric' designates the entirely unique and new relationship that is established in Jesus Christ as being both fully human and fully divine: God and man as cooperating for the benefit of the whole creation, not separated and yet not mixed, not confused and yet in full harmony."

been called "the real Father of Byzantine theology."[36] Maximus's treatises, *The Mystagogia, The Ascetic Life,* and *The Four Centuries on Charity,* will be essential to examining his contribution to the Eastern doctrine of theosis.

According to Maximus, God is everything in all things, the sustaining link between the spiritual and the material, the harmonious presence in the universe.[37] The relationship between God and each thing is prior to all other relationships, not because it negates them, but because it is their cause and sum. The possibility of sacrament arises from the immanency implied by this hierarchy of relationships. Because the sum is present in the parts, the parts, or the created order, can reveal the sum, or the sacred.

The taming and even obliteration of the passions is essential to knowing the divine, an essential aspect of theosis. For if the soul is tangled in desires for things of the flesh, it is blinded to the transcendent beauty of spiritual things. Only self-mastery will allow the soul to recognize its own dignity and transfer "its whole longing onto God."[38]

Purification is necessary because knowledge of God is of a completely different order from knowledge of things of the world. Here the relevance of the attempt to know God to the notion of theosis is crystallized: knowledge entails union. When the soul approaches divine ineffability through a process of removal, it enters into close union with God. In this state the soul contemplates God in its own self and God holds all things in himself. Created things with understanding partici-

36. John Meyendorff, *Byzantine Theology* (New York: Fordham University Press, 1974), 37.

37. "With His foreknowledge He links both spiritual and material things to each other and to Himself; as their cause, beginning, and end, He keeps all things in his close control, though they are widely different in nature. Just by the force of their relationship to Him as their beginning, He disposes them to each other; by this force all things are led into a harmony of motion and existence." Maximus the Confessor, *The Mystagogia,* trans. Julian Stead (Still River, Mass.: St. Bede's Publications, 1982), 65.

38. *Four Centuries on Charity* III 72, in *Maximus Confessor: Selected Writings,* trans. George C. Berthold, Classics of Western Spirituality (New York: Paulist Press, 1985), 71.

pate in God in their very being because God has communicated to them the divine attributes of being, eternal being, well-being (which is wisdom), and goodness. The first two attributes constitute the *image* of God. The latter two are the *likeness.*

Behind this dichotomy between the presence of God about which we can speak and the silence in which God resides is the Dionysian cataphatic-apophatic dynamic. The God who manifests is also inscrutable, beyond knowledge and participation. In *The Four Centuries* Maximus argues that God is beyond both goodness and wisdom, as well as all contraries. In *The Mystagogia,* the crucial distinction between God and creatures is their differing modes of existence. More than just a matter of being caused or uncaused, created existence differs from divine existence because the latter is inscrutable.

Since the divine infinity is impenetrable, the altar that is the point of contact between God and man is the silent mind. Maximus elaborates on the relationship between reason and mystical silence:

> When he uses the power of reason to contemplate nature, he offers to God purely as if his soul were a sanctuary, the ideas drawn from sense perception circumcised in the spirit from matter. And he calls through an eloquent and musical silence from the altar of his mind, to that other oft-sung silence in the hidden shrines of the Godhead.[39]

While the body is like the nave of the church, the place where morality is exemplified, and the soul is the sanctuary where natural contemplation occurs, the mind is the place of mystical theology. The mind leaves good and evil, and, in fact, all things behind when entering into the divine ineffability.

The doctrine of theosis demands that the movement of cataphatic-apophatic-supereminent theology sketched above become Christological. In contrast with much of Western thought, where Christology is demanded by human sin, for the Greek fathers, Christology is an origi-

---

39. *Mystagogia,* 72.

nal divine intention, built in to the creation.[40] Theosis is the direct line between creation and the re-creation of redemption, and, for Maximus, has a distinctly Christological character. The tension between the theological concern that would preserve the distinction between the divine and human natures of Christ and the soteriological concern that would unite them parallels the more fundamental tension between divine transcendence and immanence. Just as theology is defined by *relationship* with God, deification is defined by *union* with God.

Maximus has a basic understanding of theosis as a calling, gift, and task of human beings. *Four Centuries on Charity* distinguishes between the man who in charity pursues the path to which he was ordained and the man who seeks fulfillment in inferior, created things. The former lives a life of burning love for God and is not attached to creaturely things. The latter is trapped in a world of passion and self-love. In accordance with his origins, the human being is called to the divine infinity, and the response to this calling is love. The one who does not embrace patience and kindness "makes himself a stranger to love, and the one who is a stranger to love is a stranger to God, since 'God is love.'"[41]

The soul's essence was created in God's image and intended in deification to become a "pure mirror" of God.[42] Although it is created *for* this pure state, the soul is not originally created *in* it. Instead, the soul exists in limitation and contingency and must reach its divinely intended self by a reciprocal process of imitating God and being lifted up by

40. The term "supereminent" in relation to this move in Pseudo-Dionysius, Eriugena, and Cusanus suggests a third way, beyond affirmation and negation. It is a third step that literally reduplicates negation, indeed negates both affirmation *and* negation. Dionysius's *Mystical Theology* V is an excellent example of this. However, in a Thomistic context the term may suggest analogical predication and hence a "supereminent" affirmation, something not found in Cusanus.

41. *Four Centuries* I 38, Berthold, 39. Polycarp Sherwood's translation of this passage in *The Ascetic Life: The Four Centuries on Charity* (Westminster, Md.: Newman Press, 1955) makes the point even more clearly: "Being alien to charity is being alien to God since *God is love*."

42. *Mystagogia* 23, 101.

God. Christ's total theandricity awakens ours, which is complete now only in ontological nature, and not yet in existential likeness.[43]

Humankind was created for unity with God, but whether it actually does share in God's wisdom and goodness is determined by the human will. Its movement toward God in free choice is a response to God's movement toward man in Christ. Man's nature is given, but his existence unfolds according to his pursuit or avoidance of the life of charity. In arguing for the abandonment of worldly things and the concentration on things above, Maximus says that it is in *not* acting according to nature that one's soul is impure.[44]

The Byzantine emphasis on the continuity between nature and grace is in evidence here. When one is led astray by the passions, one's natural orientation to the source of all things is abandoned. Thus, it is not human nature that is fallen, but human existence that is polluted. This pollution or impurity is not an inherited condition, but is a sickness that occurs when the movement toward deification is halted.

Theosis is an ontological claim that God has made on us. This claim is rooted in our creaturehood and fulfilled in theosis by our entering into divine charity. It is a gift, not in the Western sense of "by grace alone," but in the awareness of the creature that, despite the role of human action, there is a total dependence on God. The synergy of theosis never approaches Pelagianism because of the intentional aspect of theosis. It is not a question of mankind vainly trying to restore a lost unity with God by his own power. Rather, it is a divinely ordained movement in which human action is wrapped up in God's action. But this focus on love of God alone and detachment from things of this world does not mean than the universe itself is left behind in deification.

43. For a complete discussion of this topic in relation to the major theologians of the Eastern Church see *The Mystical Theology of the Eastern Church* (Crestwood, N.Y.: St. Vladimir's Seminary Press, 1976), chapter 6: "Image and Likeness" by Vladimir Lossky.

44. "Passion is a movement of the soul *contrary to nature* either toward irrational love or senseless hate of something or on account of something material." *Four Centuries* II 16, Berthold, 48. Italics mine.

Indeed, the groundwork for the Christological theosis of Maximus the Confessor is found in his dynamic notion of the cosmos. Theosis as an intended destiny for the world, rather than as a repair to a plan gone wrong, is Maximus's aim in his formulation of the motion of the cosmos.[45] Creation originates in God's action and moves toward a fixed state of perfection. Deification is not an Origenist return of disembodied souls to an original ideal state, the fall from which was an aberration. Instead, it is a movement inclusive of the physical world that parallels the divine movement itself and results in the theandric Christ.

The motion of the cosmos is affirmed by its reflection of an originally Trinitarian motion. In the thirteenth of the *Questions to Thalassius* Maximus writes, "Through a wise contemplation of creation we receive the idea of the holy Trinity, i.e., concerning the Father, and the Son, and the Holy Spirit."[46] The inter-Trinitarian motion is adumbrated by the motion of the created order. Thus, God is the source and goal of the movement of all things.[47]

Maximus is, of course, arguing against Origen's doctrine of movement as evil and salvation as a return to a perfect, purely spiritual state.[48]

45. In finding Trinitarian adumbrations in creation, Maximus was influenced by Gregory of Nazianzus. For more, see Thunberg, *Man and the Cosmos,* 45–46. Maximus's reversal of Origen's fixity-motion-becoming (*mone-kinesis-genesis*) triad to becoming-motion-fixity (*genesis-kinesis-stasis*) gives the entire created order a foundation within the divine purpose. For a comparison of Origen and Evagrius with Maximus the Confessor on the Trinity see Polycarp Sherwood's commentary in *The Ascetic Life,* 37–45.

46. Patr. Gr. 90, 296 B.

47. The movement of rational souls is especially attributed to God's goodness: "God is the beginning, middle, and end of beings in that he is active and not passive, as are all others which we so name. For he is beginning as creator, middle as provider, and end as goal, for it is said, 'From him and through him and for him are all beings.' There is no rational soul which is by essence more valuable than another rational soul. Indeed, God in his goodness, creating every soul to his image, brings it to be self-moving." *Chapters on Knowledge* I 10–11, trans. Berthold, in *Maximus Confessor: Selected Writings,* 130.

48. Although Maximus owed much of his understanding of Origen to Justinian, he had also read Origen's own texts. See Hans Urs von Balthasar, *Cosmic Liturgy: The Universe according to Maximus the Confessor,* trans. Brian Daley (San Francisco: Ignatius Press, 2003), and Polycarp Sherwood, O.S.B., *The Earlier Ambigua of Saint Maximus the Confessor and His Refutation of Origenism* (Rome: Orbis Catholicus, Herder, 1955).

Maximus's arguments against "the Greek philosophers" who "affirm that the substance of beings coexisted eternally with God" not only emphasize God's infinity, but also underline the source of all things in an original divine movement.[49] Even the substances of things did not preexist, but were created from nonbeing by an *active* God. Theosis, for Maximus, is therefore not a retrieval of a state that should never have been lost, but the fulfillment of a process that originated in God.

As for the matter of the moving cosmos, here too Maximus follows Gregory of Nyssa and does not view it as evil. While he does privilege the spiritual over the material, he never suggests that detachment is motivated by an evil inherent in the material world. The asceticism in *Four Centuries on Charity* is motivated by a desire to return to the source of all things, not by revulsion at their materiality. Created things are shunned because of their inadequacy rather than their debased nature.

Because the embodiment of souls was a divine intention, human beings are not engaged in an escape from physical creation, but share in its total transformation. The movement of created beings in theosis is no less a movement toward perfection than the movement of God himself. Thus, the economy of salvation is no mere afterthought, but is linked to the original plan and being of God. This position is, of course, not so distant from earlier thinkers such as Gregory of Nyssa.[50]

49. *The Third Century* 28, Berthold, *Maximus Confessor: Selected Writings,* 65.

50. Maximus, however, accuses the Cappadocian of having "abused" the doctrine of *apocatastasis,* or universal restoration. Literally signifying a return to a previous position, apocatastasis highlights the tension in Christianity between the universality of Christ's salvific work and the punishment of sinners resulting from God's judgment. If God's perfect mercy and goodness is expressed in the sacrifice of Jesus Christ, it is inconceivable that any soul could remain outside of that mercy, no matter how sinful it is. At the same time, Scripture speaks of eternal punishment. Polycarp Sherwood calls this the "problem of the concrete solidarity of the human race" (*The Earlier Ambigua,* 209). The promise that, just as all fell with the first Adam, all will be restored with the second Adam, contradicts the reality of divine judgment and the significance of the human sin that precipitates it. The abuse with which Gregory of Nyssa is charged is an extreme view of universal salvation that would restore all sinners, and eventually even Satan him-

Maximus's doctrine of the Trinity supports his view of universal restoration *(apocatastasis)*. God's action in the historical Christ, his revelation, emerges out of the silent enigma of the Trinity.[51] Maximus emphasizes the unconfused union; Trinity in no way follows Unity, neither temporally nor ontologically. The mysterious light of the Trinity, at once both one and threefold, is received by the soul.

The significance of his understanding of the Trinity for theosis is that it places the Christological element at its very heart. The Son was present at the creation, at the moment when the world was made for deification. He is not a secondary level of divinity with his own ontological status whose purpose was to retrieve a fallen human spirit. Instead, he is himself both the one who destined human being for theosis

---

self, to divine communion. While Maximus's opinion of Gregory's interpretation is evident, his own doctrine is less so. Because Maximus is not only navigating between the two poles of universal salvation and eternal damnation mentioned above, but also trying to avoid the cyclical restoration of the henad from Origenistic myth, his position is a delicate one. Traditionally, Maximus has been interpreted as adhering to a doctrine of apocatastasis. Von Balthasar finds that eternal punishment is, for Maximus, a threat that may well be nullified by God's mercy *(Cosmic Liturgy)*. Jerome Gaith *(La Conception de la Liberté chez Grégoire de Nysse* [Paris: Libraire Philosophique J. Vrin, 1953]) interprets both Gregory of Nyssa and Maximus as adhering to a strong doctrine of apocatastasis in which there will be no exceptions to God's salvation. Maximus divides apocatastasis into three restorations: those of the virtuous individual, of nature, and of the sinful powers of the soul. It is the restoration of the latter that is problematic. Sherwood, however, takes the better supported view that while even sinners are restored to a clear knowledge of God, they do not achieve the same communion with God that those who have led lives of virtue do. Thus, there is a finality to punishment since sinners must eternally experience a certain separation from God, but sins themselves pass away. He maintains that Maximus thus preserves the tension between the two poles. It should be added that it is Maximus's notion of theosis that protects his doctrine of apocatastasis from Origen's cyclical reconstitution of the henad. The fragmentary nature of Maximus's doctrine of apocatastasis may also be due to his sense of mystery regarding the tension between universal salvation and eternal punishment. Though Von Balthasar and Sherwood disagree on the frequency of texts dealing with "esoteric silence," both agree that Maximus refers to the dangers of attempting to interpret doctrines that are best honored in silence. Recognizing the pitfalls of privileging universal restoration over the finality of divine judgment, or vice versa, Maximus prefers to let the tension rest in mystery.

51. Nicholas of Cusa will later extend this mystery to cover the being of all of creation. Thus, an ever-widening circle of mystery develops.

and the vehicle for the realization of that destiny. There is no gap between the God of creation and the God of redemption.

Through the practice of charity or love, human beings unite themselves, and through themselves the whole world, with both the Christ of history and the Son of the Trinity. The divine call to theosis is realized in Christ whose human nature represents the entire cosmos. And the human imitation of the Son is microcosmic in its own right since it participates in the return of all finite things to God. The divine-human reciprocity is love itself, the proper mode of human existence in the world.

Maximus thus develops Gregory's doctrine of the openness of creation to deification along Christological lines. It is not merely that the cosmos is oriented toward theosis at the moment of creation, but that theosis is based in the divine-human activity of God himself. Creation is called to participate in its original destiny and does so in a way that realizes its true nature. That is, it is neither abstracted from its embodied self nor presented with a soteriological gift that is foreign to itself. Rather, it is enabled by God to participate in its own salvation in a synergistic manner.

Maximus's distinctly Eastern approach thus avoids the pitfalls of Neoplatonic idealism, as well as the Western soteriological disjunction between creation and redemption and its attendant questions about "pure nature" that the lack of a doctrine of theosis involves. On the one hand, the material world is affirmed. On the other hand, a straight line of divine purpose is traced from creation to redemption. This approach will later be adopted by Nicholas of Cusa.

The unified action of divinity and humanity in Christ is a consequence of the divine plan since humankind was created with the capacity for participating in Christ's action. Maximus agrees with Gregory of Nyssa that the created world was intended by God from the beginning and is not simply a reaction to the fall. Incarnation and redemption are no less part of God's purpose than creation, and the created order has an eschatological dimension from the beginning.

Thus, Maximus exhibits a reverence for the harmony between the material and the spiritual/intellectual that is not nullified by the necessity of detachment from passion. The intellect's privileged position arises out of its unique likeness to God, not out of a perception of the world as evil. If theosis occurs primarily *by means of* the mind for human beings, Maximus denies that only the mind is deified. Human beings and the universe itself were created with a fundamental openness to divinity, a destiny for deification.

As we will see, Nicholas of Cusa develops concepts, such as negative theology and cosmic deification, found in both Maximus and Gregory of Nyssa. He echoes Gregory of Nyssa's positive understanding of the material world as well as his emphasis on illumination by the light of God. Moreover, his focus on Christ as the meeting place of divine and human is reminiscent of Maximus's theandric Christ. His discussion of the creative Word is similar to Maximus's notion that the Son was present at creation and the corresponding notion that there is no gap between the God of creation and the God of redemption. Although his familiarity with the primary texts of Gregory of Nyssa and Maximus the Confessor is a matter of contention, the resemblance is strong.

"THE GREAT DIONYSIUS"

The major problem with which the Greek fathers dealt was not how to express theological truths in philosophical terms, but how to keep pagan philosophy from subverting religious truths when this was done. They did not, for example, adhere to Tertullian's belief that the pursuit of philosophy could lead only to heresy. The discipline of philosophy did not itself violate their religious precepts. A genuinely Christian synthesis of Greek philosophy and the Christian religion would use Neoplatonic language and might even express itself in unusual ways not traditionally associated with biblical revelation. However, these expressions would not surrender the basic religious truth to the philosophical presuppositions of the language.

We have seen that Gregory of Nyssa and Maximus the Confessor contributed to the development of a rich tradition of theosis. Although we do not know if Nicholas of Cusa had direct access to some of these Patristic texts, the influence of another thinker, Pseudo-Dionysius, is undisputed. Many of the philosophical constructions that Nicholas of Cusa uses are Neoplatonic and directly drawn from Pseudo-Dionysius's works. An analysis of Pseudo-Dionysius's important contribution to Cusanus's thought will show that Cusanus developed a genuine synthesis of Christian theology and Neoplatonic philosophy. Both Pseudo-Dionysius and Cusanus held to a doctrine of theosis that was in line with the tradition of the Eastern Christian Church, rather than a capitulation to Neoplatonism.

Additionally, it is noteworthy that the tradition of contemplation and of the mind's union with God had been established in Christianity prior to Pseudo-Dionysius. Golitzin argues, in particular, that the pseudonymous author was strongly influenced by Origen, Gregory of Nyssa, and Evagrius.[52] Although the issue of Pseudo-Dionysius's debt to earlier Christian thinkers is beyond the scope of this work, it is further evidence of the historical background of Cusanus's own doctrine.

Cusanus's citations of the pseudonymous author's works are too numerous to list. He refers to him as "the great Dionysius" and "the greatest Dionysius," often mentioning him in company with "the divine Plato."[53] Areas of Cusanus's thought that show indebtedness to Pseudo-Dionysius include his concept of negative and supereminent theology, the notion of the inadequacy of the symbol, the idea that the unit comprehends both oneness and multiplicity, limit concepts, and the theory of participation. For our purposes, however, we will concentrate on areas that are directly relevant to theosis.

---

52. Golitzin, *Et Introibo ad Altare Dei,* chs. 6–8.

53. *De docta ignorantia* 1.17 h 48, trans. H. Lawrence Bond as "On Learned Ignorance," in *Nicholas of Cusa: Selected Spiritual Writings,* 109. Hereafter abbreviated as *DDI.*

Et in hoc aperitur intellectus magni Dionysii dicentis essentiam rerum incorruptibilem et aliorum, qui rationem rerum aeternam dixerunt; sicut ipse divinus Plato.

Pseudo-Dionysius maintains a tension between the manifesting God and the God beyond all manifestation that avoids making the created world a necessary emanation of God. This balance of the mysterious *ousia* (essence) and the divine *dunameis* (energies) plays itself out both in the mystical presence and absence of God's self in creation and in the apophatic and supereminent theology that reflects upon it. *The Divine Names* explores the way in which God, as the author of all creation, can be named, and *The Mystical Theology* expresses God's supereminence. While it is true that much in *The Mystical Theology* surpasses and even contradicts his earlier statements, Pseudo-Dionysius never indicates that the paradox is resolved in favor of either immanence or transcendence. The Creator as Creator is mysterious for Pseudo-Dionysius because of the double movement of manifestation and hiddenness inherent in the creative movement.

Here Pseudo-Dionysius evinces a basic difference with Neoplatonic thought. While the dialectic between an ineffable One and the many in which it pours itself out is inherited from Neoplatonism, the religious rather than philosophical intent of Pseudo-Dionysius's construction is clear. The One is not posited as a rational explanation of the many, but is mysterious in its very relationship with the many. Nor do the levels of hierarchy function as static forms, the Neoplatonic *kosmos noetos*. As Vladimir Lossky points out, Pseudo-Dionysius's elimination of the Neoplatonic hierarchy, and, therefore, of emanation, is essential to his refusal to let Neoplatonic philosophy dominate the Christian mystery.[54]

The divine principles of being, life, and intellect are not located hi-

---

54. Vladimir Lossky, *The Vision of God*, trans. Ashleigh Moorhouse (London: Faith Press, 1963), 99–110. Also "La Notion des 'Analogies' chez Denys le Pseudo-Areopagite," *Archives d'histoire doctrinale et litteraire du Moyen Age* 5 (1931): 279–309. The former reference in particular dates the essence/energies distinction as far back as the New Testament and thus portrays Pseudo-Dionysius as adhering to an already established tradition.

erarchically between God and creation with their own degree of reality. Nor is theophany a necessary descent from God through various levels of existence through which the mind ascends to reach God.[55] The principles are divine Providence itself, God in his self-manifestation.

The balance between the divinity as total source of all creation and the voluntary nature of the creative act is based within God himself. The divine forms are at once within God and apart from him in creation, but they never stand alone. They are within him insofar as they are creative principles and in creation insofar as he is their cause.[56] But they are not levels of existence prior to creation and differentiated from God and, thus, are not Neoplatonic emanations.

All that is, is rooted in the mystery of divinity; it is not rationally mediated through a series of emanations.[57] In placing the forms or

55. Speaking of the divine names, Pseudo-Dionysius writes: "I do not promise to express the absolutely transcendent goodness, being, life, and wisdom of that Godhead beyond all which, as scripture tells us, has its foundation in a secret place above all goodness, divinity, being, wisdom, and life. What I have to say is concerned with the benevolent Providence made known to us." *The Divine Names* V.2 816C, trans. Colm Luibheid in *Pseudo-Dionysius: The Complete Works* (New York: Paulist Press, 1987), 97. Hereafter abbreviated as *DN*.

56. "The name 'Being' extends to all beings which are, and it is beyond them. The name of 'Life' extends to all living things, and yet is beyond them. The name 'Wisdom' reaches out to everything which has to do with understanding, reason, and sense perception, and surpasses them all." *DN* V.1 816B, Luibheid, 96–97.

57. The Areopagite is careful not to go beyond the Trinity to a Godhead at rest and totally without differentiation. Because there is Trinitarian relationship within the One, apart from all creation, it is not the Trinity as such that is mysterious. That is, the Trinity is not the main object of apophatic theology. The negative and supereminent terminology applies to God's names in the theophany of creation, not internally. The focus of negative theology for Pseudo-Dionysius is the undifferentiated names of God that try to express the undifferentiated super-essence and are based on creation. The differentiated names of God (Father, Son, and Holy Spirit) are likewise symbolic. Yet, because they depend on revelation and express distinctions within the One, they are not negated in the way that the other names are. While the Trinity is mysterious, its mystery is not so much internal and between the persons, as it is external in its relation as a whole to creation. Trinity is defined as "transcendent fecundity" (*DN* I.4 592A, Luibheid, 51) and aligned with terms like "the One" (*DN* I.4 593B, Luibheid, 53), "the Superunknowable" (*DN* I.4 593B, Luibheid, 53), and "the Transcendent" (*DN* I.4 592B and 593B, Luibheid, 52–53). Thus, Pseudo-Dionysius refuses to let even the persons of the Trinity be turned into

principles within the One, he has done away with the Neoplatonic hierarchies and put the impetus toward multiplicity within the One itself. Pseudo-Dionysius is careful to say that this does not mean that there is multiplicity in the Godhead and finds that in God, wisdom, life, and being are merely names for the acts of God vis-à-vis creation. They are neither descriptions of God apart from his creativity nor separate causes within God.

Given the prominence of hierarchy in Pseudo-Dionysius's thought, more must be said about its uniquely Christian soteriological role. It may be that it acts just as the Plotinian hierarchy of rational principles expressing the natural order of things, though costumed in Christian garb. However, scholars such as Golitzin point to the specifically Christian function of the Dionysian hierarchy. The latter argues that Dionysius has "succeeded in transforming the Neoplatonists' series of causes into a ladder of icons."[58] Because an icon makes present its referent, the levels of hierarchy are incarnations.

Rather than each level *causing* each succeeding level, each *reveals* God in its own way. The goal, then, is not to intellectually ascend the order of rational principles, becoming disincarnate on the way, but to unite in grace with the incarnate Christ. While Plotinus also used the word "icon," Pseudo-Dionysius intended more by the term than a natural manifestation of the image of higher levels in the lower levels they produce.[59] God's productive goodness, his providence, is a free act. The iconic nature of the created order is a result of divine grace.

---

emanations that can be surpassed by the One in a Neoplatonic fashion. We will find that Pseudo-Dionysius's understanding of Trinity is significant for purposes of contrast with a thinker who did surrender more of his Christian concerns to Greek ones, i.e., Meister Eckhart.

58. Golitzin, *Et Introibo ad Altare Dei,* 164.

59. Stephen Gersh, *From Iamblichus to Eriugena: An Investigation of the Prehistory and Evolution of the Pseudo-Dionysian Tradition* (Leiden: E. J. Brill, 1978), 81, also n261. Plotinus uses the term *eikwn* or *eidwlon* in the following places: *Enneads* I.6.2, II.9.8–9, III.2.1, III.3.18, III.4.3, IV.3.11, V.8.1 (trans. S. MacKenna [London: Penguin Books, 1969]).

The way that Pseudo-Dionysius deals with the hierarchical principles is, thus, indicative of his views regarding the mysterious balance between the God who manifests and the God who is hidden beyond manifestation.[60] It also illustrates how this thinker, who so influenced Nicholas of Cusa, distinguished his own understanding of mystical union with God from a Neoplatonic intellectual ascent. Along with validating the material world, the vision of hierarchy as icon indicates that theosis, too, is a matter of unification by grace. Against the contention by Rist that Pseudo-Dionysius adhered to a theory of a natural power of ascent, divine theophany in an iconic order replaces an ascent of rational principles with an encounter with the incarnate God.[61]

Here the doctrine of grace finds its place in the Areopagite's theology. Consistently using the passive voice, he writes, "We, in the diversity of what we are, are drawn together by it and are led into a godlike oneness, into a unity reflecting God."[62]

Along with finding a precursor to Nicholas of Cusa's "learned ignorance" in the Areopagite's "foolish 'Wisdom,'" we discover here a repudiation of an approach to God through the power of human reason.[63] More than simply a repetitive reference to the theme of negative

60. R. Roques notes the reciprocity of ekstasis in this balance. The intellect is no longer itself when it meets God in mystery, and God is no longer God in himself when he creates. See the introduction to *La Hierarchie Celeste, Sources Chretiennes* 58, 2nd ed. (Paris: Janvier, 1970), v–xcvi, and "Symbolisme et theologie negative chez le Ps.-Denys," *Bulletin de l'association Guillaume Bude* (1957): 97–112. We noted a similar parallel movement in Chapters 1–3 regarding the notions of theophany and theosis in Nicholas of Cusa.

61. J. M. Rist, "Mysticism and Transcendence in Later Neoplatonism," *Hermes* 92 (1964): 213–225.

62. *DN* I.4 589D, Luibheid, 51. In a lengthier passage (*DN* VII.1 865C–868A, Luibheid, 106) he writes: "The human mind has a capacity to think, through which it looks on conceptual things, and a unity which transcends the nature of the mind, through which it is joined to things beyond itself. . . . We should be taken wholly out of ourselves and become wholly of God, since it is better to belong to God rather than to ourselves. Only when we are with God will the divine gifts be poured out onto us. Therefore let us supremely praise this foolish 'Wisdom,' which has neither reason nor intelligence and let us describe it as the Cause of all intelligence and reason, of all wisdom and understanding." In *The Celestial Hierarchy* IV.4 181B (Luibheid, 158) Dionysius refers to the "gift of knowledge."

63. Cusanus remarks in *Apologia doctae ignorantiae discipuli ad discipulum,* 50, "Diony-

theology, this passage portrays deification as the immediate unity with God that follows from self-transcendence. Moreover, the latter is a result of divine gifts, not of an ascent through a series of causes. Indeed, *God* is specifically referred to as "the Cause of all intelligence and reason," "wisdom and understanding."

Pseudo-Dionysius admits that before we are perfectly united with God and our "understanding is carried away," we do attempt to raise our minds to God through symbolism and analogy.[64] But, in the end,

> We leave behind us all our own notions of the divine. We call a halt to the activities of our minds and, to the extent that is proper, we approach the ray which transcends being. Here, in a manner no words can describe, preexisted all the goals of all knowledge and it is of a kind that neither intelligence nor speech can lay hold of it nor can it at all be contemplated.[65]

The natural human capacity for reason, itself a divine gift, is used to approach God as far as it is able. Eventually, however, the mind is stilled when it is struck by the "blazing light" of God.[66] Deification is a result of the engulfing fire of divine love, not of philosophical discipline. God, "because of his love for humanity . . . has deigned to come down to us and . . . like a fire, he has made one with himself all those capable of being divinized."[67] Only because of this is the human being able to grow into divine likeness.

Here the Areopagite's repudiation of the Neoplatonic hierarchy of emanation comes into its full importance. Given the ultimate impotence of the mind to truly know God on its own, one might argue that the pursuit of knowledge of any kind is futile. After all, no exercise of the mind, however sophisticated, can bring deification. A kind of pro-

---

sius says to Gaius that most perfect ignorance is knowledge." He is referring to Epistola 1: "To Gaius" (Dionysiaca 1, 607). Cf. Cusanus's remarks in *De possest* 53.1 h 4.

64. *DN* I.4 592C, Luibheid, 52–53.

65. *DN* I.4 592D, Luibheid, 53.

66. *DN* I.4 592C, Luibheid, 53.

67. *The Ecclesiastical Hierarchy* 2, II.1 393A, Luibheid, 201.

grammatic skepticism would result. On the other hand, if, as Pseudo-Dionysius seems to indicate, the attempt to know God *is* still a worthwhile pursuit, one might ask what knowledge the mind actually attains. If, before the mind is engulfed in the divine light where God cannot be named, naming has any validity at all, what is it that is named? If not to God, then to what do the names apply?

A Neoplatonist would answer that they apply to the divine emanations. While the mysterious One is not known, the lesser hierarchies can be known. Pseudo-Dionysius, however, has an entirely different answer. Instead of distinguishing among a series of ever-increasing levels of divinity, he makes the distinction between God-in-himself *(in se)* and God in his processions *(proodoi)*. About the name "Being," for instance, Pseudo-Dionysius writes,

> But I must point out that the purpose of what I have to say is not to reveal that being in its transcendence, for this is something beyond words, something unknown and wholly unrevealed, something above unity itself. What I wish to do is to sing a hymn of praise for the being-making procession of the absolute divine Source of being into the total domain of being.[68]

In his processions, God can be known and named, though in himself he is unknowable and unnamable. Insofar as God has externalized himself in creation, he is approachable by the human intellect. Without this approachability, such a gulf would exist between Creator and creature that atheism would be the only reasonable human response. Instead, the divine self-manifestation provides accurate, though limited, knowledge of God and the promise of deification.

With this the difficulties of the paradox between the natural drive

---

68. *DN* V.1 816B, Luibheid, 96. Later he reiterates, "I must speak now of those names which tell of the Providence of God. I do not promise to express the absolutely transcendent goodness, being, life, and wisdom of that Godhead beyond all which, as scripture tells us, has its foundation in a secret place above all goodness, divinity, being, wisdom and life." *DN* V.2 816C. Luibheid, 97.

to know God and his ultimate unknowability are resolved. It is not that the names of God are deceptions, giving false information about him. Neither are they only partially true, losing their accuracy as one moves up the levels of hierarchy. And, finally, they are not exercises in futility, just as easily pursued as not. Instead, they are completely accurate and worthy of pursuit insofar as they apply to God as he has proceeded out from himself. In-himself, in his super-essence, he is, however, still hidden.

A final consequence of a careful interpretation of the divine processions as icons rather than as emanations is an understanding of their distinction from the person of the Trinity. Only with this can the essential place that is opened up for Christ in Pseudo-Dionysius's thought be seen. Scholars such as Rorem and Gay who see Dionysius's Christ as a cosmetic decoration of an otherwise Neoplatonic system overlook the fact that the persons of the Trinity are not emanations of the One.[69]

Pseudo-Dionysius stresses that "in scripture all the names appropriate to God are praised regarding the whole, entire, complete divinity rather than any part of it, and that they all refer indivisibly, absolutely, unreservedly, and totally to God in his entirety."[70] He follows this with a lengthy explanation of how the terms "good," "life," "Lord," and the like are applied to the Father, the Son, and the Spirit. The Incarnation is not a "logical fulfillment and completion of the neo-Platonic hierarchy of being,"[71] but a mysterious and crucial act of God.

Many of the constructs in Cusanus's thought can be directly traced to Pseudo-Dionysius. Not only does Nicholas depend on the Areop-

---

69. Paul Rorem, "The Uplifting Spirituality of Pseudo-Dionysius," in *Christian Spirituality: Origins to the Twelfth Century,* ed. B. McGinn, J. Meyendorff, and J. LeClercq (New York: Crossroad, 1988), 144. John Gay argues that "The Incarnation is no paradox, but is the expected fulfillment of a complex structure of reflection and emanation . . . Dionysius . . . assumes an alien neo-Platonism which eliminates the mystery by reducing the dualism of the world and God to a monistic naturalism." "Four Medieval Views of Creation," *Harvard Theological Review* 56, no. 4 (1963): 258.

70. *DN* II, 1, 636C, Luibheid, 58.

71. Gay, "Four Medieval Views of Creation," 258.

agite's theory of naming God, but he also develops the notion of reason as a divine gift. And, finally, there is be no question of the centrality of Christ to Nicholas of Cusa's doctrine of theosis. Because of Pseudo-Dionysius's influence on Nicholas, including frequent references to and quotations of his texts, the extent to which Pseudo-Dionysius himself can be accused of unorthodoxy is important. However, it is evident that there are crucial differences between the Areopagite's thought and Neoplatonism. Given both his creative use of Neoplatonic philosophy and his essential orthodoxy, it is no wonder that Pseudo-Dionysius has enjoyed such influence in the development of mystical and Greek Christian thought.

With the previously existing tradition of theosis in mind, it is now possible to turn to Nicholas of Cusa's own doctrine. We will find that his theory of deification, while not contradicting the earlier doctrine, is a unique addition to the development of the term.

2

THEOPHANY AS

SELF-COMMUNICATION

THE IMPLICATIONS OF
THEOPHANY FOR GOD

Theosis and Theophany

In the Christological theology of Cusanus's later texts, especially *De filiatione Dei* and *De dato patris luminum,* theosis is identified with divine Sonship. This chapter, however, is concerned with the broader issue of divine manifestation, or theophany, in creation as a background for Nicholas's ultimately Trinitarian notion of theosis. His Christology, central to theosis, will be dealt with primarily in my fourth chapter and only briefly in this background discussion of theophany.[1] Theophany, in Cusanus's thought, is expressed through the use of various metaphysical locutions. Each of his texts tends to focus on a particular schema: *De*

---

1. See below in this chapter, "A Christological Theophany," on the *maximum contractum,* chapter 3 on oneness, equality, and union, and the entirety of chapter 4.

docta ignorantia on the coincidence of opposites and *complicatio-explicatio;*[2] *De coniecturis* on participation and *unitas-alteritas;*[3] and *Trialogus de possest* on Actualized-possibility, or *possest.*[4] This study will avoid discussing the significance of Cusanus's shifts among models by moving topically, without, however, ignoring the chronological progression of his thought.[5]

While it is true that in Cusanus's epistemology, difference or utter transcendence is prior to immanence, for the purposes of this examination of theosis, the latter will be studied first. His primary text on the divine transcendence, *De docta ignorantia,* written in 1440, precedes his main works on immanence or identity by many years. (*De visione Dei* was written in 1453 and *De li non aliud* in 1462.) However, because theosis is a *metaphysical* rather than an epistemological category, the or-

2. Translated as "enfolding-unfolding," *complicatio-explicatio* refers to the way in which God *enfolds* all things in himself such that, in God, they are God, and to the parallel unfolding of God's self in the world. The schema is expressive of the way that Cusanus perceives the relationship between the one God and the multiplicity of the universe.

3. *Unitas,* or unity, and *alteritas,* or otherness, are Neoplatonic terms that in Cusanus's thought involve the notion of participation. Unity generally denotes God or being that communicates or participates itself, not in itself or it would replicate itself, but in otherness. Thomas McTighe has shown that a difference between Cusanus and Neoplatonist thought is that for the former *alteritas* is the multiplicity while for the latter it is a principle that accounts for multiplicity. See Thomas McTighe, "*Contingentia* and *Alteritas* in Cusa's Metaphysics," *American Catholic Philosophical Quarterly* (Winter 1990): 55–71.

4. *Possest* is the combination of the two terms *posse,* to be possible, and *esse,* the infinitive of the verb *sum,* to be or exist. It is also the union of the words of the phrase "Possibility exists" *(posse est).* Translated by Jasper Hopkins as "Actualized-possibility," *possest* is a name for God that refers to the fact that God is the actuality of every possibility and that not even possibility precedes or escapes him. God is the *Posse-Est,* the "Can-Is," the actuality of every possibility. Cf. *De venatione sapientiae* 13, trans. Jasper Hopkins, "On the Pursuit of Wisdom," in *Nicholas of Cusa: Metaphysical Speculations* (Minneapolis: Arthur J. Banning Press, 1998).

5. J. Koch argues that Cusanus actually moves from one metaphysical system to another, while Rudolf Haubst sees his later thought as a natural progression from his earlier works. Others, such as Thomas McTighe, take the more middle road of finding new elements in his later texts, but no significant breaks from his previous thought. The difficulty of proceeding systematically through his metaphors or schemas is his own shifting employment of them. He moves freely from one rubric to another, often using a set of terms yet undeveloped in a particular text to buttress or elucidate terms he has been using all along.

der of priority is reversed, both actually and methodologically. It is only because of God's self-manifestation and presence in creation that the movement of theosis can occur. That is, theosis as a metaphysical category is based on divine theophany and is, therefore, fundamentally different from the epistemological project of knowing God that typically assumes a movement from the human to the divine. In proceeding to examine Cusanus's metaphysics first, we are, in fact, justified by his own Platonic persuasion. In *De docta ignorantia* he writes: "With regard to its own operation, understanding, therefore, follows being and living, for through its own operation, it cannot give being or living or understanding. But with regard to the things that are understood, the intellect's understanding, through similitude, follows being and living and nature's understanding."[6]

There are, of course, epistemological ramifications of his metaphysics. For instance, that God is mysterious is not surprising given the absolute difference between God and creation. But the fact that this mystery is ultimately extended to creation itself *is* remarkable since this is the realm in which human powers of comparison, and thus of knowledge, are at work. The mystery of the universe that Cusanus describes in Book II of *De docta ignorantia* is directly predicated on the universe's affinity to its source.[7] Thus, transcendence anchors the whole metaphysical scheme, but it is not strictly prior to immanence and manifestation from the perspective of the theotic destiny of creation.

6. *DDI* 2.6 h 126, Bond, 144.

Sequitur igitur intelligere esse et vivere, quoad operationem suam, quoniam per operationem suam nec potest dare esse nec vivere nec intelligere; sed intelligere ipsius intellectus, quoad res intellectus, sequitur esse et vivere et intelligere naturae in similitudine.

7. "Indeed, our intellect, which cannot leap beyond contradictories, does not reach the being of the creation either by division or by composition, although the intellect knows that this being originates only from the being of the maximum. Derived being, therefore, is not understandable, just as the incidental being of an accident is not understandable if the substance to which it is incidental is not understood." *DDI* 2.2 h 100, Bond, 132.

Noster autem intellectus, qui nequit transilire contradictoria, divisive aut compositive esse creaturae non attingit, quamvis sciat eius esse non esse nisi ab esse maximi. Non est igitur ab esse

Nicholas's early text *De docta ignorantia* offers an initial perspective on the foundational role that theophany plays in the metaphysics of the created order. While this work is primarily concerned with the question of human knowledge of God, the issue of definition is applicable to both the epistemological and metaphysical realms. Occasionally, he even refers to the fact that it is precisely because we participate in God that our minds are drawn to seek knowledge of him. In the passage below, the infinite straight line represents God. The curve in its various degrees stands for human beings (and possibly all things in the created order). The perfection of a curved line, its maximum or minimum, is a straight line. The latter both constitutes the being of the former and negates it. Thus, Nicholas writes:

> Furthermore, our insatiable intellect, stirred by this discussion, seeks with care and great delight, to know how it can more clearly see this participation of the one maximum. And once again with the example of the infinite straight line to assist us, it tells us the following. A curve, which admits a greater and a lesser, cannot be a maximum or a minimum, nor is a curve as curve anything, for it is a falling away from what is straight. Therefore, the being which is in a curve comes from its participation of straightness, since maximally and minimally a curve is only what is straight. Hence, the less a curve is a curve (as is the circumference of a larger circle), the more it participates straightness: not that it takes a part of it, for infinite straightness cannot be divided into parts.[8]

Here is found a clear explanation of the link that Nicholas perceives between knowing and being, as well as, perhaps, a foreshadow-

---

intelligibile, postquam esse, a quo, non est intelligibile, sicut nec adesse accidentis est intelligibile, si substantia, cui adest, non intelligitur.

8. *DDI* 1.18 h 52, Bond, 110–11.

Amplius, non satiabilis noster intellectus cum maxima suavitate vigilanter per praemissa incitatus inquirit, quomodo hanc participationem unius maximi posit clarius intueri. Et iterum exemplo infinitae rectitudinis linealis se iuvans ait: Non est possibile curvum, quod recipit magis et minus, esse maximum aut minimum; neque curvum ut curvum est aliquid, quoniam est casus a recto. Esse igitur, quod in curvo est, est ex participatione rectitudinis, cum maxime et minime curvum non sit nisi rectum. Quare, quanto curvum est minus curvum, ut est circumferential maioris circuli, tanto plus participat de rectitudine; non quod partem capiat, quia rectitudo infinita est impartibilis.

ing of the direction that his later thought will take. His early emphasis on the "learned ignorance" of the human mind will shift to a focus on "the vision of God," a mystical identity of God and creation, and later on God himself as "Not-other" than the created order. Our intellect is stimulated by the fact that "[t]herefore, no thing exists in itself except the maximum, and everything exists in itself as it exists in its essence, because its essence is the maximum."[9] It is stimulated to the point of insatiability by the fact that this same Maximum is "incomprehensible." The mind's quest is predicated upon a particular metaphysical condition, the fact that created being participates in the Uncreated Maximum. It is thus with Nicholas's metaphysics that this study will begin.

In order to understand Nicholas of Cusa's use of the key notion of theophany, it is necessary to view it from two directions: from the divine toward the created order and from the created order toward the divine. In other words, theophany has different implications for God than it has for creation, and both sets of implications are significant for theosis. Given that Cusanus focuses so often on human ignorance about God, it is perhaps daring to begin this study with God rather than with creation. And yet, his most original name for God, the Not-other, suggests that it is not inappropriate in metaphysical studies to begin there, and that, indeed, we cannot proceed without an examination of the implications of theophany for God. From the side of the divine, theophany is linked to definition or knowledge of God, notions that can be developed in terms of both causality and presence.

To begin with, it is important to note what theophany does *not* mean. In the above passage, Nicholas explicitly warns against the conclusion that divine self-manifestation implies that God is "partible." Here Cusanus is drawing attention to the difference between "participation" and "partition." Participation is the paradoxical theory in which the identity and difference of God and the universe are both main-

---

9. *DDI* 1.17 h 50, Bond, 110.

Nulla igitur res est in seipsa nisi maximum, et omnis res ut in sua ratione est in seipsa, quia sua ratio est maximum.

tained. Neither increased nor diminished by the world's creation, God informs the world by being at one with it, while at the same time maintaining his transcendence. Partition, on the other hand, is the idea that God is divided up or scattered into his creation. In Cusanus's eyes, the infinity of God rules out the idea that God could be partible. Thus, he makes it clear that theophany as participation does not mean that God is diminished in any way. In fact, the opposite is true. As will be shown, the concept of participation strengthens God's absoluteness and extends his infinity.

The Not-Other and Ontological Priority

Cusanus also insists that, despite the many paradoxes he employs, theophany is not irrational. In the text *On God as Not-Other,* he makes the acceptance of his ideas contingent upon their reasonableness. Ferdinand must be "compelled by reason" or reject all that Nicholas has to say.[10] This condition is important because of the unusual terminology that Cusanus employs. As will later be explained more fully, the paradoxes and negative theology that pervade Nicholas's theology are not a mark of irrationality, but are essential to the presentation of truth that would otherwise be inexpressible. The first thing, of course, that Ferdinand wants explained is how the one and triune God can be called "Not-other," a name that eclipses the ordinary categories of definition.[11]

Many other metaphors describe theophany for Cusanus, such as the coincidence of opposites, *complicatio-explicatio,* and Actualized-possibility.

---

10. *Directio speculantis seu de Non Aliud* 1 h 2, trans. Jasper Hopkins, "On God as Not-Other," in *Nicholas of Cusa on God as Not-Other: A Translation and an Appraisal of De Li Non Aliud* (Minneapolis: University of Minnesota Press, 1979), 33. Hereafter abbreviated as *DNA*.

Nicolaus: Dicam et tecum, Ferdinande, hoc pacto colloquar: quod omnia quae a me audies, nisi compellaris ratione, ut levia abicias.

11. Naming God will prove, for Nicholas, to be at once a highly problematic and consequential act. For a detailed discussion of this topic, see chapter 3 on negative theology.

All of these include, to at least some degree, the same ramifications for God that Not-other does. Not-other is, however, Nicholas's most mature formulation of the identity side of theophany and its significance for God. It is, thus, for simplicity's sake the one I have chosen to focus on in this section. The other metaphors will not be neglected, but will be examined in detail in the second half of this chapter.

The first explanation that Nicholas gives of the term "Not-other" develops the concept of God's *self*-referentiality. Not-other is not other than Not-other, that is, than itself. God is not a different thing from himself. The second explanation refers to the created order or the "other." What is other is not other than other.[12] Both formulations illustrate that "Not-other" is, in fact, the quintessential term for theophany viewed from the side of the divine.

Inasmuch as "Not-other" describes the relationship between God and creation as one of divine self-manifestation, it establishes one side of the crucial equation that balances God's participability and imparticipability. God is Not-*other* than his creation. Nicholas's idea that the created order is a theophany, an expression of God's very self, is underlined by his favorable reference to David of Dinant's view that "the visible world is the visible God."[13] It is an oft-remarked fact, especially among Pseudo-Dionysian scholars,[14] that without both identity and difference between God and the world, there is a danger of sliding into either dualism or monism. When God is referred to as the Not-other, the presence of God's self in creation is maintained, and thus the danger of the former is avoided.

This divine presence is at once the basis and motivation for the

---

12. Note that the other is not equal to the Not-other. The two formulations are significant in their difference. Nicholas is not merely confusing terminology here, but is obeying the law of noncontradiction.

13. *DNA* 17 h 81, Hopkins, 123.

Ferdinandus: David igitur de Dynanto et philosophi illi quos secutus is est, minime errarunt, qui quidem deum hylen et noyn et physin, et mundum visibilem deum visibilem nuncuparunt.

14. Nicholas himself notes Dionysius on this point. *DNA* 1 h 5.

movement of the created order toward God. According to Cusanus, "Therefore, each thing desires that which is not *other* than itself. But since Not-other is not *other* than anything, all things supremely desire it as the beginning of being, the conserving means, and the rest-giving terminal goal."[15] The Not-other is the source, the conservation, and the goal of the other. Though it is evident from his insistence on divine immanence that Cusanus is not a dualist, he has been charged with both dualism and monism.

These are serious charges because both monistic and dualistic systems lose the possibility of relationship between God and the world. In the case of the former, the two are identified and the prerequisite autonomy of relating terms is absent. In the case of the latter, the absolute separation of the two terms entails a lack of commonality, also a requirement for relationship. A metaphysical construct in which God is absolutely different from the created order sets the world against him and negates the possibility and reason for the movement of each term toward the other, thus leading, for all practical purposes, to a state of total isolation or atheism. In both cases, the traditional theological goal of discovering the manner in which God deals with the created order and the way in which creatures should react to God is undermined.

Nicholas's development of a divine immanence that protects his thought against dualism has been explored. In addition, he strongly maintains divine *transcendence,* a concept that will be examined in the next chapter, resulting in a sharp *difference* between the created and divine orders. Such difference is, of course, the key to arguing against charges of monism. There is more at stake here than mere theological speculation. The problem is that the neglect of either side of the equation, absolute identity or absolute difference, threatens the self-identity

---

15. *DNA* 9 h 35, Hopkins, 73.

Hoc igitur quodlibet desiderat quod ab ipso est non aliud. Non-aliud vero cum ab aliquo non sit aliud, ab omnibus summopere desideratur tamquam principium essendi, medium conservandi, et quiescendi finis.

either of God, of creation, or of both. God would not be infinite and absolute, that is, would not be himself, if the world existed utterly apart from him. And the created order would not have its own being if it were absorbed into a monist system.

When God is called "Not-other," the identification between him and creation is clearly indicated. The other half of the paradox, God's absolute transcendence, is indicated by Nicholas's references to the *Mystical Theology* of Dionysius and the fact that "all the names of God signify a participation in Him who cannot be participated in."[16] However, it is not as evident here as in the strongly paradoxical language and negative theology that Nicholas uses elsewhere. This does not mean, however, that the language of Not-other alone indicates monism. Rather, embedded within it is a strong defense against such an interpretation: the foundational role that Not-other plays for all of creation. Cusanus writes, "Hence, it is evident to anyone that God, though unnamable, names all things; though infinite, defines all things; though limitless, delimits all things; and likewise for everything else."[17]

God, therefore, is definitive for all of creation, that is, is fundamental to the definition and being of all things. God can also be called "the First" that is itself defined through no other but itself. God's foundational character is itself the reservoir of his absolute difference from the world. No other thing can claim such status. This is, in fact, an enduring theme in Nicholas's thought. *De visione Dei,* for instance, focuses not on *achieving* union with God, but on God's priority and an already realized union. Yet, no term expresses this idea as clearly as "Not-other."

Nicholas has given the philosophical concern for definition a theological meaning surpassing even that endowed by Scholasticism. He has,

---

16. *DNA* 16 h 79, Hopkins, 121.

Ex quo video quod omnia nomina divina imparticipabilis participationem significant.

17. *DNA* 6 h 21, Hopkins, 57.

Ferdinandus: Nemo est qui quidem, mentem applicans, haec tecum non videat. Ex quo constat unicuique deum innominabilem omnia nominare, infinitum omnia finire, interminum omnia terminare, et de omnibus eodem modo.

in fact, turned the entire project of definition on its head. It is God who defines, not the human mind. It is impossible to overestimate the importance of definition for Plato; he attacks problems of knowledge and even ethics by seeking definitions of terms. While Nicholas follows Plato (and later Neoplatonists) by saying that the divine is the most real or is truly real, he differs from him in a significant way. Unlike Platonic essentialism that sees definitions as characterizing the Forms, for Nicholas, the ultimate Form, or God, cannot be described, but instead itself does the defining. And though Cusanus, like Aristotle, attempts definition by exploring causality, it is not a causality that makes use of substantial forms.

His anti-Aristotelian position means that Cusanus avoids Aquinas's method of using the philosophical tools of definition for theological purposes. He is not interested in approaching God using human categories based on analogy and a corresponding difference in the meaning of theophany for God. For Cusanus, there is a reversal, not of the importance of definition, but in the use that is made of it. Nicholas does understand that definition implies causality, but he uses the metaphor of coldness and ice to describe the absolute causality of God. If coldness ceased, ice, but not water, would also cease. But, if the being (of the ice and water) ceased, then ice and water would too. Still, the possibility-of-being-water would continue to exist. If that too ceased, there would yet remain intelligible nothing that would presumably contain the possibility of other things creatable by Omnipotence. "However, if Not-other ceased, all the things it precedes would immediately cease. And so, not only would the actuality and the possibility of the beings which Not-other precedes cease, but so also would the not-being and the nothing of these beings."[18]

The causality aspect of the theophany involved in the term "Not-other" illustrates both the absoluteness of divine causation and what

---

18. *DNA* 7 h 23, Hopkins, 61.

Verum si ipsum non-aliud cessaret, statim omnia cessarent quae ipsum non-aliud antecedit. Atque ita non entium solummodo actus cessaret ac potentia, sed et non-ens et nihil entium, quae non-aliud antecedit.

one could call its intimacy. God is not the cause merely of the actual being of things, nor is he merely an efficient cause. Rather, he underlies the very possibility of all things, including nothingness. Both facts point toward the infinity and omnipotence of God.

This, then, is an implication that theophany has for God correlative to that of God's self-manifesting presence in creation: a unique aspect to the traditional notion of God's infinity—that is, his ontological priority. Despite Nicholas of Cusa's insistence on God's immanence and on the possibilities for the divinization of created being, the Christian understanding of God is not threatened. What has traditionally been called God's transcendence or infinity is refined to the point where immanence and manifestation in particularity do not undermine the original intent of the theological construct.

This is further illustrated by the manner in which theophany entails a divine presence in creation. Again, the concept of the Not-other is most useful in eliciting the significance of presence for God. In Not-other "we see clearly how it is that in Not-Other all things are Not-other antecedently to being themselves and how it is that in all things Not-other is all things."[19] The divine presence to and in the created order is so intense that it is an identity: "in all things Not-other *is* all things." Nevertheless, this intimacy is founded upon the priority of the divine because in Not-other, before being themselves, all existing and nonexisting things are Not-other. Nicholas clarifies his point by comparing the Not-other to the *ratio* or "Constituting Ground" of all things: "Through this Constituting ground the sky is constituted as the sky; and in the sky this Constituting ground is the sky. Therefore, it is not the case that the perceptible sky (1) is from an other that which it is or (2) is anything *other* than the sky."[20]

19. *DNA* 6 h 22, Hopkins, 57.
Nam cum ipso non-aliud cessante omnia quae sunt quaeque non sunt, necessario cessent, clare perspicitur quomodo in ipso omnia anterioriter ipsum sunt et ipsum in omnibus omnia.
20. Ibid.
Tunc enim ratio cur caelum caelum et non aliud prioriter in ipso est, per quam constitutum est

Divine priority does not suggest, however, that God can be known apart from the created order. Cusanus is in no way leading up to a secret gnosis or to a kind of decreation, a path to God that leaves the universe completely behind. It is precisely the presence of the Not-other in creation, the presence entailed by theophany, that illuminates this other aspect of the divine: the fact that God manifests. The character of Ferdinand observes that "the Creative Will, which is Not-other, is desired by all things and is called Goodness."[21] Despite the fact that God transcends the world and that understanding him is a process of learned ignorance (see chapter 3), divine manifestation is an incontrovertible and irreversible fact. There is no going behind it to understand God, and even the intellectual darkness that is brought by learned ignorance is not final. The foundational role of the Not-other for the created order means that negative theology does not triumph.

Cusanus's epistemology is, thus, a clear reflection of his metaphysics. Although the strictly epistemological questions of negative theology and learned ignorance will be dealt with elsewhere, a brief excursus is here necessary to show how issues of paradox and analogy are involved in the concept of theophany and involve divine ontology.

The Coincidence of Opposites and the Question of Analogy

Nicholas's justification for learned ignorance regarding God is developed in his doctrine of God as the coincidence of opposites, the idea that in God all oppositions meet. Ordinarily, unknown things are judged by their likeness to things that are known, as when a vast distance is measured by a series of known lesser distances. The problem is that God, as Absolute Maximum and Minimum, is infinite and im-

---

caelum sive quae in caelo est caelum. Sensibile igitur caelum non est id quod est ab alio aut quid aliud a caelo, sed ab ipso non-aliud, ab aliquo quod vides ante nomen, quia omnia in omnibus est nominibus et omnium nullum.

21. *DNA* 9 h 35, Hopkins, 73.

Ferdinandus: Optime ista sic esse contemplor, et video voluntatem, quae non-aliud, creatricem ab omnibus desiderari et nominari bonitatem.

measurable. It is as when a polygon is inscribed in a circle to measure it. The circle is true; the polygon is an approximation of truth. The polygon can gain more and more angles in order to become more and more similar to the circle, but it can never exactly measure the circle until and unless it becomes the circle itself. It is not the human mind that can do such measuring, but rather, God, in whom not just the knowledge but the being of all things coincides.[22]

Using objects and concepts from the finite universe to attempt analogically to reach a knowledge of the infinite God is useless. If we do not recognize that theophany is the primary disclosure of God, we try to measure the infinite with the finite and we seek direct analogies of God in vain. (Of course, there is a secondary kind of analogy present in the cognitive process that Nicholas calls "conjecture" or "surmise.")[23]

It is clear that Cusanus's apophatic approach is based on his theology of mystical causality and divine presence. God simply cannot be analogized in a proportional manner. In God, all things are enfolded and he is unfolded in all things. Thus, creation has only derived being and is nothing in itself, because when God is removed, nothing remains. There is nothing in the created order that can provide a foothold for an analogical approach to God. There is nothing that exists alongside of God and to which he can be compared. In *De visione Dei,* Nicholas addresses God:

22. The difference between Cusanus and nominalist thinkers is highlighted by the *coincidentia oppositorum.* In his early works, Cusanus believes that God contains the coincidence of opposites, while in his later works he finds that God transcends it. In contrast, the nominalists believed that the law of noncontradiction had jurisdiction over *potentia absoluta,* the absolute power of God.

23. The human mind is like God, the Creator of the world, in the way that it constructs the conjectural world. But this analogy is an analogy of proportionality or relation, not a direct analogy of proportion. God is not directly compared to humanity; rather his relationship to Creation is compared to humanity's relationship to the conceptual world. No knowledge, therefore, is gained about God's attributes, but only about his relations. Moreover, this particular analogy is itself dependent on an original human ignorance since the human mind can construct only what is not already there for it to discover. Whereas direct analogy depends on what one already *knows,* the analogy be-

> You are, therefore, O God, the opposition of opposites, because you are infinite, and because you are infinite, you are infinity itself. In infinity the opposition of opposites is without opposition. Lord, my God, strength of the weak, I see that You are infinity itself. Therefore, there is nothing that is other than, or different from, or opposite you. . . . Absolute infinity includes and embraces all things. . . . Nothing, therefore, exists outside it.[24]

Thus, the most basic requirement for analogy, opposition or distinction between two things, is removed by God's absoluteness, including both his absolute identity and his absolute difference from the created order.

God's infinity thus abolishes the possibility of attributing human characteristics to him, even if they are infinitely described. For instance, one cannot say that because humans possess rationality, God must possess it infinitely. This absence of analogy is also an absence of the traditional hierarchy of being. While it still may be argued that Cusanus saw varying degrees of development in the universe, human beings, for example, as more developed than lions or stones, his primary model of God as the coincidence of opposites reemphasizes God's infinity, absoluteness, manifestation, and mystical presence to all things.

Nicholas cites Plato's forms (although not their multiplicity) as parallel to the way in which the Not-other grounds the created order. This

---

tween the creative mind and the Creator God admits that the mind does *not* know any given concepts and so must create them for itself. See below and chapter 2.

24. Nicholas of Cusa, *De visione Dei* XIII h 54–55, trans. H. Lawrence Bond, "On the Vision of God," in *Nicholas of Cusa: Selected Spiritual Writings* (New York: Paulist Press, 1997), 259–60. Hereafter abbreviated as *DVD*.

Es igitur tu, deus, oppositio oppositorum, quia es infinitus. Et quia es infinitus, es ipsa infinitas. In infinitate est oppositio oppositorum sine oppositione. Domine deus meus, fortitudo fragilium, video te ipsam infinitatem esse. Ideo nihil est tibi alterum vel diversum vel adversum. Infinitas enim non compatitur secum alteritatem, quia cum sit infinitas, nihil est extra eam. Omnia enim includit et omnia ambit infinitas absoluta. . . . Est igitur infinitas et complicat omnia, et nihil esse potest extra eam.

Another translation by Jasper Hopkins, *Nicholas of Cusa's Dialectical Mysticism: Text, Translation, and Interpretative Study of De Visione Dei* (Minneapolis: Arthur J. Banning Press, 1985) is also available.

connection between the divine presence that occurs with theophany and the fact that the Not-other is the ontological foundation of the created order will be for Nicholas a justification for negative theology and will later even lead him to speculate that Plato attained knowledge of things through revelation.[25] Nicholas's Platonic background in the area of Form or Measure will be discussed at length in the chapter on negative theology. However, here it is important merely to note that his understanding of the notion was indeed Platonic and not Aristotelian.[26] Due to an illegitimate imputation of substantial form to Cusanus, thinkers such as Rudolf Haubst and John L. Longeway have attributed a Thomistic analogy of being to Cusanus. Haubst believes that Nicholas's notion of conjecture can be identified with the Scholastic *analogia entis*,[27] while Longeway agrees, he argues that Cusanus denied only epistemological analogy and not metaphysical analogy.[28]

The key to a refutation of the idea that Nicholas accepted the possibility of metaphysical but not epistemological analogy between God and creation is his distinction between enfolding and unfolding.[29] Giv-

25. "Now what is posterior exists by means of participation in what is prior. Hence, what is the first (by participation in the first all things are what they are) is seen prior to intellect; for it is not at all the case that all things participate in intellect. Therefore, intellect does not attain to 'what is earlier or older than intellect itself'—to use his Proclus' words. Wherefore, I think that Plato mentally viewed the substance, or the beginning (*principium*), of things by way of revelation—in the manner in which the Apostle tells the Romans that God has revealed Himself to them." *DNA* 20 h 92, Hopkins, 135.

Posterius autem prioris partiipatione subsistit. Primum igitur (cuius participatione omnia id sunt quod sunt) ante intellectum videtur, cum omnia intellectu nequaquam participent. Intellectus igitur "anterius sive senius se ipso," ut verbis eius utamur, non attingit. Ex quo Platonem reor rerum substantiam seu principium in mente sua revelationis via percepisse—modo quo apostolus ad Romanos dicit deum se illis revelasse.

26. He did, however, adhere to the nominalist position that universals exist only in the mind. *Idiota de mente* XI.

27. "analogy of being"

28. See Rudolf Haubst, "Nikolaus von Kues und die analogia entis," in *Streifzuege in die Cusanische Theologie* (Muenster: Aschendorff 1991), 232–242, as well as John L. Longeway, "Nicholas of Cusa and Man's Knowledge of God," *Philosophy Research Archives* 13 (1967–68): 289–313.

29. These constructs were originally used by Boethius and Thierry of Chartres.

en in terms of actuality and possibility, his explanation of them in *De possest* is one of the most clear to be found in any of his works. Although he sometimes uses the language of formal causality, it is evident that he is far from the Thomistic analogy that these thinkers attribute to him. Since the dialogue begins by attempting to unravel the meaning of Paul's statement in Romans 1:20 that the invisible things of God can be known in creation, the question of formal causality arises immediately. Does Paul simply mean that one can move from the forms of things to their origin in God, the Beginning? Is enfolding just another version of analogy in which things are traced by their likeness back to their existence in the Creator? No, Nicholas clearly intends something very different. Completely avoiding the language of intellectual abstraction of forms, the cardinal answers by leading his questioners to an understanding of the meaning of the idea that God is actually every possible thing. It is not merely that all things exist in God, but that enfolded in God, all things are God. Since God is the life and essence of things, he can be called the Form of their forms. In fact, things can be said to exist more truly in the Form of forms than they do in themselves. But these are not the Aristotelian substantial forms of Aquinas.

It makes much more sense to answer the objection "warum Cusanus das Wort *analogia* kaum gebraucht"[30] by taking Nicholas's own statements at face value than to hypothesize about his desire to avoid controversy. Given the daring nature of some of his theological language, it hardly seems likely that he would shy away from borrowing accepted Scholastic language or that such usage would be the focus of controversy. It is his *un*-Scholastic position, including his notions about the imprecision of finite knowledge and his positing of extreme immanence, that aroused the ire of fellow theologians such as John Wenck, not his use of traditional theological terminology.

The fact that Nicholas is not talking about a removal of things from

---

30. Haubst, *Streifzuege,* 240.

their contingent creaturehood or simply referring to a divine archetype can be seen by his metaphor of the line. In both cases, he emphasizes the inclusive infinity of God rather than his formal transcendence. Unlike human beings, God is *possest,* Actualized-possibility; he *is* everything he *can be.* (It should be noted that the term *possest* is ambiguous and difficult to translate. Jasper Hopkins's choice of "actualized-possibility" captures one range of meanings but is too static a noun to avoid missing the more active, verbal connotations of potency, power, and creative energy.) If a line had actualized-possibility, it would extend everywhere; there would be no shape or figure that was not bounded by it since everything that it could trace, it would trace. At the same time, it would extend minimally, since it would actually fulfill the possibility that it extended nowhere. All figures, no matter how different, how great or how small, would thus be made through it and embraced by it and could be seen in it.[31]

But the text that Haubst himself uses to prove his point can also be used against him. *De coniecturis* links conjecture to the participation between the four unities. Just as the senses' otherness occurs in the unity of rationality, so does rationality's otherness occur in the unity of the intellect, and that of the intellect in the divine unity. But each of these unities experiences its otherness as conjecture, since it can only *participate* in what is a higher unity than itself and can never fully comprehend it.[32] Based on this same passage, Haubst argues that Cusanus can be translated into Scholastic terminology to the effect that human knowledge is always only in an analogy of proportion or participation to reality.[33]

31. According to Mahnke, Nicholas here evinces a clear difference from the Plotinian doctrine of unity, in which infinite multiplicity is potentially found in infinite unity. For Cusanus, God, both potentiality and actuality, is the infinite unity that actually contains infinite multiplicity. Dietrich Mahnke, *Unendliche Sphaere und Allmittelpunkt* (Halle: Max Niemeyer Verlag, 1937), 86.

32. *De coniecturis* 1.4 h 13, trans. Jasper Hopkins, in *Complete Philosophical and Theological Treatises,* vol. 1 (Minneapolis: Arthur J. Banning Press, 2001), 168–69. Hereafter abbreviated as *DC.*

33. Haubst, *Streifzuege,* 237.

Haubst is correct that there is a second-order analogy specifically cited by Cusanus in the text. Just as God has created the universe of real things *(realia)*, the human mind is the creative source of the world of rationality *(rationalia)*. But the kind of relational analogy found in *De coniecturis* never approaches the direct analogy of the Scholastic analogy of being. Even in combination with the citations of *De venatione sapientiae* that use the term "analogy" and the references to Cusanus's fondness for mathematical terminology in *De docta ignorantia* and elsewhere, Haubst's case is weak. The kind of parts-to-whole analogy mentioned in the former is not an example of *analogia entis;* nor can Cusanus's mathematical metaphors, predicated upon ignorance rather than likeness, be interpreted as the proportion between copy and original as Haubst supposes.

This is not to say, however, that Cusanus's avoidance of analogical language is the result of an inherent monism in his thought. While Rudolf Haubst outlines a *Seinsmetaphysik* that admits analogy, Joseph Koch finds both a *Seinsmetaphysik,* in *De docta ignorantia,* and an *Einheitsmetaphysik,* in *De coniecturis.* The latter denies analogy on the basis of the ultimate unity of all things and the impossibility of taking the step that precedes analogy, that is. differentiation. Nicholas, however, does not commit himself to either metaphysical schema. From the side of God, Nicholas clearly avoids monism by his insistence on divine autonomy. From the side of creation, monism is denied as Nicholas focuses on the break between the created and divine orders that engenders negative theology, a topic that will be examined in the next chapter.

Despite Cusanus's emphasis on divine inclusivity and immanence, a Neoplatonic influence, he was able to preserve the notion of divine freedom vis-à-vis creation by emphasizing God's role as *Creator.* God's autonomy is not threatened by theophany. Nicholas's replacement of the Neoplatonic opposition between the One and nothingness and the classical celestial-terrestrial difference with the Creator-creation distinction is the key to his defense of divine volition. (Of course, the latter distinction is expressed as *Unitas/alteritas, complicatio/explicatio,* and

Non-aliud/aliud, rather than in the language of creation.) Nicholas's denial of levels of hierarchy progressively more distant from the one is a crucial step in his alteration of Neoplatonic emanation. The elements are just as intermingled in the celestial realm as they are in the terrestrial, making the celestial no more a pure emanation from the One than its earthly counterpart. In fact, the created order *in its entirety* is God unfolded, though contingent, and unnecessary to him. Cusanus thus wiped out the notion of a necessary emanation from the divine and the possibility that it could be conditioned by creation.

It is interesting to note that Cusanus does not use the traditional ex nihilo formulation in his philosophical and theological texts (though it does appear in his sermons) to emphasize divine freedom, but instead reverts to the theme of God's reconciliation of oppositions within himself. Nicholas evidently intends not-being to be as empty a concept as possible and equal to nothingness since he says that it is not itself a created thing.[34] Though the world has no being apart from God, not-being is itself comprehended by God. The enfolding of God is to be understood in such a way that all opposites are reconciled, including that of being and not-being.

> Absolute possibility is not able to exist prior to actuality—unlike the case where we say that some particular possibility precedes its actualization. For how would absolute possibility have become actual except through actuality? For if the possibility-of-being-made made itself actually exist, it would actually exist before it actually existed. Therefore, absolute possibility, about which we are speaking and through which those things that actually exist are able actually to exist, does not precede actuality. Nor does it succeed actuality; for how would actuality be able to exist if possibility did not exist? Therefore, absolute possibility, actuality, and the union of the two are coeternal. They are not more

---

34. *Trialogus de possest* 5, trans. Jasper Hopkins, "On Actualized-Possibility," in *A Concise Introduction to the Philosophy of Nicholas of Cusa,* 3rd ed. (Minneapolis: University of Minnesota Press, 1980), collected in *Complete Philosophical and Theological Treatises,* vol. 1 (Minneapolis: Arthur J. Banning Press, 2001), 916. Hereafter abbreviated as *DP.*

than one eternal thing; rather, they are eternal in such way that they are Eternity itself.[35]

To Cusanus, "nothing" is that which has no being, that is, not-being. Whatever lacks actual being has at least the possibility of being. Even absolute nothingness cannot escape being encompassed by God or absolute possibility.

The coincidence of the opposites of actuality and possibility in God means that not even that which has no being is distinct from the infinity of God. When things are brought from not-being into being they move from a state of possibility into a state of actuality through divine Power. But since God is absolute possibility, all things, even not-being itself, exist in God and, in God, are God. The example of the authorship of a book helps clarify Nicholas's idea.[36] A book's author has both the active ability to write it and the passive ability of the book's being written. His ability to write the book thus comprises the not-being of the book because its existence or not-existence is in his power. In the same way, nothingness and all things that come from nothingness are enfolded in the possibility that is God. Instead of the traditional emphasis on the person of God creating ex nihilo, this formula points toward divine freedom by indicating that the important distinction is between God and creation since not-being or possibility is encompassed by, rather than opposed to, God. God is not bound by a necessary emanation into nothingness.

The divinization of the created order is predicated upon an original divine manifestation. Theosis rests on theophany. Theophany, however, is not a limited, "momentary" occurrence, that leaves the Absolute

35. *DP* 6, Hopkins, 916–17.

Possibilitas ergo absoluta, de qua actu antequam actu esset. Possibilitas ergo absoluta, de qua loquimur, per quam ea quae actu sunt actu esse possunt, non praecedit actualitatem neque etiam sequitur. Quomodo enim actualitas esse posset possibilitate non exsistente? Coaeterna ergo sunt absoluta potentia et actus et utriusque nexus. Neque plura sunt aeterna, sed sic sunt aeterna quod ipsa aeternita.

36. *DP* 29, Hopkins, 929.

and the created orders isolated and autonomous. Rather, it is a lasting theophany and presence that has consequences for both divine and created ontology. The parallel consequences for the world are linked to the former by the second person of the Trinity, the divine Word. Intrinsic to God "in himself" is the outward movement of the Incarnation. Although Cusanus primarily discusses Christology in terms of theosis (indeed in *De filiatione Dei* he defines *filiatio* as such), his understanding of theophany is thoroughly Christological in its own right.

A Christological Theophany

Nicholas of Cusa begins his earliest Christological text, the third book of *De docta ignorantia,* by a rehearsal of the nature of contracted, that is, multiple and embodied, things. By virtue of its particularity, "no thing coincides with another," nor can any contracted thing "participate precisely the degree of contraction of another."[37] No contracted thing can be the maximum, the minimum, or the limit of either its genus or species because before it reaches that point, "it is changed into another."[38] What Cusanus is arguing for is the impossibility for any particular created thing to be the perfection or summit of its species and the total incommensurability between God as Maximum and the created order.[39] There is always the possibility for higher and lower, greater and less, among contracted things.

37. *DDI* 3.1 h 183, Bond, 170.

Nullum igitur contractum gradum contractionis alterius praecise participare potest, ita ut necessario quodlibet excedat aut excedatur a quocumque alio. Consistunt igitur inter maximum et minimum omnia contracta, ut quocumque dato possit dari maior et minor contractionis gradus, absque hoc quod hic processus fiat in infinitum actu, quia infinitas graduum est impossibilis, cum non sit aliud dicere infinitos gradus esse actu quam nullum esse, ut de numero in primo diximus.

38. *DDI* 3 h 187, Bond, 171. Maximum and minimum are taken from the language of fourteenth-century physics.

Non igitur descendit species aliqua, ut sit minima alicuius generis, quoniam antequam ad minimum deveniat, commutatur in aliam; et pariformiter de maxima, quae commutatur in aliam, priusquam maxima sit.

39. Note that this is in contrast to the universe as a whole that he describes as a "contracted maximum." See further discussion below.

Nevertheless, he then explores the possibility of a *maximum contractum,* that, as "God and creature would have to be both absolute and also contracted" and "could exist in itself only by existing in absolute maximumness."[40] Such a thing would "actually be all the things that in the power of that genus or species are able to be" and would in itself join God and all things.[41] It would be neither a commingling nor a composition of God and creature, nor would either divinity or contraction vanish into the other.

Still speaking hypothetically, Cusanus explores the nature of the contracted maximum. His Christology will rest on the dual notion that the universe is the concrete maximum and that human beings are the middle term of that creation. If God chooses to unite Himself with an individual of a species then that individual would exist as the contracted maximum individual and "such a thing would have to be the fullness of that genus and species."[42] Humanity contains both a lower nature (sensible nature) and a higher nature (intellectual nature). Nicholas writes, "Indeed, it is human nature that is raised above all the works of God and made a little lower than the angels. It enfolds both intellectual and sensible nature and embraces all things within itself, so that the ancients, with reason, called it a microcosm or miniature world."[43] Hu-

---

40. *DDI* 3.2 h 192, Bond, 173–74.

Neque etiam ipsum tale ut contractum Deus, qui est absolutissimus, esset; sed necessario foret maximum contractum, hoc est Deus et creatura, absolutum et contractum, contractione, quae in se subsistere non posset nisi in absoluta maximitate subsistente.

41. *DDI* 3.2 h 190, Bond, 173.

Amplius adiciam, si maximum contractum ad speciem actu subsistens dabile esset, quod tunc ipsum secundum datam contractionis speciem omnia actu esset, quae in potentia generis aut speciei illius esse possent.

42. *DDI* 3.2 h 191, Bond, 173.

Quapropter, si aliquod dabile foret maximum contractum individuum alicuius speciei, ipsum tale esse illius generis ac speciei plenitudinem necesse esset ut via, forma, ratio atque veritas in plenitudine perfectionis omnium, quae in ipsa specie possibilia forent.

43. *DDI* 3.3 h 198, Bond, 176.

Humana vero natura est illa, quae est supra omnia Dei opera elevata et paulo minus angelis minorata, intellectualem et sensibilem naturam complicans ac universa intra se constringens, ut microcosmos aut parvus mundus a veteribus rationabiliter vocitetur.

manity does not exist as an abstraction, but only in concrete form. It would thus be necessary for a real human being to rise up to God and for God to lower himself to the human form. If mankind is a microcosm of the created universe, then the *maximum contractum* would be the perfect microcosm.

The contracted maximum would be located squarely within the principle of divine theophany:

> But as the equality of being all things, God is the creator of the universe, since the universe has been created according to God. It is to this highest and maximum equality of being all things absolutely that the nature of humanity would be united. As a result, through the assumed humanity, God would, in the humanity, be all things contractedly, just as God is the equality of all things absolutely.[44]

Through the contracted maximum, God's immanence would be given a contracted mode in addition to its absolute mode. Moreover, since it is the first-born, the equality of being all things, that is the creative principle of God and since this principle, or God the Son, exists prior, not temporally, but ontologically,[45] to God-and-man, or the incarnation, there is a creative movement within the Godhead that is completely apart from creation itself. And here Nicholas has switched from the hypothetical to the assertive: this contracted maximum individual is Jesus Christ. Theophany as incarnation means that God is fundamentally creative and, as the fourth chapter will show, conciliatory.

---

44. *DDI* 3.3 h 200, Bond, 176–77.

Deus autem, ut est aequalitas essendi omnia, creator est universi, cum ipsum sit ad ipsum creatum. Aequalitas igitur summa atque maxima essendi omnia absolute illa esset, cui ipsa humanitatis natura uniretur, ut ipse Deus per assumptam humanitatem ita esset omnia contracte in ipsa humanitate, quemadmodum est aequalitas essendi omnia absolute.

45. *DDI* 3.3 h 202, Bond, 177–78.

THE IMPLICATIONS OF THEOPHANY
FOR CREATION

The implications of divine self-manifestation in creation *for creation* are not easily expressed by a single schema. Because of the richness that theophany imparts to the world, it is here that the variety of constructs used in Nicholas's many texts are so valuable. The presence of the Infinite in the finite has great significance for creation in its own right, for creation vis-à-vis God, and, finally, for God in creation. The circle is thus completed as a focus on creation returns us once again to God. As occurs so often in Cusanus's thought, nothing finite can be considered in complete isolation, but all things eventually must refer to the Infinite.

The Affirmation of Individuality

One of the most interesting aspects of theophany in regard to the created order is the way in which it affirms the uniqueness of individual things and mitigates the rigid hierarchy traditionally found in medieval cosmologies. This aspect is expressed by the *complicatio-explicatio* schema found in *De docta ignorantia*. The plurality of things in the universe receives its being from the One, but there is no multiplication of the One.[46] Nevertheless, things are given their variety by virtue of the fact that, while united as one in the Divine Mind, they are understood

46. Plurality does not mean a multiplication of sameness, according to *DDI* 2.3 h 108, Bond, 135–36. "Therefore, just as number arises from our mind by virtue of the fact that we understand as individually many that which is commonly one, so the plurality of things arises from the divine mind, in which the many exist without plurality because they exist in enfolding unity. As things cannot participate equally the equality of being, so God, in eternity, understood one thing in one way and another in another way. Consequently there arose plurality, which in God is unity."

Sicut igitur ex nostra mente, per hoc quod circa unum commune multa singulariter intelligimus, numerus exoritur: ita rerum pluralitas ex divina mente, in qua sunt plura sine pluralitate quia in unitate complicante. Per hoc enim, quod res non possunt ipsam aequalitatem essendi aequaliter participare, Deus in aeternitate unam sic, aliam sic intellexit, ex quo pluralitas, quae in ipso est unitas, exorta est.

in different ways. But, Nicholas reminds us, "God's understanding is God's being."[47] The variety of creation is, thus, directly attributable to the fact that it is enfolded in the very being of God.

God's unfolding of himself in creation does not curse it with monist uniformity, nor replicate God. Though Oneness is the source of plurality, it is not itself multiplied, a fact that surpasses understanding and is the subject of learned ignorance. Neither does it set up a system of decreasing perfection as one moves from complex, rational creatures to simple, nonsentient things. The self-identity bestowed upon created individuals is distinct, both in regard to God and in regard to other members of the created order. The former avoids pantheism and monism, and the latter avoids the kind of hierarchy that is the source of much criticism among feminist philosophers today. An examination of some specific texts concerning his views of individuality is in order.

Nicholas shows a modern appreciation for individual uniqueness of humans very clearly when he says that

> Since no one person is like another in any thing, not in sense or imagination, or intellect, or in an activity, whether writing, painting, or a craft, even if for a thousand years someone zealously attempted to imitate another in anything, one would never arrive at precision, although at times a perceptible difference may go unnoticed.[48]

In Cusanus's thought, there is no hint of the substantial definition of things found in Plato. What makes someone him*self* is not the inherence in him of impersonal form, but a unique personality inclusive of

47. *DDI* 2.3 h 109, Bond, 136.
Si pergis ad numerum similitudinem considerando, quomodo numerus est unius communis per mentem multiplicatio, videtur, quasi Deus, qui est unitas, sit in rebus multiplicatus, postquam intelligere eius est esse.

48. *DDI* 2.1 h 94, Bond, 129.
Quoniam nemo est ut alius in quocumque—neque sensu neque imaginatione neque intellectu neque operatione aut scriptura aut pictura vel arte—etiam si mille annis unus alium imitari studeret in quocumque, numquam tamen praecisionem attingeret, licet differentia sensibilis aliquando non percipiatur.

individual characteristics. The reality of someone, or something, is his contracted individuality because it is in this individuality that God has manifested.[49] Theophany is therefore the crux of Cusanus's theological anthropology.

But it is not just human beings who are granted an individuality apposite to their own selves. Precisely because the Absolute manifests in plurality, each member of the plurality has its own proper character. In a lengthy, but illuminating, passage Cusanus explains:

> Every creature is, as it were, a finite infinity or a created god, so that it exists in the way in which this could best be. It is as if the Creator had spoken: "Let it be made," and because God, who is eternity itself, could not be made, that was made which could be made, which would be as much like God as possible. The inference, therefore, is that every created thing as such is perfect, even if by comparison to others it seems less perfect. For the most merciful God communicates without difference and envy, and what God communicates is received in such a way that contingency does not permit it to be received otherwise or to a higher degree. Therefore, every created being finds its rest in its own perfection, which it freely holds from the divine being. It desires to be no other created being, as if something else were more perfect, but rather, it prefers that which it itself holds, as if a divine gift, from the maximum, and it wishes its own possession to be perfected and preserved incorruptibly.[50]

49. Contraction is the delimitation of a species or universal to an individual thing. It is the concretization of a generality into a particular, which has the effect of locating it in space and time and making it finite.

50. *DDI* 2.2 h 104, Bond, 134.

Quoniam ipsa forma infinita non est nisi finite recepta, ut omnis creatura sit quasi infinitas finita aut Deus creatus, ut sit eo modo, quo hoc melius esse possit; ac si dixisset creator: "Fiat", et quia Deus fieri non potuit, qui est ipsa aeternitas, hoc factum est, quod fieri potuit Deo similius. Ex quo subinfertur omnem creaturam ut talem perfectam, etiam si alterius respectu minus perfecta videatur. Communicat enim piissimus Deus esse omnibus eo modo, quo percipi potest. Cum igitur Deus absque diversitate et invidia communicet et recipiatur, ita quod aliter et alterius contingentia recipi non sinat, quiescit omne esse creatum in sua perfectione, quam habet ab esse divino liberaliter, nullum aliud creatum esse appetens tamquam perfectius, sed ipsum, quod habet a maximo, praediligens quasi quoddam divinum munus, hoc incorruptibiliter perfici et conservari optans.

Every created thing is what it is because it has freely received its being from God, not because God poured only a limited amount of himself into it. Each individual thing is as much like God as possible; nothing can be said to be more perfect than another.

But if Nicholas did not argue for complete uniformity, what is the source of the difference between things? Although, divine theophany is *self*-manifestation, Nicholas did not hold that God could remake himself, due to the fact that "making" implies temporality, or at least finitude. The antithesis of making and eternity meant that God could manifest only in something less than himself, in "contingency." Lest "contingency" and "received" suggest that the created order had some sort of autonomous being, however negative, prior to creation or that the difference between things is a result of such autonomy, Nicholas argues just a few paragraphs later that there are no vacant spaces: "No one, therefore, understands how God, whose unity of being does not exist by the intellect's abstracting from things nor as united to or as immersed in things, is unfolded through the number of things. If you consider things apart from God, they are nothing, as number is nothing apart from unity."[51]

Cf. *De dato Patris luminum* 2 h 102. Trans. Jasper Hopkins, "The Gift of the Father of Lights," in *Nicholas of Cusa's Metaphysic of Contraction* (Minneapolis: Arthur J. Banning Press, 1983), 121: "Yet, provided our construal be sound, we can accept Hermes Trismegistus's statement that God is called by the names of all things and that all things are called by the name of God, so that a man can be called a *humanified god* and so that, as even Plato claimed, this world can be called a *perceptible god*" (italics mine). Hereafter abbreviated *DPL.*

Et quamvis sic deus sit omnia in omnibus, non est tamen humanitas deus, licet posset sano intellectu Hermetis Trismegisti dictum admitti deum omnium rerum nominibus et res omnes dei nomine nominari, sic quod homo nominari posit deu humanatus, et hic mundus deus sensibilis, ut et Plato voluit.

The notion that the created world is the most perfect world possible and that its deficiencies arise from its limitations (for Plato, matter; for Cusanus, possibility of being) is Platonic. Cf. Plato *Timmaeus* 29e ff.; Plotinus *Enneads* II 9, 17; and *DDI* 2.8 h 139, Bond, 149–50.

51. *DDI* 2.3 h 110, Bond, 136–37.

Deus igitur, cuius esse unitatis non est per intellectum a rebus abstrahentem neque rebus unitum aut immersum, quomodo explicetur per numerum rerum, nemo intelligit. Si consideras res sine eo, ita nihil sunt sicut numerus sine unitate.

When God is removed, nothing remains. There are no empty receptacles. God creates in nothing and is the very being of things. The finite plurality's difference stems entirely from the Absolute unity itself. If it did not, it would, indeed, suggest an ordinary Thomistic hierarchical system. If some things simply did not possess as much of God as other things, the latter could be improved and one could move nearer to God as one moved up the ladder of reception of divine being. Contingency is not a limiting thing, but is a criterion of theophany itself, a demand of divine self-revelation in otherness.

This is not to say that Nicholas does not see a ranking of higher and lower beings (angels over humans, for instance) or gradations of nature (such as intellectual vs. sensible).[52] It is merely to place the origin of this hierarchy in God's fecundity and distinguish its legitimate use as a revelation of the latter, from other views rooted in Neoplatonism that would see such a ranking as comparative within the order of creation and would make use of it for an ascent to God. And, while it is true that Nicholas appears to use Aristotelian and Thomistic language when he speaks of a created thing as a *deus occasionatus* (occasioned God) and a woman as a *vir occasionatus* (occasioned man), the context of this language, including his use of the term "image" immediately before this, suggests that he does not mean "inferior" as much as "presence."[53]

52. In *De coniecturis* I, 10, h 44–53 he differentiates between things according to a superiority or inferiority of unity. Note, however, that he is here talking about unity as a function of the numbering process of the human mind, not about Unity or God as Absolute Oneness. For a detailed discussion on this process see Clyde Lee Miller, "Nicholas of Cusa's *On Conjectures (De coniecturis),*" in *Nicholas of Cusa: In Search of God and Wisdom,* ed. Gerald Christianson and Thomas Izbicki (New York: E. J. Brill, 1991), 119–40. Likewise, though his discussion "on the difference of individual things" refers to their various degrees of "nobility," he is comparing things within their species, not to things of other species and then to God. Even his language in chapter 10, "On the Differences of Beings Composed Out of the Soul and the Body," revolves around degrees of sentiency, not around consequent degrees of nearness to God.

53. *DDI* 2.2 h 104, Bond, 134.

Quis ista intelligere posset, quomodo omnia illius unicae infinitae formae sunt imago, diversitatem ex contingenti habendo, quasi creatura sit Deus occasionatus sicut accidens substantia occasionata et mulier vir occasionatus?

Furthermore, God imparts him*self,* not with "envy and difference," but "freely." Precisely because it is his very (indivisible) self that is communicated, it is impossible to attribute to Cusanus the entirety of the traditional notion of the created order in which "order" implies a ranking of ever more perfect things. Though he is viewed as part of the dawn of modernity, Nicholas saw himself as firmly embedded in the medieval tradition. In no way, then, does he do away with hierarchy. He does, however, present it in a new light that softens its harsher implications. Every created thing *qua created thing* is perfect. It is not perfect in its place or perfect in subservience to other more lofty creatures, but simply perfect as a created thing and as an aspect of unfolded Oneness. Clearly, the plurality and variety of the created order are a result of divine fecundity, not of the filling in of the slots of a hierarchy that reflects medieval society.

The Universe: Infinite, Eternal, Unified

A further implication of the theophany of the absolute is its endowing of the universe with an infinity and eternality that reflect the absolute Infinite and Eternal. Long before Copernicus, Nicholas hypothesized about discarding the idea of the fixed and central position of the earth in a finite universe in favor of an unbounded and moving one. "But since the universe embraces all the things that are not God, the universe cannot be negatively infinite, although it is boundless and thus privatively infinite."[54] The universe is not strictly infinite because, of course, it is not God, but it is not bounded by anything other than God and is, therefore, "privatively infinite." Granted, the universe has

---

54. *DDI* 2.1 h 97, Bond, 130–31.

Universum vero cum omnia complectatur, quae Deus non sunt, non potest esse negative infinitum, licet sit sine termino et ita privative infinitum; et hac consideratione nec finitum nec infinitum est.

For a thorough treatment of Nicholas's understanding of the physical makeup of the universe, see Dorothy Koenigsberger, "Universality, the Universe and Nicholas of Cusa's Untastable Foretaste of Wisdom," *European History Quarterly* 17 (Jan. 1987): 3–33.

only a limited infinity and, at least, an eternality in the divine being, but these concepts nevertheless herald the dawn of a new science.

On the controversial point of the universe's eternality, Nicholas identifies God's being with the being of creation and asks, "If, therefore, God is all things and if this means creating, how can one understand the creation not to be eternal, since the being of God is eternal, indeed, is eternity itself?"[55] Nevertheless, in *De dato Patris luminum* he remarks, "I notice how *cautiously* the Apostle (James) states that in the Giver every creature is eternal and is eternity itself. The omnipotence of the Giver coincides with His eternity, for the Omnipotent was always able to give. Therefore, every gift was eternally with the Father from whom it descends when it is received."[56] Cusanus is not negating the doctrine of creation here, but arguing for an "originated eternity" in which creation can be compared to whole numbers. The series of whole numbers begins with oneness but does not end. Hence, the theotic destiny of creation is prefigured in the concept of originated eternity as creation attains infinite perfection and eternal duration in God.

Furthermore, the creation reflects the trinity of God insofar as it is contracted. "The unity of the universe, therefore, is threefold, for it is from the possibility, the necessity of connection, and the connection, which one can designate as potentiality, actuality, and connection."[57] God the Father is possibility, God the Son is actuality, and God the Holy Spirit is the union of the two. This incipient Trinitarian character

55. *DDI* 2.2 h 101, Bond, 132.

Si igitur Deus est omnia et hoc est creare, quomodo intelligi hoc poterit, quod creatura non est aeterna, cum Dei esse sit aeternum, immo ipsa aeternitas?

56. *DPL* 3 h 104. Translation and italics mine.

Amplius adverto, quam caute apostolus exprimit omnem creaturam in datore aeternam atque ipsam aeternitatem esse. Omnipotentia enim datoris coincidit cum ipsa aeternitate, semper enim omnipotens potuit dare. Fuit igitur omne datum in aeternitate apud patrem, a quo dum recipitur, descendit.

57. *DDI* 2.7 h 130, Bond, 146.

Est igitur unitas universi trina, quoniam ex possibilitate, necessitate complexionis et nexu, quae potentia, actus et nexus dici possunt.

to God vis-à-vis creation will be more fully developed in the notion of incarnation and will come to its full flowering in Cusanus's understanding of theosis.

In a return to more philosophical concerns, upon the plurality derived from the theophany depends the oneness of the universe. "Universe indicates universality, that is, a unity of many things."[58] It is because the One reveals itself in multiplicity that the universe is indeed a *uni*-verse. Although the Absolute Quiddity of the sun is identical to the Absolute Quiddity of the moon, because, of course, the Absolute Quiddity of each is God, their contracted quiddities are diverse. The One God who is absolutely identical to each and every thing is contracted actually in difference. The divine manifestation of Unity into difference allows for the created order's existence as a united, singular thing. Thus, to divine Unity can be traced the self-identity of the diversity of things and their incorporation into the universe.

The unfolding of God in creation and the enfolding of creation in God means that there is an interdependence within the created order itself that Cusanus expresses by the phrase "each thing is in each thing."[59]

> The universe, as most perfect, has preceded all things in the order of nature, as it were, so that it could be each thing in each thing. In each creature, the universe is the creature, and each receives all things in such a way that in each thing all are contractedly this thing. . . . If therefore, all things are in all things, all things are seen to precede each thing. All things, therefore, are not many things, since plurality does not precede each thing.[60]

---

58. *DDI* 2.5 h 115, Bond, 139.
Universum dicit universalitatem, hoc est unitatem plurium.
59. *DDI* 2.5 h 117, Bond, 140.
Si acute iam dicta attendis, non erit tibi difficile videre veritatis illius Anaxagorici 'quodlibet esse in quolibet' fundamentum fortassis altius Anaxagora.
60. Ibid. *Universum enim quasi ordine naturae ut perfectissimum praecessit omnia, ut quodlibet in quolibet esse posses. In qualibet enim creatura universum est ipsa creatura, et ita, quodlibet*

Because God unfolds himself immediately in the entire universe, the relationship between each created individual and the universe is a limited parallel of the relationship between each created individual and God. To this extent, it means that particular individuals cannot be considered on their own, even at this "non-theological," or secular, level. Metaphysically, the whole comes before the part, and "all things, therefore, are at rest in each thing, because one degree could not exist without another."[61] Cusanus's sense of a coherent, interdependent whole is not, then, merely a theological concept, something between the orders of the divine and the universe. It is also intra-universal.

The above idea that the One is unfolded immediately in each individual of the multiplicity has other consequences for the created order. Most importantly, it gives it real, but dependent, ontological status, avoiding both Platonic unreality and Neoplatonic emanation. Created things are not shadows of what is truly real, nor is their being mediated through emanations that proceed from the One. Thus, they are not merely attenuated versions of divine realities, but they have status in their own right. A detailed comparison of Neoplatonism with Nicholas of Cusa and a look at its influence on his thought will be undertaken in chapter 4. At this point, it is sufficient merely to outline Cusanus's position. The distinction between it and that of Platonic and Neoplatonic thought is important at this stage primarily because of the reference he makes to the latter and his frequent use of the Neoplatonist terminology. A cursory reading of his work could lead to the mistaken evaluation of him as either a Platonist or a Neoplatonist.

The *complicatio-explicatio* formula itself makes clear that Nicholas has

---

recipit omnia, ut in ipso sint ipsum contracte. Cum quodlibet non posit esse actu omnia, cum sit contractum, contrahit omnia, ut sint ipsum. Si igitur omnia sunt in omnibus, omnia videntur quodlibet praecedere. Non igitur omnia sunt plura, quoniam pluralitas non praecedit quodlibet. Unde omnia sine pluralitate praecesserunt quodlibet ordine naturae. Non sunt igitur plura in quolibet actu, sed omnia sine pluralitate sunt id ipsum.

61. *DDI* 2.5 h 121, Bond, 141–42.

Quiescunt igitur omnia in quolibet, quoniam non posset unus gradus esse sine alto, sicut in membris corporis quodlibet confert cuilibet et omnia in omnibus contentantur.

not merely dressed a Platonic ontology in Christian clothes. While he is adamant that the divine order is that which is most real and definitive for all else, he is just as convinced that the actual world is not a shadowy order cast by Form. The fact that God has unfolded himself in creation and that creation is, originally and now, enfolded in God is sufficient to dispel all doubts as to its ontological status. The very foundational character of God, his primacy in all respects, is exactly that which gives the created order its reality. In various ways, Nicholas repeats the idea that in God, created things are God, and, in creation, God is creation.

Nicholas's elaboration of this concept in the language of actuality and possibility of *De possest* is one of the most clear to be found in any of his works. Cusanus's refusal to ascribe completely to the Platonic scheme is detailed in the answer to the question posed by John: "How can it be the case that all things are enfolded in Actualized-possibility?"[62] (The interlocutors are rehearsing between themselves the explanation of Actualized-possibility that the Cardinal has just given.)

> *Bernard:* Because by "possibility" in an unqualified sense, every possibility is meant. Hence, if I were to understand that every possibility is actual, I would understand that nothing more would be left over. For if anything were left over, surely this thing would be possible to exist.
>
> *John:* You speak correctly. For if the possibility-to-be does not exist, then nothing exists; on the other hand, if the possibility-to-be does exist, then all things are-what-they-are in it, and nothing remains outside it. Therefore, necessarily, all created things have existed in it from eternity. For what-was-created always existed in the possibility-to-be, in whose absence nothing was created. Clearly, Actualized-possibility is all things and includes all things.[63]

62. *DP* h 16, Hopkins, 922.
Quomodo intelligis in possest omnia complicari?
63. Ibid.
Quia posse simpliciter dictum est omne posse. Unde si viderem omne posse esse actu, utique nihil restaret amplius. Si enim aliud aliquid restaret, utique hoc esse posset; ita non restaret, sed prius non fuisset comprehensum.

It is, once again, the theophanic character of God in relation to the created order that gives this order its own, albeit dependent, ontology. The actuality of all things is enfolded in Actualized-possibility since not even the possibility of all things can exist apart from it.

But Cusanus is just as clear that there are no quasi-divine ontological levels mediating between God and the world. Thus, despite his frequently Neoplatonic language, he successfully avoids the ancient Greek version of emanation. This is the point at which the meaning of theophany for the created order vis-à-vis itself and the meaning of theophany for creation vis-à-vis God meet. Here the two are intertwined and cannot be separated. It is only, for instance, because the world is not separated from God by hierarchical principles of emanation that it has a direct relationship with God, and it is precisely this direct relationship that endows it with its own metaphysical reality.

Although, as previously discussed, Cusanus asserts the priority of the universe as a contracted maximum over particular things, he is quick to deny that this kind of priority establishes it as a mediating level between the Absolute Maximum and the world.

> Since we have said that the universe is only the contracted first, and in this respect a maximum, clearly the whole universe came forth into being by a simple emanation of the contracted maximum from the absolute maximum. But all the beings that are parts of the universe, without which the universe, because it is contracted, could not be one, whole, and perfect, came forth into being together with the universe, and not as Avicenna and other philosophers would have it, with intelligence first, the noble soul next, and then nature.[64]

64. *DDI* 2.4 h 116, Bond, 139–40.

Quoniam vero dictum est universum esse principium contractum tantum atque in hoc maximum, pates, quomodo per simplicem emanationem maximi contracti a maximo absoluto totum universum prodiit in esse. Omnia autem entia, quae sunt partes universi, sine quibus universum—cum sit contractum—unum, totum et perfectum esse non posset, simul cum universo in esse prodierunt, et non prius intelligentia, deinde anima nobilis, deinde natura, ut voluit Avicenna et alii philosophi.

The priority of the universe is not a priority of origination, but a priority involving the encompassing nature of divine theophany. It is not the case that a semi-divine and immaterial "Universe" ideally containing all particulars emanated from the Absolute and then that actual particulars emanated from this intermediate principle. Rather, Nicholas's use of the language of priority in reference to the universe as a whole is designed to illustrate the fact that the richness of the universe is a reflection of the infinite richness of God. For Cusanus, by definition, theophany demands a presence in variety and multiplicity. And, he makes it very clear, it is a total presence in each and every member of that multiplicity, not a gradual attenuation of presence through levels of emanation.

The fact that Nicholas is well aware of his distinction from the Neoplatonists (he calls them "Platonists") is illustrated by his detailed outline of their position in chapter 9 of *De docta ignorantia* II. Among other things, he notes the concept of the world-soul, which, as "connecting necessity," precedes and enfolds all things. Thus, the Platonists "did not want forms as they exist in matter to be other than those that exist in the soul of the world; rather, forms exist according to different modes of being; in the soul of the world they exist as true and in themselves, but in matter they exist as resemblances, not as in their purity but in shadow."[65]

Although "many Christians acquiesced in this Platonistic approach,"[66] Cusanus finds contradiction in the very notion of world-soul because it "has its existence only together with possibility, through

---

65. *DDI* 2.9 h 144, Bond, 151.

Et ita modus essendi in anima mundi est, secundum quem dicimus mundum intelligibilem. Modus essendi actu per determinationem possibilitatis actu per explicationem, ut iam dictum est, est modus essendi, secundum quem iste mundus est sensibilis secundum eos. Neque voluerunt illas formas, ut sunt in materia, esse alias ab ipsis, quae sunt in anima mundi, sed tantum secundum modum essendi differenter, ut in anima mundi veraciter et in se, in material verisimiliter, non in sua puritate, sed cum obumbratione.

66. *DDI* 2.9 h 146, Bond, 152.

Multi Christianorum illi viae Platonicae acquieverunt.

which it is contracted."[67] The distinction between forms, which exists in the world-soul, requires both possibility and contraction, but these two terms are antithetical. He concludes this excursion into Neoplatonism by writing:

> The necessity of connection, therefore, is not, as the Platonists determined, a mind inferior to the begetting mind, but it is the Word and Son equal with the Father. . . . God alone is absolute; all else is contracted. Between the absolute and the contracted there is no intermediate, as those imagined who believed the soul of the world to be a mind subsequent to God and prior to the contraction of the world. For God alone is the soul and mind of the world.[68]

Cusanus recognizes the validity of seeking a connection between the Unity and the multiplicity, or, in traditional terms, the One and the many. In his view, however, it is the One itself that provides that connection, not a mediating level that is at once plural and uncontracted. God is Absolute Unity, while at the same time enfolding all multiplicity.

But Cusanus is not just indulging in complicated and contradictory statements. He has a particular metaphysical principle in mind according to which the relationship between Unity and multiplicity can be explained, the principle of participation. Participation will, in fact, prove to be a condition for the possibility of relationship between the transcendent and the created order. An examination of this concept is furthered by moving from the *complicatio-explicatio* schema to one in which its inner structure is more clearly expressed. It is not that the early *com-*

67. *DDI* 2.9 h 148, Bond, 153–54.
Anima igitur mundi non habet esse nisi cum possibilitate, per quam contrahitur, et non est ut mens separata a rebus aut separabilis.
68. *DDI* 2.9 h 149–50, Bond, 154–55.
Unde necessitas complexionis non est, ut posuerunt Platonici, scilicet mens minor gignente, sed est Verbum et Filius aequalis Patri in divinis, et dicitur logos seu ratio, quoniam est ratio omnium. . . . Solus Deus est absolutus, omnia alia contracta. Nec cadit eo modo medium inter absolutum et contractum, ut illi imaginati sunt, qui animam mundi mentem putarunt post Deum et ante contractionem mundi. Solus enim Deus anima et mens mundi est eo modo, quo anima quasi quid absolutum, in quo omnes rerum formae actu sunt, consideratur.

plicatio-explicatio couple lacks or is contrary to participation. (*De docta ig-norantia* does in fact use the term in some passages, and the latter text occasionally refers to the forthcoming *De coniecturis,* where the term is discussed in detail.) It is simply that it is better developed elsewhere.[69]

Participation

Our larger topic, theosis, means a process of divinization that is predicated upon a divine self-manifestation that brings with it an essential participatory relationship between God and creation. Without participation, there would be total difference between the two terms that might allow for sudden transformation or reabsorption into God, but not true theosis. Similarly, a metaphysical scheme in which difference is always absolutely prior to identity would undermine divinization by implying that, at bottom, participation is really only a cover for the above interpretations. Thus, it is necessary that God and creation both retain their individual and separate self-identities and that they possess a closeness that can only be defined as *participation,* a construct involving both identity and difference. Identity is required as the impetus for relationship; total difference would result in isolated terms lacking both the basis and the motivation for interaction. Nevertheless, complete similitude is itself unsatisfactory as it would abolish the plurality of terms that is necessary for relationship, and the structure would lapse into monism. The distance brought by dissimilitude is also essential. The logic of participation is its provision for a true Creator-creation dynamic.

In *De coniecturis,* Cusanus moves back and forth between the participation of things in unity (*unitas* of any kind) or precision and the participation in what he variously calls divine Unity or actuality or Intellect. The former kind of participation is, of course, a model of the latter, and serves to illustrate it. In both cases, not merely similitude, but

---

69. For a discussion of the significance of the role that participation, expressed as *unitas* and *alteritas,* plays in Cusanus's thought see McTighe, "*Contingentia* and *Alteritas* in Cusa's Metaphysics."

otherness *(alteritas)* and imparticipability are central to the performance of participation in Cusanus's thought. In other words, participation is much more complex than the explanation of one thing by its similarity to another, original thing. As the following study will show, participation depends on the dynamism of both the imparticipability of Absolute Unity in itself and its participability in otherness. If the above analysis is correct, this should come as no surprise. An examination of several passages will elucidate his development of the term.

First it is necessary to understand what he means by *unitas,* or "oneness": "Since for oneness to be oneness is for it to exist precisely and as it is, you see adequately and very clearly that oneness is identity that is unimpartible, inexplicable, and—as it is in itself—unattainable. For just as in its own being every existent is present as it is, so in another being it is present in a manner other than it is in itself."[70] Nicholas equates unity with a thing being precisely what it is, a self-identity that is unduplicatable. Certainly the thing itself can be duplicated, but it will not be the self-same thing; rather, it will exist in another. He calls this communication of unity from one thing to another "participation."

But it is a leap from this kind of statement about particular things to the formula that the relationship between Unity and all things is parallel. The move from the participation of unity among things to the participation of divine Unity is made via an epistemological route. That is, if one's intellect is not and cannot be identical to an intelligible thing, the thing cannot be understood precisely as it is. Total comprehension requires total likeness. Since all things exist through the divine intellect, it alone comprehends all things. He writes, "And since the Divine Mind is the most absolute preciseness of all things, it happens that all created minds partake of it differently and in terms of otherness-of-variation. However, in and of itself the ineffable Divine Mind remains unable to

---

70. *DC* 1.11 h 54, Hopkins, 188.

Quoniam unitatem unitatem esse est ipsam praecise atque, uti est, esse, satis tibi atque clarissime constat unitatem esse ipsam identatem incommunicabilem, inexplicabilem atque, uti est, inattingibilem. Sicut enim omne ens in propria sua entitate est, uti est, ita in alia aliter.

be partaken of, since the condition of the participants causes this varied result."[71] And he continues, "For absolute Oneness, which is also Super-ineffable Truth, remains unable to be partaken of as it is in and of itself. Now the nature of intelligence is to understand, i.e., to partake of Truth. But Truth as it is in and of itself cannot be partaken of by intelligence; rather, Truth remains eternal, and altogether absolute, Infinity."[72]

Absolute Unity is at once participable and imparticipable. In itself, it is imparticipable and incommunicable precision. In "the condition of the participants," that is, their otherness, it is participable. Its imparticipability is the guarantor of its participability, anchoring the separateness that establishes a relationship of participation between two different things. Its participability is the out-working of that relationship.

But, as McTighe points out, this does not entail a Proclean Unity with two levels, the highest imparticipable, the lowest participable. *Alteritas* does not mean a principle of otherness, a substrate principle that accounts for multiplicity. Rather, it designates the multiplicity itself, the unfolded *(explicata)* members of a plurality.[73] Otherness simply *is,* as he explains, the participation. It is not as though there is imparticipable unity alongside an other that then performs the action of participating in the unity. Participation *is* the existence of otherness. According to McTighe, participation is horizontal, not vertical. Participation exists horizontally among the members of the multiplicity. It is not vertical, since the antecedent unity is unparticipable.[74] It is important, then,

---

71. *DC* 1.11 h 55, Hopkins, 189.

Et quoniam divina ipsa mens omnium est absolutissima praecisio, ipsam omnes creatae mentes in alteritate variationis differenter participare contingit illa ipsa ineffabili mente imparticipabili perdurante, condicione participantium hoc agente.

72. *DC* 2.6 h 104, Hopkins, 215.

Assis hic totus, Iuliane, nam unitas ipsa absoluta, quae est et veritas superineffabilis, uti est, imparticipabilis remanet. Intelligentiae autem esse est intelligere, hoc est quidem veritatem participare. Non est autem ipsa, uti est, participabilis, sed remanet aeterna ipsa atque absolutissima infinitas, nec est in alteritate nostrae rationis participabilis, cum ratio nostra sit intelligentiae alteritas.

73. McTighe, "*Contingentia* and *Alteritas* in Cusa's Metaphysics.

74. Ibid. McTighe also contrasts Cusanus with Aquinas on this issue. Cf. above, "Theosis and Theophany."

not to think of participation as an action that occurs in spite of its impossibility, but as the existence of Unity in otherness. It is a metaphysical circumstance, not an event that challenges the coherence of absolute Unity.

Out of divine theophany and its corresponding participatory-nonparticipatory relationship between God and world arises an intense sacramentalism expressed in Cusanus's text of a decade later, *De visione Dei*. Despite the span of time between the two works, there are indications in *De coniecturis* that Cusanus was already thinking of divine vision as a metaphor for the orientation of the created order to the divine. In the second part of the early text, for instance, he identifies absolute Unity with absolute Necessity and absolute vision.[75] It is the metaphor of the vision of God that traces the connection between the relationship of the divine to the created order and the divine to itself, that is, the return of God to himself.

The Vision of God

Rather than a programmatic text aimed at disseminating a method for achieving a vision of God, *De visione Dei* is a reflection upon an already existing divine vision of the world and consequent human vision of God. The title itself hints at the closeness between God's vision, where God is subject, and the vision of God, where God is object.[76]

Cusanus introduces his vision metaphor as follows: "In the effort to transport you to divine things by human means, I must use some kind of similitude. But among human works I have found no image more suitable for our purpose than that image of an all-seeing figure. Through the painter's subtle art its face is made to appear as if looking on all around it."[77] The image is an icon, hung on a wall, that gives one the feeling that no matter where one moves in the room the eyes

---

75. *DC* 2.1.

76. Hopkins, *Nicholas of Cusa's Dialectical Mysticism,* 17. "Dei" is both the subjective and objective form of the genitive case of "Deus."

77. *DVD* h 2, Bond, 235.

Si vos humaniter ad divina vehere contendo, similitudine quadam hoc fieri oportet. Sed inter

follow. Seeing all, "the face looks unfailingly on all who walk before it even from opposite directions."[78] Paradoxically, however, Nicholas of Cusa calls this face "the unmovable face" and "the unchangeable gaze."

Nicholas's theological anthropology is largely shaped by the presence of God represented by the metaphor of the divine gaze. The immediate effect of God's omnivoyance is the existential security of the individual, the affirmation of him, no matter what his station in life:

> And while the brother observes how this gaze deserts no one, he will see that it takes diligent care of each, just as if it cared only for the one on whom its gaze seems to rest and for no other, and to such an extent that the one whom it regards cannot conceive that it should care for another. He will also see that it has the same very diligent concern for the least creature as for the greatest, and for the whole universe.[79]

The divine gaze combines impartiality with essential closeness. God's attention is not diverted from one person (or thing) to another, but pursues each one to the utmost degree without being divided or scattered. This means that the individual has an existential connection with God that is ultimate and lasting.

But what about an ontological closeness or identity with God? Does the divine Icon's gaze follow every aspect of the individual's existence because of a prior condition of unity with God? Indeed, the one who is the "absolute being of all" is the foundation of all things.[80] Addressing God, Cusanus writes, "Your being, Lord, does not desert my

----

humana opera non repperi imaginem omnia videntis propositio nostro convenientiorem, ita quod facies subtili arte pictoria ita se habeat quasi cuncta circumspiciat.

78. *DVD* h 3, Bond, 236.

Et ita revelatione relatoris perveniet ut sciat faciem illam omnes, etiam contrariis motibus, incendentes non deserere.

79. *DVD* h 4, Bond, 236–37.

Et dum attenderit quomodo visus ille nullum deserit, videt quod ita diligenter curam agit cuiuslibet, quasi de solo eo, qui experitur se videri, et nullo alio curet, adeo quod etiam concipi nequeat per unum, quem respicit, quod curam alterius agat. Videbit etiam quod ita habet diligentissimam curam minimae creaturae quasi maximae et totius universi.

80. *DVD* IV h 9, Bond, 239.

Ita enim tu, absolutum esse omnium, ades cunctis, quasi non sit tibi cura de quocumque alio.

being, for I exist only insomuch as you are with me. And since your seeing is your being, therefore, because you regard me, I am, and if you remove your face from me, I will cease to be."[81] The gaze of the icon/ God is not merely the source of the experience of union with God, but is also the source of that union itself and the source of the existence of all things included in that union. Again, there is a shifting of perspective, this time from creation vis-à-vis God to creation in reference to itself. God's seeing is equated with his being and is linked to the being of all other things. The metaphor is inverted as Cusanus explains that the icon (God) is the exemplar of all observing faces so that each one recognizes its own truth when looking at it.

An image hung on a wall can immediately show itself. It can refer to other things (i.e., what it is an image of) only secondarily. God, however, presents himself and all things to the one who sees him. Cusanus addresses God with this in mind:

> O God, You have led me to that place in which I see your absolute face to be the natural face of all nature, the face which is the absolute entity of all being, the art and the knowledge of all that can be known. . . . And how will you give yourself to me if you do not at the same time give me heaven and earth and all that are in them? And, even more, how will you give me yourself if you do not also give me myself?[82]

God so imparts himself to all things, including the self, that knowledge of him brings knowledge of all these things. Theophany gives the universe back to itself, allows it a glimpse of itself as well as of God. Indeed, the immanence of God provides for an innate sacramentalism in

---

81. *DVD* IV h 11, Bond, 239–40.

Esse tuum domine, non derelinquit esse meum. Intantum enim sum, inquantum tu mecum es. Et cum videre tuum sit esse tuum ideo ego sum quia tu me respicis. Et cum videre tuum sit esse tuum, ideo ego sum quia tu me respicis. Et si a me vultum tuum subtrasxeris.

82. *DVD* VII h 24–25, Bond, 246.

O deus, quorsum me perduxxistik, ut videam faciem tuam absolutam esse artem et scientiam omnis scibilis. . . . Et quomodo dabis tu te mihi, si non pariter dederis mihi caelum et terram et omnia quae in eis sunt? Immo quomodo dabis tu te mihi, si etiam me ipsum non dederis mihi?

which the divine presence both indicates and, as will later be shown, brings about the theosis of the created order.

The intimacy of theophany and theosis in this respect is indicated by Werner Beierwaltes, who writes,

> Analogous to thought and self-recognition, in the sight of God, the countenance of the human being is not rendered contourless or denied; its individuality is not extinguished. Instead, it is in God as *God himself,* just as the intellect . . . is only then able to then recognize itself. . . . The *visio facialis* is thereby to be understood as *filiatio* or *theosis,* in which human reason grasps itself and everything else with a simple glance in the sight of God.[83]

Rather than being extinguished or made featureless by the vision of God, the self is affirmed in itself as God's vision becomes its vision. Likewise, all of the created order is encompassed by the simplicity of the divine vision. In the mystical vision, God's vision and one's own vision coalesce. Since God's "sight *is* an eye, i.e., a living mirror, it sees all things in itself. Even more, since it is the cause of all that can be seen, it embraces and sees all things in the cause and reason of all, that is, in itself."[84]

The observer of the icon sees, first of all, his own self, as he gazes on the icon. But the dialectic does not lapse into a pure projection of subjectivity because he realizes that it is the Observer (my term) who

---

83. Werner Beierwaltes, *Visio Facialis: Sehen in Angesicht,* Bayerische Akademie der Wissenschaften Philosophische-Historische Klasse Sitzungsberichte 1988, Heft 1 (Munchen: Verlag der Bayerischen Akademie der Wissenschaften, 1988), 27. Translation mine. "So ist—analog zum Denken und zur Selbsterkenntnis des Intellekts—das Angesicht des Menschen im Sehen Gottes nicht negierend konturlos gemacht, nicht als individuelles ausgeloescht, sondern es ist *in* Gott als *es selbst Gott,* so wie der Intellekt (die Vernunft als 'intellectualis viva dei similitudo') sich nur dann *selbst* zu erkennen imstande ist . . . 'visio facialis' ist damit als 'filiatio' oder 'theosis' zu begreifen, die mit *einem* 'einfachen Blick' im Sehen Gottes sich selbst und Alles Andere durch diesen selbst erfasst."

84. *DVD* VIII h 30, Bond, 249.

Sed visus tuus, cum sit oculus seu speculum vivum, in se omnia videt. Immo quia causa omnium visibilium, hinc omnia in causa et ratione omnium, hoc est in se ipso, complectitur et videt.

constitutes his being and that of all other things. Thus, the observer's vision of the icon becomes the Observer's vision of the observer, and, finally, the Observer's vision of himself. The active human performance of seeing becomes the passive role of being mirrored. Addressing God, he writes,

> Thus, what you seem to receive from one who looks on you is your gift, as if you were the living mirror of eternity, which is the form of forms. While anyone looks into this mirror, one sees one's own form in the form of forms, which is the mirror. And one judges the form which one sees in the mirror to be the image of one's own form since this is the case with a polished material mirror. Yet the contrary is true. For that which one sees in this mirror of eternity is not an image but what one sees is the truth of which one who sees is an image.[85]

The Image and the image have been inverted; it is the created order that is the ontological reflection of the divine. This point is all the more powerful as it is expressed in visual metaphors that ordinarily imply that the one who sees is the subject. Nicholas's careful dissection of the mystical vision turns what is typically the epistemological subject, the one who sees, into the metaphysical object. Here the implications of theophany for God, his absolute primacy and total immanence, meet those of theophany for creation.

It is, in fact, in Nicholas's epistemology that the counterpart of divine immanence will emerge. In the doctrine of negative theology and the concepts of *ratio* (reason) and *intellectus* (intellect) the crucial view of God and the universe as absolutely separate and different will be developed. This aspect of Cusanus's thought is essential to his total vision of the Creator-creation relationship; it will be examined next.

85. *DVD* XV h 63, Bond, 263–64.

Et ita id quod videris ab intuente recipere, hoc donas, quasi sis speculum aeternitatis vivum, quod est forma formarum. In quod speculum dum quis respicit, videt formam suam in forma formarum, quae est speculum. Et iudicat formam quam videt in speculo illo esse figuram formae suae, quia sic est in speculo materiali polito—licet contrarium illius sit verum, quia id quod videt in illo aeternitatis speculo non est figura sed veritas, cuius ipse videns est figura.

3

TRANSCENDENCE AS THE DISTANCE BETWEEN KNOWER AND KNOWN

THE EPISTEMOLOGY OF CUSANUS

Transcendence and Immanence

In Cusanus's thought, the paradoxical counterpart of the divine presence in the created order that results from theophany is divine transcendence. The mystical union afforded by the intimacy of God's manifestation is balanced by God's distance. Cusanus's epistemology is thus infused with a sense of divine mystery and is evidence that he was not a monist. This chapter will treat the mystery of God, the Trinity, and creation.

Beginning with Aristotle and Theophrastus and developed by Plotinus and later Neoplatonists, true knowledge of something, especially of immaterial things, was not mere sensation but union with it. The modern assumption that knowledge of one thing by another requires a distance between the two, a distance allowing for observation and measurement, was unheard of. To know something was to encompass it completely, not to observe it dispassionately.

Cusanus, too, adhered to the notion that "unless the intellect becomes like the putatively intelligible object, it does not understand it."[1] "For assuredly, every thing of which there is a concept is encompassed by that concept."[2] Because God is the "absolute Concept" he enfolds everything conceivable and is himself held by no concept. The Concept or Word is therefore *inconceivable*, and all names for conceivable things must be removed from it. Given this tradition of knowing something as becoming one with it, divine transcendence would, one would think, endanger union with God by removing it as a cognitive possibility. That is, this pole of Nicholas's metaphysical scheme would seem to undermine the primary path to theosis, the path of the mind.

It would thus appear that his metaphysics destroys his epistemology (vis-à-vis God) and, thus, for all practical purposes, also destroys itself. What use would an ontological union with God be if God could not be thought of, contemplated, spoken to, or made relevant to the life of the mind? An utterly unconscious union would be no union at all. The dilemma of negative theology is that it negates the basis for theology itself, God's expressiveness. In an effort to pay homage to God's transcendence, he is venerated out of existence. Therefore, the main issue in the discussion of transcendence is its implications for human relationship with God, and especially relationship as worked out through the processes of human thought. In this context, then, it is knowledge, not as theoretical definition, but as unitive contemplation, that is important. For Nicholas of Cusa and many of his Neoplatonic predecessors, defining God was more than a philosophical exercise. It was a religious act that itself was the axis of unitive relation.

---

1. *DP* 18, Hopkins, 923.

Nisi enim intellectus se intelligibili assimilet, non intelligit, cum intelligere sit assimilare et intelligibilia se ipso seu intellectualiter mensurare.

2. *DP* 40, Hopkins, 934.

Omne enim cuius conceptus est aliquis, utique in conceptu clauditur.

If transcendence, the polar opposite of theophanic immanence, is to be understood, it must be in the dual context of on the one hand divine Supereminence and paradox, and on the other, human *ratio* and intellect. As in the previous chapter, this chapter will focus first on God (his transcendence and unapproachability) and then with increasing specificity on the created order. And also similar to the previous chapter, this one will end with a return to God. An examination of the above concepts will reveal that Nicholas's understanding of the mystical union that culminates in theosis is not obviated by his insistence on the absolute distance of God. Building on the Dionysian tradition of negative theology, he is able to provide for a profound union that is situated in the intellect rather than in human reason. The epistemological consequences of transcendence do not undermine theophany or its goal, theosis, but serve to underscore them in a new way. They also help Nicholas maintain his orthodoxy by providing a bulwark against those who, focusing on his emphasis on union, have accused him of monism. It is precisely the manifestation of the transcendent God in the intellect that allows for a unique divinization of humanity and its centrality in the theotic movement of the entire universe.

Knowledge of God has been attempted, in the history of Christian thought, through the exercise of naming him. The conjunction of positive predicates with the subject *God*—for example, "God is being"—originates in the ontological intimacy stemming from divine self-manifestation. The case for such intimacy in the thought of Nicholas of Cusa is strong, as became clear in the first chapter of this book. The absolute is describable because it is the absolute that determines and constitutes the particular. Names referring to the multiplicity can, to a certain extent, be transposed to the One. The problems with such transposition, however, also are evident: the danger of pantheism and the limitations of human definition. Too great an identification of God with the world results in the idea that the world simply *is* God, that they are one without distinction. And, indeed, Nicholas of Cusa has been accused by thinkers such as Dermot Moran of holding pantheistic and monist views.[3]

A second problem with cataphatic theology is that of the opposition between divine infinity and human limitation, including limitation of the human mind. More than hubris, it borders on sacrilege to suggest that the Infinite can be defined by the finite. Moreover, even if the theologian is aware of this problem and is content with simply describing God as God exists *for human beings,* there is an exclusion of God's existence *in Himself* that is unsatisfactory. The problem of the disparity between God-in-Himself and God-for-me is thus highlighted by the use of cataphatic theology. It seems that, whether or not it can be accurately spoken about, God's existence independent of creation ought at least to be considered. It is these difficulties that Nicholas and others such as Pseudo-Dionysius and the Greek fathers sought to avoid through the use of negative theology.

It is the problem of juxtaposition, of conceptually placing the divine and created orders together in any way, that evokes negative theology. Thinkers in the Neoplatonic tradition sought to establish the abrupt ontological difference they saw as necessary for anchoring first creation, and then its result, the intense closeness of the mystical union. That is, the act of creation requires an Actor, a Creator, who is absolutely different from the created order. A God who was of the same metaphysical "stuff" as the creation, albeit greater or the greatest, would not answer the criterion of being the Ultimate. One would always be driven to ask the further question, "Who created God?" It is not, then, merely a question of veneration that drives the postulate of total disjunction between the two orders, but a question of theological necessity. Nicholas of Cusa avoided the problem of juxtaposition by not using analogy as a primary theological construct.[4] Instead of operating

<hr>

3. Dermot Moran, *The Philosophy of John Scotus Eriugena: A Study of Idealism in the Middle Ages* (New York: Cambridge, 1989).

4. He does, however, freely use metaphors and likenesses, but these are predicated

primarily in the realm of cataphatic theology, as did the Scholastics, he took refuge in apophatic theology in order to express the incomprehensible transcendence of the divine.

No better articulation of Nicholas's thoroughgoing apophaticism exists than the following:

> Hence wisdom[5] . . . is known in no other way than through the awareness that it is higher than all knowledge and is unknowable and inexpressible by any speech, incomprehensible by any intellect, unmeasurable by any measure, unlimitable by any limit, unboundable by any bounds, disproportionable in terms of any proportion, incomparable in terms of any comparison, unbefigurable by any befiguring, unformable by any forming, immovable by any movement, unimaginable by any imagining, unsensible by any sensing, unattractible by any attracting, untasteable by any tasting, inaudible by any hearing, unseeable by any seeing, inapprehensible by any apprehending, unaffirmable by any affirming, undeniable by any negating, undoubtable by any doubting, inopinionable by any opining. And because Wisdom is not expressible by any expression, the intended object of these expressions cannot be thought, for Wisdom is unthinkable by any thought—Wisdom, through which and in which and from which are all things.[6]

Clearly, Cusanus is adamant about the impossibility of positive language about God, in spite of the immanence established by theophany. No human means of sensation or comprehension can approach God.

---

upon an original *disjunction* between Creator and creature. He refers to them as "remote" or distant parallels, and they are not used with the same confidence, so to speak, as analogical ascent language traditionally is. His early sermons are also cataphatic. For more on this, see "The Epistemology of Cusanus" in this chapter, on the *ratio.*

5. "From *Ratio* to Intellect" in this chapter shows that Wisdom is identical to God.

6. Nicholas of Cusa, *Idiota de sapientia* I, 10, trans. Jasper Hopkins, "The Layman on Wisdom," *Nicholas of Cusa on Wisdom and Knowledge* (Minneapolis: Arthur J. Banning Press, 1996), 99.

Unde sapientia . . . non aliter scitur quaam quod ipsa est omni scientia altior et inscibilis et omni loquela ineffabilis et omni intellectu inintelligibilis et omni mensura immensurabilis et omni fine infinibilis et omni termino interminabilis, et omni proportione improportionabilis et omni comparatione incomparabilis et omni figuratione infigurabilis et omni formatione informabilis et in

The Mystery of Creation

Another point to note is the impact of the intersection of inexpressible transcendence and divine manifestation upon the knowability of creation. The result of the unknowable God's self-manifestation in the created order means that learned ignorance does not have as its object God alone. Ineffability extends from God in Trinity, to the Incarnation, to the created universe. This deepening sense of the divine mystery depends on Nicholas's understanding of the being of creation as the being of God and as destined for theosis. As he titles the second chapter of *DDI* III, "That the Being of a Creature Comes from the Being of the First in a Way That Cannot Be Understood."[7] The counterpart of the *visio facialis,* the glance into the omnivoyant face in which one sees one's own self, in which dependent being knows itself, is the nonintelligibility of the hidden God. Creation's origin and goal in the mystery of God means that unless it knows God it cannot know itself, but that this too is bathed in learned ignorance. The more the implications of God's mystical causality, of the mystery of God himself, are drawn out, the wider becomes the reach of apophatic theology.

The dependence of creation on God, a dependence in which creation is informed by the *immanent* God, means that some of the same difficulties we have in naming God are present in attempts to name the universe. He explains:

> Derived being, therefore, is not understandable, since the being from
> which it exists is not understandable, just as the incidental being of an

---

omni motione immobilis et in omni imaginatione inimaginabilis et in omni sensatione insensibilis et in omni attractione inattractabilis et in omni gustu ingustabilis et in omni auditu inaudibilis et in omni visu invisibilis et in omni apprehensione inapprehensibilis et in omni affirmatione inaffirmabilis et in omni negatione innegabilis et in omni dubitatione indubitabilis et in omni opinione inopinabilis. Et quia in omni eloquio est inexpressibilis, harum locutionum non potest finis cogitari, cum in omni cogitatione sit incogitabilis, per quam, in qua, et ex qua omnia.

7. *DDI* 2.2 h 98, Bond, 131.

Quod esse creaturae sit inintelligibiliter ab esse primi.

accident is not understandable if the substance to which it is incidental is not understood. The creation as creation, therefore, cannot be called "one," since it descends from unity; nor "many," since it takes its being from the One, nor both "one and many" conjointly.[8]

Here the usual construct that God is mysterious because he is the One, the Source, or Cause, while creation is knowable, is reversed. Creation partakes in the divine ineffability. Its descent from Oneness is not a descent into comprehensibility but into an extension of Infinite mystery.

Nicholas's interpretation of knowledge as comparison found early in the text on learned ignorance already hints at the mystery of even nonspiritual things. Because comparison indicates agreement as well as otherness, it necessarily involves number. He underscores the inseparability of number and knowledge by his reference to the Pythagorean position that everything is composed and known through number. But, he says, "the precise combinations in corporeal things and the congruent application of known to unknown so far exceed human reason" that even Socrates knew only that he did not know.[9] Nicholas includes Solomon and Aristotle in a list of those who perceived the difficulty of gaining knowledge of things and even their utter inexplicability. Thus, for Nicholas, the mystery of the universe is not completely a result of its divine referentiality. Lurking in comparative knowledge is ignorance of its object.

Cusanus asserts that because of its relationship to God, it is difficult even to locate the created order in terms of being. The universe is not

---

8. *DDI* 2.2 h 100, Bond, 132.

Non est igitur ab esse intelligibile, postquam esse, a quo, non est intelligibile, sicut nec adesse accidentis est intelligibile, si substantia, cui adest, non intelligitur. Et igitur non potest creatura ut creatura dici una, quia descendit ab unitate; neque plures, quia eius esse est ab uno; neque ambo copulative.

9. *DDI* 1.1 h 4, Bond, 88–89.

Praecisio vero combinationum in rebus corporalibus ac adaptatio congrua noti ad ignotum humanam rationem supergreditur, adeo ut Socrati visum sit se nihil scire, nisi quod ignoraret, sapientissimo Salomone asserente cunctas res difficiles et sermone inexplicabiles; et alius quidam divini spiritus vir ait absconditam esse sapientiam et locum intelligentiae ab oculis omnium viventium.

God, who is being, nor is it nothing, but somewhere in between. "It seems, therefore, neither to be, since it descends from being, nor not to be, since it is before nothing, nor a composite of both."[10] Human reason simply cannot pass beyond the contradictories inherent in the created order.

The form of divine mystery known as Supereminence also extends to the things of the created order insofar as they are in God. Cusanus develops this idea in *De possest.* The notion of actualized-possibility can, through symbolism, lead one to the Almighty. There one can behold "all the things which you understand to be able to be, and to be able to be made—behold them above every name by which what-is-able-to-be is nameable. Indeed, you behold them above being and not-being."[11] Enfolded in the Infinite Power, the created order is beyond every name and enters into the Supereminent nature of God.

It is important to note, however, that Nicholas's assertion of the mystery of the universe is not a call to a retreat from contemplation of it. He is in no way advocating a suspicion of empirical knowledge or suggesting a purely Platonist approach. Indeed, his text is suffused with an admiration of the world in all of its particularity. Here is one place where he hovers on the divide between traditional and modern thought. His position on the mystery of the universe is born of an ancient theological concern for the transcendence of God. Yet his wonder at the complexity and beauty of the world is thoroughly modern.

Neither is Cusanus's use of the *via negativa* an indication that he was unaware of the role of analogy and comparison in the cognitive process. In fact, he begins *De docta ignorantia* by remarking that "all who in-

---

10. *DDI* 2.2 h 100, Bond, 132.

Videtur igitur neque esse, per hoc quod descendit de esse; neque non esse, quia est ante nihil; neque compositum ex illis.

11. *DP* h 25, Hopkins, 927.

Quia possest absolute consideratum sine applicatione ad aliquod nominatum te aliqualiter ducit aenigmatice ad omnipotentem, ut ibi videas omne quod esse ac fieri posse intelligis supra omne nomen quo id quod potest esse est nominabile—immo supra ipsum esse et non-esse omni modo quo illa intelligi possunt.

vestigate judge the uncertain proportionally by comparing it to what is presupposed as certain."[12] He also understands the internal structure of using the similarity of things to come to knowledge. "[P]roportion expresses agreement in some one point and also expresses otherness."[13] All ordinary knowledge, according to Cusanus, is reached by moving from what one already knows to what is yet unknown but similar in some respects and different in others. Understanding is not reached in a void without reference points but occurs by analogy with one's previously established cognitive location.

However, the citizen of *Idiota de sapientia* strikes a Socratic pose as he argues for the necessity of humility in the pursuit of wisdom. The confidence instilled in us by our knowledge of this world must not blind us to our ignorance about God. Analogy gives us only more knowledge about ourselves, not fresh knowledge about God. Thus, the way of comparative knowledge is soundly rejected by Cusanus in the case of knowledge of God. The Infinite "escapes comparative relation" because there is simply no comparison that can be made between what is finite and what is infinite. Cusanus gives the name "maximum" to "that beyond which there can be nothing greater,"[14] another name for which is the "absolute one."[15] As usual, he does not name God arbitrarily but has a distinct purpose in mind.

12. *DDI* 1.1 h 2, Bond, 87–88.

Omnes autem investigantes in comparatione praesuppositi certi proportionabiliter incertum iudicant; comparativa igitur est omnis inquisitio, medio proportionis utens.

13. *DDI* 1.1 h 3, Bond, 88.

Proportio vero cum convenientiam in aliquo uno simul et alteritatem dicat, absque numero intelligi nequit.

14. *DDI* 1.2 h 5, Bond, 89.

Maximum autem hoc dico, quo nihil maius esse potest.

For quotations I have used the more recent translations by H. Lawrence Bond. While he does not capitalize terms that refer to God, such as "maximum," or to Christ, such as "equality of all being," the earlier translations by Jasper Hopkins do. In my own writing, I have retained the capitalization of terms that clearly refer to the divine in an effort to distinguish between the various levels of meaning in Cusan terminology.

15. The notion that quantitative terms such as "great" or "Maximum" and qualitative terms such as "good" can be applied to God while not implying that there actually is a quantity or a quality to him is also found in Augustine's *De Trinitate*.

The Absolute Maximum

Nicholas articulates his rejection of the possibility of analogical language about God in terms of the interdependent relationship of divine transcendence and immanence. That which is absolutely one, Maximality, is "fullness" insofar as it comprehends everything. Analogy, however, requires the opposition of one thing to another, the juxtaposition of the two, in order for the determination of greater or lesser to be made. But everything of which it can be said that it is lesser or greater is a finite thing.

God as Absolute Maximum is infinite, and comparison between him and a finite thing is impossible given the coinciding of the Maximum with all things. Because "such unity is completely free from all relation and contraction, it is clear that because it is absolute maximumness, nothing is opposed to it."[16] This, then, is his justification for the inability to approach God through the ordinary mental process of analogy or the comparison of the unknown with the known. According to Cusanus, "Nor can the most penetrating intellect conceive that which is infinite, boundless, and one, and which is both all things and that in which there is no diversity of opposition."[17]

For the human mind, transcendence results in the mystery of God and the inability to speak of him in an ordinary manner. Language that measures the infinite by the finite can never lead us to God. He explains, "Because it is evident that there is no proportion between the infinite and the finite, it is very clear that where we encounter a greater and a lesser, we do not reach the simply maximum. . . . A finite intel-

---

16. *DDI* 1.2 h 5, Bond, 89.

Coincidit itaque maximitati unitas, quae est et entitas; quod si ipsa talis unitas ab omni respectu jhet contractione universaliter est absoluta, nihil sibi opponi manifestum est, cum sit maximitas absoluta.

17. *DP* h 17; my translation.

Nec altissimus intellectus concipere potest infinitum interminum et unum quod omnia atque ipsum, ubi non est oppositionis diversitas.

lect, therefore, cannot precisely attain the truth of things by means of a likeness."[18] Truth can never be measured by something that is not itself truth because the truth of the Maximum is infinite and indivisible. The infinity of the Maximum can always be approached more nearly; it is always beyond one's grasp and thus is incomprehensible.

Nicholas's apophatic approach can be further elucidated by a look at the similar way that the alternative concept of *possest* (Actualized-possibility) functions in this context. Actualized-possibility, a name for God, is that which *is* actually all that it is possible to be. The difficulty in naming Actualized-possibility some*thing* lies in the fact that all things, aside from Actualized-possibility itself, have the potential to be something that they are not. For instance, one cannot call *possest* "quantity" because quantity "is able to be greater than it is or something other than it is."[19] Actualized-possibility, however, cannot be increased in magnitude or decreased in magnitude, "for possibility itself is actually the completest possibility."[20]

It is important to note that Nicholas's negative theology is rooted in more than the traditional notion of an infinite God. It is not merely transcendence, but an inclusive transcendence that grounds his negative theology. It is, therefore, his doctrine of God that transforms what would otherwise be ignorance *(ignorantia)* into *learned* ignorance *(docta ignorantia)*. Only through an understanding of the limits of our understanding, only in learning our ignorance, can we come to any knowl-

18. *DDI* 1.3 h 9–10, Bond, 90–91.

Quoniam ex se manifestum est infiniti ad finitum proportionem non esse, est et ex hoc clarissimum, quod, ubi est reperire excedens et excessum, non deveniri ad maximum simpliciter, cum excedentia et excessa finita sint . . . Dato igitur quocumque, quod non sit ipsum maximum simpliciter, dabile maius esse manifestum est . . . Non potest igitur finitus intellectus rerum veritatem per similitudinem praecise attingere.

19. *DP* h 30. Hopkins, 929–30.

Ideo quantitas non est. Quantits enim cum posit esse id quod non est, non est possest. Putaq potest esse maior quam est aut aliud quam est; sed non sic possest, cui nec maioritas quae esse potest aut quidquam quod esse potest deest. Ipsum enim posse actu perfectissimum.

20. Ibid.

edge of God. This is done not through a simple denial of human intellectual capacities, but through further development of his doctrine of God and an exploration of the consequent ways in which God confounds human understanding.

The incomprehensibility of God originates in the notion of God's infinity and his manifestation in the (privatively) infinite universe. God transcends the universe, but the universe, as theophany, is a limited infinity. Infinity is not, therefore, a flat concept, but is given texture by its explication as the Maximum-minimum couple. We have seen above in Cusanus's articulation of the Absolute Maximum its comprehensive character. He agrees with Hermes Trismegistus that if God is to be named, either he would have to be called by every name or else all things would have to be called by God's name.[21] But the counterpart of Maximum, the Minimum, is necessary to establish the total mystery of God. Nicholas explains the concept of the Minimum in the following passage:

> Since the absolutely maximum is all that can be, it is completely actual. And just as there cannot be a greater, so for the same reason there cannot be a lesser, since it is all that can be. But the minimum is that than which there cannot be a lesser. Because the maximum is also of this sort, it is obvious that the minimum coincides with the maximum.[22]

Since the Maximum is all that there can be, nothing surpasses it and it is called "Maximum." But if it does envelop all possibility of being within itself, nothing can be less than it either and it therefore also earns the appellation "Minimum." The two terms are alternate designations for the Infinite; they coincide.

---

21. *DDI* 1.24 h 75, Bond, 121.
22. *DDI* 1.4 h 11, Bond, 91–92.

Excedit igitur maxima aequalitas, quae a nullo est alia aut diversa, omnem intellectum; quare maximum absolute cum sit omne id, quod esse potest, est penitus in actu; et sicut non potest esse maius, eadem ratione nec minus, cum sit omne id, quod esse potest. Minimum autem est, quo minus esse non potest. Et quoniam maximum est huiusmodi, manifestum est minimum maximo coincidere.

Cusanus articulates the internal logic of this coincidence when he points out that it rules out an opposition between Maximum and Minimum. Given the inclusivity of the Maximum, it is inconceivable that anything should oppose it, and no-*thing* does, as we have argued above. But it is not even permissible that the inverse concept, the Minimum, should rival it; this too must be accounted for in some way that rules out a fixed polarity that would threaten the Infinite with either limitation or dualism. The construct of the coincidence of opposites is the solution, a solution reached through an unpacking of what it means for the Maximum to be altogether actual.

The coincidence of opposites is integral to the notion of learned ignorance. It is not just that God is too much for our understanding (implicitly leaving open the possibility that some day we might know *enough* to reach him), but that he totally confounds us by his very nature. It is the way in which God has dis-closed himself that has closed us to precise knowledge of him. "Therefore, because the absolutely maximum is absolutely and actually all that can be, and it is without opposition to such an extent that the minimum coincides with the maximum, it is above all affirmation and all negation. It both is and is not all that is conceived to be, and it both is and is not, all that is conceived not to be."[23] The coincidence of opposites is thus the vehicle of Cusanus's move from a simple negative theology that denies the possibility of language based on similitude to a theology of first, paradox, and later, supereminence.

Cusanus seems to recognize not only the danger that a strictly apophatic approach will erase all relationship with God, but also the related issue of the comparative nature of this kind of theology. Negative theology does not escape an analogical approach, although it is an anal-

---

23. *DDI* 1.4 h 12, Bond, 92.

Quia igitur maximum absolute est omnia absolute actu, quae esse possunt, taliter absque quacumque oppositione, ut in maximo minimum coincidat, tunc super omnem affirmationem est pariter et negationem. Et omne id, quod concipitur esse, non magis est quam non est; et omne id, quod concipitur non esse, non magis non est quam est.

ogy that denies commonality between the two terms. The *via negativa* is trapped in a self-referentiality just as much as analogy is. Its consequent inability to tell us anything about God, but ability only to tell us about ourselves is indicated by Cusanus's explanation of this approach as the pathway of "removing boundaries," a pathway *"within yourself."*[24] In negative theology, one conceives of God, implicitly compares him with oneself and one's world, and then removes predicates such as corporeality, sensation, the imagination—in short, all points of comparison between God and self. Nicholas, however, wants to avoid the absolute silence that a strictly negative theology would entail. The fact that one need not stop with the rejection of all predicates, but can move to the coincidence of all predicates and their denials, as well as beyond this coincidence, means that ignorance about God is not bare silence but is *learned*.

Paradox and Metaphor

The coincidence of the opposites of Maximum and Minimum is just one example of his pervasive paradoxical language. Paradoxes and metaphors nearly breaking under the weight of their contradictory components are at the heart of Nicholas's theology because they avoid the pitfalls of purely apophatic language. This type of language asserts that if God is good (or has any other quality), since goodness is equivocal in relation to God and man, it cannot be predicated of God in a way that is comprehensible by man or meaningful to him. This approach has the advantage of respecting God's infinite power as well as being theologically beautiful. It is, however, ultimately unsatisfactory given certain Christian tenets. That is, if one holds that God *manifests* and that he created human beings for relationship, a relationship for which he was in-

---

24. Nicholas of Cusa, *De quaerendo Deum* V h 49, trans. H. Lawrence Bond, "On Seeking God," *Nicholas of Cusa: Selected Spiritual Writings* (New York: Paulist Press, 1997), 30–231.

Est denique adhuc via intra te quaerendi deum, quae est ablationis terminatorum.

carnated, it is unlikely that he would leave them in the abyss of ignorance. And if the world is God's creation, it must certainly say something about its Creator that has positive content. In addition to this problem of the endangering of the logic of theophany and the possibility for relationship with God, it can be criticized as itself a form of analogy. Insofar as it too uses the language of similitude and the denial of the same, it can never tell us anything about God, but only about ourselves. On the other hand, the language of coincidence opens up new possibilities for religious language. By the very fact that it tells us about the limits of our own reason, it speaks of God himself, of his absoluteness and our relationship to him.

Nicholas refuses to be caught in one-dimensional, truth-falsehood terminology, focusing instead on the fullness of God. Sometimes Cusanus's paradoxical language is clothed in symbols such as the icon and its beholders. These symbols are more than mere analogies because they are so altered that their very definitions are undermined. For instance, an image is hung on a wall and surrounded by observers. The power of seeing that image and the meaning of that image reside with the observers, not with the image. The image cannot make itself seen, and its meaning and existence are dependent on the observers. It is an *image,* not an exemplar. Yet, Cusanus inverts all of these relationships in his metaphor, making the icon the source of knowledge and being and the observers the true images. It is paradoxical that God's eyes follow and yet do not follow, that the beholder sees himself and yet not himself, that God is object and yet supremely subject, that God is immanent and yet transcendent, and so on.

Nicholas introduces visual metaphors in an effort to break the impasse of rational propositional discourse about God. Propositional language cannot escape its anthropocentric and limited perspective, but the metaphor that opens up a paradox can. The metaphor is still a human construction, but it is not one-dimensional. Whether Cusanus is using the metaphor of the icon or other contradictory images, he uses both implied and explicitly paradoxical language to speak of God. He finds the metaphor useful as a starting point, yet unable to completely hold the fullness of his philosophical and theological concepts of God.

Still using the language of "sight," he writes:

> Formerly you appeared to me, O Lord, as invisible by every creature since you are a hidden, infinite God. Infinity, however, is incomprehensible by every means of comprehending. Later, you appeared to me as visible by all, for a thing exists only as you see it, and it would not actually exist unless it saw you. For your vision confers being, since your vision is your essence. Thus, my God, you are equally invisible and visible.[25]

Since God is Absolute Being, the being of all things, he is visible in his world. Yet, he is still the unknown, invisible, incomprehensible God. Cusanus sees a fluid dialectic in which the top term (God) informs the bottom term (the world and all of its elements). The two terms are more imposed upon one another than hierarchically situated. "Hence, I experience how necessary it is for me to enter into the cloud and to admit the coincidence of opposites, above all capacity of reason, and to seek there the truth where impossibility confronts me."[26]

The paradoxical notion of the coincidence of opposites is but one form of the unresolvable and incomprehensible tension that pervades Cusanus's philosophy of religion. Although terms such as "Maximum and Minimum," *possest,* and Infinite Equality are derived from philosophical speculation, Cusanus sees contradictory language as more than a philosophical issue. Whether expressed in mathematical terms or in the symbol of the icon, it is deeply embedded in the Christian theo-

---

25. *DVD* XII h 47, Bond, 256.

Appararuisti mihi, domine, aliquando ut invisibilis ab omni creatura quia deus absconditus infinitus. Infinitas autem est incomprehensibilis omni modo comprehendendi. Apparuisti deine mihi ut ab omnibus visibilis quia intantum res est, inquantum tu eam vides, et ipsa non esset actu nisi te videteret. Visio enim praestat esse, quia est essentia tua. Sic, deus meus, es invisibilis pariter et visibilis.

26. *DVD* IX h 36, Bond, 251.

Unde experior quomodo necesse est me intrare caliginem et admitere coincidentiam oppositorum super omnem capacitatem rationis et quaer ibi veritatem ubi occurrit impossibilitas.

logical tradition. Paradox is pervasive in Meister Eckhart, for instance. In Cusanus's case, it is difficult to know whether he originally developed the notion from his studies of theology or from his education in philosophy and mathematics.[27] Most likely the concept caught his eye in both areas and his studies mutually reinforced each other. Regardless, it is important to see how the pervasiveness of contradictory language extends learned ignorance far beyond abstract concepts of God to the traditional tenets of the Christian faith, Trinity and Christology.

The doctrine of the Trinity is directly related to the inability of the human mind to grasp the Infinite and is a further example of divine transcendence. Nicholas's treatment of the Trinity thus finds a logical place in *De docta ignorantia.*[28] It is not a silent God that is reached through learned ignorance, but the fecund Trinity. In the same way that we attain knowledge of the Maximum triangle, we learn of the Trinity. In an infinite or Maximum triangle, the sides would all be infinite,

> since the sum of two sides of a triangle cannot be smaller than the third. . . . And since there cannot be more than one infinite, you understand, in a transcendent way, that an infinite triangle cannot be composed of more than one line, although it is the maximum and truest triangle . . . the one infinite line must be three lines and these three must be one most simple line. The same is true of angles.[29]

27. There is an unconfirmed tradition that early in his life Nicholas studied with the Brothers of the Common Life in Deventer. If this is true, it would suggest that the theological tensions of Trinity and Christology were the first to come to his notice. Erich Meuthen disputes this (*Nikolaus von Kues, 1401–1464. Skizze einer Biographie* [Muenster: Aschendorff, 1992]), however. Nicholas of Cusa's later education is more certain and included canon law, mathematics, science, philosophy, and theology. Although his most extensive formal philosophical and theological work occurred last, from 1425 to 1426 in Cologne, the possibility remains that his early university work in Heidelberg in 1416 may have included some as well. See Duclow, "Nicholas of Cusa."

28. A detailed discussion of the notion of Trinity in Nicholas of Cusa is found in Rudolf Haubst's work *Das Bild des Einen und Dreieinen Gottes in der Welt nach Nikolaus von Kues.* Trierer Theologische Studien 4 (Trier: Paulinus, 1952).

29. *DDI* 1.14 h 37, Bond, 104–5.

Deinde constat—quoniam omnia duo latera cuiuslibet trianguli simul iuncta tertio minora esse non possunt—trianguli, cuius unum latus est infinitum, alia non esse minora. Et quia quae-

This identity language about the parts of an infinite triangle takes on new depths when applied to the Trinity.

> Consequently, from this consideration we come to know the true triangle and the most simple line in the way possible to a human being, and from this knowledge, therefore, we shall, in learned ignorance, attain to the Trinity. . . . The example also shows us that the angles of the triangle cannot be numbered "one," "two," and "three," since each angle is in each angle, for as the Son says: "I am in the Father, and the Father in me."[30]

The circular movement that is implied by the identity of the engendering Father with the engendered Son is reminiscent of the theology of Jan van Ruusbroec.[31] Learned ignorance does not end in transcendent knowledge of a silent Godhead, but in mystical union with an ever-expressive, Trinitarian God.

For Cusanus, the Trinity is explained in the linking of the general terms of oneness, equality, and union with the theological terms of Father, Son, and Spirit.[32] He argues in Book I that not only is oneness eternal but so are equality and union. In arguing that oneness is eternal because it precedes the mutability of otherness, Cusanus is making the Neoplatonic move of identifying multiplicity with changeability. One-

---

libet pars infiniti est infinita, necessarium est omnem triangulum, cuius unum latus est infinitum, alia pariformiter esse infinita. Et quoniam plura infinita esse non possunt, transcendenter intelligis triangulum infinitum ex pluribus lineis componi non posse, licet sit maximus verissimus triangulus, incompositus et simplicissimus; et quia verissimus triangulus, qui sine tribus lineis esse nequit, erit necessarium ipsam unicam infinitam lineam esse tres et tres esse unam simplicissimam. Ita de angulis, quoniam non erit nisi angulus unus infinitus, et ille est tres anguli et tres anguli unus.

30. *DDI* 1.19 h 57–58, Bond, 113–14.

Quare ipsum verum triangulum atque simplicissimam lineam ex praehabitis scientes, modo quo hoc homini possibile est, in docta ignorantia Trinitatem attingemus . . . Hic etiam videtur, quomodo numerari anguli trianguli per unum, duo, tria non possunt, cum quilibet sit in quolibet,—ut ait Filius: "Ego in Patre et Pater in me."

31. Jan van Ruusbroec (1293–1381), a Flemish mystic, is known for his understanding of the divine life as a movement of expansion and contraction. Human life shares in this movement as the "common life" leads the individual into the life of the Trinity. Pertinent writings include *The Sparkling Stone, The Spiritual Espousals,* and *The Seven Steps of the Ladder of Spiritual Love.*

32. Cf. similar terms in Augustine and in the theologians of the School of Chartres.

ness is eternal because otherness implies a shift away from the original oneness, and that shift forecloses eternality.

Equality is eternal for parallel reasons. Because every inequality is analyzable into an equality, equality precedes inequality and is eternal. If, in the case of two quantities, the larger quantity's excess precludes their equality, one need only remove that excess to make them equal. For Cusanus, this suggests that all inequalities can be analyzed into what is prior, that is, equality. Furthermore, union precedes separation, just as the number one precedes the number two. Nothing can be separate without having first been united or without at least presupposing union, so union is likewise eternal. Thus, the character of Eternity is itself trine, and Nicholas maintains that "Our very holy doctors" have "called Unity 'Father,' Equality 'Son,' and Connection 'Holy Spirit.'"[33]

Though Nicholas appears to have presented a logical and unmysterious Trinitarian system, this doctrine is included in learned ignorance because it is actually fraught with paradox. It is, on the most basic level, incomprehensible that one can be three and three can be one. But Cusanus's explication of the Trinity in terms of oneness, equality, and union only deepens the mystery. The cognates of oneness are immutability and eternity. But Nicholas roots equality, something that implies duality and mutability, in oneness. The notion of union would only seem to confirm that oneness has itself changed, that it is being either added to or *re*united. But Nicholas affirms that all three terms are eternal. With this background of the general terms, the ineffability of the theological construct is brought into focus. It is paradoxical that the One Father can *generate* the Son and be joined with him in Union, and yet remain both eternal and undivided. The fact that God is at once one and trine, eternal in all three persons and yet generating, generated, and united, is a matter for learned ignorance.

---

33. *DDI* 1.9 h 26, Bond, 98.

Quod autem sanctissimi nostri doctores unitatem vocaverunt Patrem, aequalitatem Filium, et connexionem Spiritum sanctum, hoc propter quandam similitudinem ad ista caduca fecerunt.

It should not be surprising that trinity bears the imprint of theophany when examined in learned ignorance. The creation itself reflects the trinity of God insofar as it is contracted, insofar as it is materially expressed. "Indeed, contraction is impossible without that which is contractible, that which contracts, and the connection that is accomplished by the common actuality of the other two."[34] To revert to the actuality–possibility schema, God the Father is possibility, God the Son is actuality, and God the Holy Spirit is the union of the two. Thus, there is a Trinitarian character to the theophanic knowledge that we do have of God: that He exists, and that His Being informs the being of the created universe.

But Cusanus does not restrict learned ignorance to the economic Trinity; it is applied to the immanent Trinity as well. The doctrine of Christ is an area where polar opposites are held in tension and can be approached only through learned ignorance. The incarnation, a union of God and man, Infinite and finite, is utterly paradoxical. It would seem impossible for a transcendent God, characterized, as we have seen, by absolute priority and nonparticularity, to lower himself and reveal himself through the form of a fleshly human being. If learned ignorance is the path to knowledge of God and if the doctrine of the Trinity holds, then we are also in ignorance concerning the way in which God the Son unites himself to mankind.

Nicholas follows the classic Chalcedonian doctrine of Christ. The unity of God and man in the person of Christ must not be viewed in such a way that it is God alone, for what is contracted does not change its contractedness. That is, union does not remove the particularity of humanity. Neither must it be viewed as purely man, because God does not let go of His divinity. It is also not true that the unity is a composite, for the essence of God and man cannot mingle with one another.

---

34. *DDI* 2.7 h 128, Bond, 145.
Non potest enim contractio esse sine contrahibili, contrahente et nexu, qui per communem actum utriusque perficitur.

According to Nicholas, "This union would be greater than all intelligible unions."[35] The incarnation is a mystery. But it is a mystery that is central to knowledge of God.

It is through the mystical union with Christ that God is revealed to mankind. To be mystically united with God is to truly know God. Nicholas writes, "Understanding, therefore, is directed by faith, and faith is extended by understanding. Where there is no sound faith, there is no true understanding. . . . But there is no faith more perfect than truth itself, which is Jesus."[36] This is not to say that becoming one with Christ clears up the mysteries of God or that learned ignorance is abolished upon being mystically united with Christ. Rather it is to say that only in Christ do we enter into the fullness of the mysteries of God. To know God is to be united with God and vice versa. If Christ unites us with God, then it is through Christ that we know God, according to Cusanus's concept of knowledge. "The greatest and profoundest mysteries of God, although hidden to the wise, are revealed by faith in Jesus. . . . Therefore, we also see that because of the immensity of his excellence he cannot be comprehended."[37]

Several questions regarding the pervasive tensions in Cusanus's

35. *DDI* 3.2 h 194, Bond, 174.
Supra omnem igitur intellectum haec unio foret.
36. *DDI* 3.11 h 244, Bond, 196–97.
Dirigitur igitur intellectus per fidem, et fides per intellectum extenditur. Ubi igitur non est sana fides, nullus est verus intellectus. Error principiorum et fundamenti debilitas qualem conclusionem subinferant, manifestum est. Nulla autem perfectior fides quam ipsamet veritas, quae Iesus est.
37. *DDI* 3.11 h 245, Bond, 197.
Maxima enim et profundissima Dei mysteria in mundo ambulantibus, quamquam sapientibus abscondita, parvulis et humilibus in fide Iesu revelantur, quoniam Iesus est, in quo omnes thesauri sapientiae et scientiarum absconditi sunt, sine quo nemo quidquam facere potest . . . Qui cum in hoc mundo non sit cognoscibilis, ubi ratione ac opinione aut doctrina ducimur in symbolis per notiora ad incognitum, ibi tantum apprehenditur, ubi cessant persuasiones et accedit fides; per quam in simplicitate rapimur, ut supra omnem rationem et intelligentiam in tertio caelo simplicissimae intellectualitatis ipsum in corpore incorporaliter, quia in spiritu, et in mundo non mundialiter, sed caelestialiter contemplemur incomprehensibiliter, ut et hoc videatur, ipsum scilicet comprehendi non posse propter excellentiae suae immensitatem.

thought must be addressed. Is his paradoxical language merely a stylistic device, or does it involve its content as well? That is, can his paradoxes be equivalently translated into ordinary discourse and still retain their meaning? And if they are untranslatable, how can they be meaningful at all? If this language of equivocity and identity is translatable into analogical language, Nicholas is not really doing anything new at all. But if he is making a nontraditional move, we must struggle to make sense of it.

In his interpretive study of *De visione Dei,* Jasper Hopkins considers the possibility of translation. First, he compares Cusanus's use of paradox to that of Charles Dickens's well-known opening lines, "It was the best of times, it was the worst of times," and remarks,

> Dickens expresses himself as he does in order to capture the attention and the imagination of the reader—in order to create a more vivid and provocative impression. Similarly, Nicholas's statement that "the finite is united to the Infinite and Ununitable" conjoins two prima facie inconsistent conceptions. And it conjoins them for two reasons: to foster in the reader's mind a sense of amazement and inquiry and to "summarize pithily," as it were, an elaborate series of nonparadoxical propositions.[38]

Hopkins appears to suggest that the paradox is merely a heuristic device, calculated to engage the reader and summarize for easy reference. The use of paradox would appear to be dictated by pedagogic concerns rather than by the immensity and incomprehensibility of the content.

Later Hopkins argues that "Nicholas shows that the paradoxical expression in question was meant to be understood as tacitly accompanied by qualifiers."[39] Then he lists some of the most central paradoxes and comments, "Each of the foregoing statements, like the ones mentioned still earlier, is *equivalently translatable* into a conjunction of nonparadoxical propositions."[40]

---

38. Jasper Hopkins, *Nicholas of Cusa's Dialectical Mysticism: Text, Translation, and Interpretive Study of De visione Dei* (Minneapolis: Arthur J. Banning Press, 1985), 36.
    39. Ibid., 37.   40. Ibid., 41; italics mine.

Most likely, Hopkins is trying to argue that Nicholas's paradoxes are content-full, not content-less, and that they can be saved from absurdity through translation. This reading is supported by Hopkins's further remarks:

> Moreover, like the earlier paradoxical utterances these too are non-self-contradictory: they merely have a surface appearance of self-contradictoriness because of their syntactical form. Even when Nicholas speaks of God as surrounded by the coincidence of contradictories, he does not mean that God acts in ways that defy all intelligibility or that He is rightly conceivable in accordance with an inconsistent description. Rather, the expression indicates that God's being is uniquely beyond all actual and conceptual differentiation, so that it cannot be truly and nonmetaphorically characterized by any predicate whose meaning is drawn from human experience.[41]

Hopkins's own position results from his attempt to interpret Cusanus in such a way that the gap between human reason that cannot abide indefiniteness and a particular form of religious language that escapes human logic is bridged. In doing so, he asserts that given qualifiers, the paradoxical language is no longer paradoxical.

However, the paradoxes are *not* equivalently translatable even when enough qualifiers are added and they are detached from their syntactical form. Jasper Hopkins's effort to deny that the paradoxes are self-contradictory jettisons the heart of Cusanus's philosophy, the notion that the finite human mind is dwarfed by God's infinity. Hopkins's last sentence in the above quote refers to the central notion that human logic, guided by the law of noncontradiction, cannot conceive of God. He has a clear grasp of Nicholas's thesis, but, ironically, his effort to defend it undermines it. Adding qualifiers that flatten the contours of the paradox robs it of its ability to astonish and point toward the divine. A reduction to ordinary discourse inevitably imports norms of

---

41. Ibid.

human rationality that fall far short of their object. On Nicholas's model there is no completely adequate substitute for paradoxical discourse, (although there may be room for an equivalent understanding of God in the realm of *experience*). Paradox and tension are not just a conjunction of positive and negative theology. It is not that "God is visible *and* invisible," but "God is visible" and "God is invisible."

He admits that in learning to know God as the coincidence of opposites, God has "given me courage to do violence to myself."[42] Shedding one's reason and entering the realm of paradox is so difficult to do that it is *violent*. But it is a "necessary" violence. It is curious that rationality, ordinarily seen as an essentially divine gift, is the very thing that must be transcended when seeking God. Cusanus admits that even to erudite philosophers, this seems impossible and absurd.

To explain himself, he uses another comparison:

> And I have discovered that the place where you are found unveiled is girded about with the coincidence of contradictories. This is the wall of paradise, and it is there in paradise that you reside. The wall's gate is guarded by the highest spirit of reason; and unless it is overpowered, the way in will not lie open. Thus, it is on the other side of the coincidence of contradictories that you will be able to be seen and nowhere on this side.[43]

Rather than a path to God, human reason is a guard that must be passed before one can reach God. God resides in paradise, on the other side of the paradoxes at which one arrives via reason. In another selection, he refers to God as "beyond the wall of the coincidence of en-

---

42. *DVD* IX h 37, Bond, 251–52.

Et animasti me, domine, qui es cibus grandium, ut vim mihi ipsi faciam, quia impossibilitas coincidet cum cum necessitate.

43. Ibid.

Et repperi locum, in quo revelate reperieris, cinctum contradictoriorum coincidentia. Et iste est murus paradisi in quo habitas, cuiuss portam custodit spiritus altissimus rationis, quis nisi vincatur, non patebit ingressus. Ultra igitur coincidentiam contradictoriorum videri poteris et nequaquam citra.

folding and unfolding" and "absolute from all that can be spoken or thought."[44]

Nicholas argues that the either-or condition imposed by the law of noncontradiction itself does not satisfy our drive to know:

> [For] if sight is not satisfied by seeing, nor the ear by hearing, then even less is the intellect satisfied by understanding. Therefore, that which satisfies the intellect, or that which is its end, is not that which the intellect understands. Nor can that which the intellect utterly does not understand fully satisfy it, but only that which it understands by not understanding. . . . [O]nly the intelligible which the intellect knows to be so intelligible that this intelligible can never be fully known can satisfy the intellect.[45]

Furthermore, he directly addresses the law of noncontradiction in *De coniecturis* when he writes:

> To state many points very briefly: nothing in mathematics can be known by means of any other root than the root-belief that a coincidence of opposites is unattainable. Whatever in mathematics is demonstrated to be true is shown to be true from a consideration of the fact that unless it were true a coincidence of opposites would be implied, and this result would constitute a going beyond reason. Likewise, everything that is shown by reason to be unattainable is unattainable on the basis of the fact that a knowledge of it would imply a coincidence of opposites.[46]

44. *DVD* XI h 46, Bond, 255–56.

Redeo iterum confisus adiutorio tuo, domine, ut te ultra murum coincidentiae complicationis et explicationis reperiam. . . . Disiunctio enim pariter et coniunctio est murus coincidentiae ultra quem existis, absolutus ab omni eo quod aut dici aut cogitari potest.

45. *DVD* XVI h 70, Bond, 266.

Video te, domine deus meus, in raptu quodam mentali, quoniam si visus non satiatur visu nec auris auditu, tunc minus intellectus intellectu. Non igitur id quod satiat intellectum, seu est finis eius, est id quod intelligit. Neque id satiare potest quod penitus non intelligit, sed solum illud quod non intelligendo intelligit. Intellibile enim quod cognoscit non satiat; nec intelligibile satiat quod penitus non cognoscit; sed intelligibile quad cognoscit adeo intelligibile, quod numquam posit ad plenum intelligi, hoc solum satiare potest.

46. *DC* 2.1 h 77, Hopkins, 200.

Although Nicholas's notion of the intellect (versus the *ratio*) will be discussed at length in the final part of this chapter, here it is sufficient to note that the human mind is most at home when it is drawn ever deeper into understanding, into an endless understanding. Complete knowledge of an object, in the sense of mastery, is not as satisfying as knowledge that overpowers as well. This endless and overpowering understanding exceeds rationality and its attachment to the principle of noncontradiction. Divine infinity is clearly the center of his position. If the Infinite wreaks havoc with human understanding, Nicholas seems to say it is purposive and divinely ordained.

However, an awareness of the limitations of human language and the capacity for understanding does not lead to abandonment of the project of knowing. Understanding that is limited and *knows* that it is limited reaches beyond itself in that very knowledge. Perspectival thought is not futile if that perspective allows for a shattering of itself. Therefore, our categories of understanding that allow for the existence of paradox, as a linguistic form and as a symbolic content, point toward the infinity of the divine. Definition and the principle of noncontradiction were never meant to restrict our knowledge, but to advance it. Allowing them to dictate reality is granting ontological status to what were intended to be tools of thought. They should be seen as descriptive of the human world, not as normative for all that is. When the laws of logic become not merely cautionary, but definitive, the possibility for union with God vanishes.

But if Cusanus cannot be discursively translated and if he is a negative theologian, can he be accused of inconsistency in formulating any theology at all? That is, if he finds God so infinite and incomprehensible, how is he justified in speaking even in paradox? One could perhaps argue that Nicholas's project is incoherent and that he should either re-

---

Et ut brevissime multa dicam, nihil in mathematicis sciri poterit alia radice. Omne, quod demonstratur verum esse, ex eo est, quia, nisi foret, oppositorum coincidentia subinferretur, et hoc esset rationem exire. Sic omne id, quod ostenditur per rationem adipisci non posse, ex hoc est, quia eius scientia esset coincidentiae oppositorum illativa.

main silent or speak logically, but certainly should not indulge himself in confusing and irrational paradoxes.

However, true nonsense is not escaping the strictures of the principle of noncontradiction, but is trying to speak in a "learned" manner about God. Given God's transcendence it is absurd to speak literally or even discursively of him. Clyde Lee Miller aptly characterizes Nicholas of Cusa's method as "dialectical thinking" as he was "out to do nothing less than think God."[47] We know God is not Father or Son or Bridegroom in any ordinary sense. Although speaking analogically does not disobey the rules of human logic, it is only partially satisfactory. Positive statements about what God is "like" never quite seem to attain the heights of God's infinity and are founded upon human characteristics. Although it is tempting to be silent, Nicholas recognizes the absurdity of silence when he is faced by the overflowing fullness of theophany. How can he observe "all beauty of visible forms, variety of colors, agreeable symmetry, splendor of precious stones, greenness of meadows, luster of gold,"[48] in short, God's manifestation without speaking? He explains that "the power of the Ineffable embraces every sayable thing and that nothing can be said in which in its mode the cause of every saying and of everything said does not shine forth."[49] For this rea-

47. Clyde Lee Miller, *Reading Cusanus: Metaphor and Dialectic in a Conjectural Universe* (Washington, D.C.: Catholic University of America Press, 2003), 1–16.

48. *De quaerendo Deum* I h 28, trans. by H. Lawrence Bond, "On Seeking God," in *Nicholas of Cusa: Selected Spiritual Writings* (New York: Paulist Press, 1997), 221. Hereafter abbreviated *DQD*.

Unde in regno summi atque maximi Regis omnis décor visibilium formarum, varietas colorum, proportio grata, respendentia carbuncularis, graminea viriditas, fulgor auri et quidquid visum delectat, et in quo visus quasi in thesauro regni sui quiescendo delectatur, in curia magni Regis pro nihilo habentur, cum sint de infimis stramentis curiae.

49. *De filiatione Dei* VI h 84, trans. H. Lawrence Bond, *On Divine Filiation* (2000), online. Available from www.appstate.edu/~Bondhl/ [accessed 12 December 2005]. Hereafter abbreviated as *DFD*.

Quando enim quicumque studiosus subtiliter considerando attendit quomodo ipsum unum omnium causa non potest non exprimi in omni expressione, sicut verbum non potest non eloqui in omni loquente, sive se dicat loqui sive se dicat non loqui, tunc sibi manifestum est virtutem ineffibilis omne dicibile ambire et nihil dici posse, in quo modo suo causa omnis dicentis et dicti non resplendeat.

son, Nicholas uses paradox and later supereminent language to speak of God.

The paradoxical language of Nicholas of Cusa affirms that grace remains at the center of being. Cusanus's thought takes account of Ockham's position that there can be no discourse about God. Likewise, it affirms the beauty and fullness of this world. God spoke and created the world. Nicholas is driven to speak and bear witness. God's speech was not silence, nor was it nonsense. Neither was Cusanus's. Thus, Nicholas gives no indication that he views his paradoxes as translatable or his mystical theology as dissolvable into discursive language, nor can one argue that his noisy silence is self-contradictory.

His deliberate choice of paradoxical language is illuminated by Michel de Certeau, who points out the astonishment that accompanies it and opens the mind to the absolute:

> The domain of surprise will be the birthplace of discourse. The absence of a visible or imaginable object serves as a prelude, still without content, empty, to the necessity of believing the speech of the other. . . . *Experiri volens:* If you will pursue the experience and continue to seek, then the possibility of a displacement that is no longer physical but intellectual will appear—that of another path that is no longer in the continuity of visual perception, but the path of *admiratio* itself, an imageless surprise, an opening to the unknown.[50]

De Certeau perceives the way in which ordinary discourse is broken open by the paradoxical metaphor. This surprise opens us to the unknown divine as well as to an encounter with others who have had the same experience. Nicholas's entire focus is on the transcendence of God and the way in which it defies human discourse. The coincidence of opposites and its corresponding paradoxes are central concepts, not summarizing shortcuts. Nowhere does he exhibit a tendency to translate his paradoxes and make them more palatable.

---

50. Michel de Certeau, "The Gaze of Nicholas of Cusa," *Diacritics* 17 (1987): 18.

In later texts, Cusanus's theology of the coincidence of opposites develops into a theology of supereminence. Influenced by Pseudo-Dionysius, he perceives that "someone who says that nothing at all exists does not say less than one who says that all the things exist that appear to. Nor does someone who says that God is all things speak more truly than the one who says that God is nothing or is not, since one knows that God is ineffable, beyond every affirmation and negation."[51] Paradox is rooted in God's dwelling beyond even the realm where affirmation and negation apply at the same time.

In *De visione Dei* the coincidence of opposites has been transformed from God himself into a wall guarded by reason. "And, therefore, to one approaching you, *now* and *then* meet in coincidence within the wall that surrounds the place where you dwell. For *now* and *then* coincide in the circle of the wall of paradise. But it is beyond *now* and *then* that you, my God, who are absolute eternity, exist and speak."[52] God resides in paradise, on the other side of the paradoxes at which one arrives via reason.

Nicholas makes himself very clear regarding the limits of human understanding in the distinction of *ratio* from intellect that he outlines in *De coniecturis*. A look at the function of *ratio*, including both its possibilities and its limits, will enable us to take Cusanus seriously instead of subjecting him to a "translation" that he never intended.

51. *DFD* VI h 84, Bond; italics mine.

Nec minus apud ipsum hic dicit, qui ait nihil penitus esse, quam ille qui ait omnia esse quae videntur. Nec verius hic dicit, qui ait deum omnia esse, quam ille, qui ait ipsum nihil esse aut non esse, cum sciat deum super omnem affirmationem et negationem ineeffabilem, quidquid quisque dicat, et hoc ipsum, quod quisque de ipso dicit non aliud esse quam modum quendam, quo de ineffabili loquens loquitur, sidcut hae duae species homo et asinus genus animalitatis vario modo exprimunt, humana etenim species rationaliter, asinine irrationaliter.

52. *DVD* X h 42, Bond, 254.

Et ideo accendenti ad te occurrunt in muroo, qui circumdat locum ubi habitas, in coincidentia. Coincidit enim nunc et tunc in circulo muri paradisi. Tu vero, deus meus, ultra nunc et tunc existis et loqueris, qui es aeternitas absoluta.

FROM RATIO TO INTELLECT

The Finite Ratio

The problem with discursive reasoning is, as we have seen, the disparity between its capacity and its object, God. The above discussion of divine transcendence and learned ignorance has shown that to whatever extent its *activity* images God, its *content* is empty of him. The question must then be asked about the value of rationality at all. If its inadequacy in being united with God through knowledge is evident, and if such union is the goal of human existence, should it not be discarded altogether? Although Cusanus does move beyond the processes of human reason to the workings of the intellect, he does not argue for an abandonment of discursive reasoning but sees it as inherently purposive.

Revaluating ignorance as *learned* carries with it a self-reflectivity that points toward the theotic destiny of human beings. Although theosis will be explored more fully in the next chapter of this book, it is important to point out that Nicholas's epistemology has a theotic dimension in the way that it moves the finite mind beyond itself, indicating its ultimate fulfillment in God. It is this theotic dimension that defends the project of knowing God against the charge of futility. The search for God beyond names in negation, then beyond negation in coincidence, and finally beyond coincidence, is not at all an empty movement toward the loss of self and the vanishing of God. Cusanus writes, "Accordingly, this name *'possest'* leads the one-who-is-speculating beyond all the senses, all reason, and all intellect unto a mystical vision, where there is an end to the ascent of all cognitive power and where there is the beginning of the revelation of the unknown God."[53]

That this path to the mystical vision is a divinely intended move-

---

53. *DP* 15, Hopkins, 921.
　　Ducit ergo hoc nomen speculantem super omnem sensum, rationem, et intellectum in mysticam visionem, ubi est finis ascensus omnis cognitivae virtutis et revelationis incogniti dei initium.

ment toward both divine disclosure and the disclosure of self *within the disclosure of God* is certainly implied by Nicholas's metaphysics of theophany, but it is spelled out early in his definitive epistemological treatise *De docta ignorantia*. The longing to know is a gift from God and is really the desire to exist in the best manner that human nature allows. However frustrated this desire may be, however parallel to the unpleasantness of hunger, it is not in vain, but is divinely ordained.[54] Rather than being a negation of human cognitivity and the human nature that is characterized by it, divine transcendence is thus their ultimate affirmation. It is the finitude of the human mind, brought into relief by its attempts to know the Infinite, that forces it to acknowledge its origins and destiny in the Infinite. Frustration and unpleasantness are transformed, if not into the eschatological satisfaction of the epistemological quest found in scholasticism, then at least into peaceful affirmation of human nature.

Again, in *De coniecturis,* Nicholas argues that the purpose and goal of the human mind is infinite rationality. The mental processes so negatively portrayed in *De docta ignorantia* are affirmed as the *imago dei* in *De coniecturis.* The human creativity embodied in the conjectural process is itself a means of uniting with that of which it is an image.[55] It is, of course, the *imaging* of divine fecundity, not the *content* of rational knowledge, that is this means. Learned ignorance means that image cannot be extrapolated into simple analogy. Thus, rationality is a path to be explored, despite the fact that it will ultimately be transcended.

Finally, his later text *De quarendo Deum (On Seeking God)* reminds us that "indeed, unless this world aided the seeker, humankind would have been sent into the world to seek God in vain. Therefore, this world must assist whomever seeks God, and the seeker must know that neither in the world nor in all that a human conceives is there anything similar to God."[56] Here Cusanus affirms two principles that are super-

---

54. *DDI* 1.2 h 1–2, Bond, 87–88.   55. *DC* 1.1.
56. *DQD* I, h 18, Bond, 217–18.

ficially incoherent, and explains their coherency. Humanity has entered this world, has been sent by God, in order to seek God, and yet discovers here no likeness to God. Since God does not act without purpose, nor does he contradict himself, it is certain that the world is "useful" in completion of the ordained task, the search for God. But, as is becoming clear, the assistance the world offers is a product of theophany and theosis, a function of the mystical presence of God, not a path signposted by likenesses.

To understand Nicholas's view of seeking God, his concepts of *ratio* and intellect must be examined. These concepts put him in dialogue with Neoplatonism, nominalist ideas,[57] and scholasticism. Some of the main points of dialogue, such as the Neoplatonic influence of knowledge as union and the scholastic issue of the law of noncontradiction, have already been mentioned. It remains to look at Nicholas's own texts to see how *ratio* functions as both the catalyst for learned ignorance and the gateway to the processes of the intellect. The primary text in which he discusses the operations of the mind is *De coniecturis,* although other texts are relevant as well.

The Conjecturing Mind

De coniecturis is ostensibly not primarily a theological text, but a "new method" in the investigative arts.[58] Though it is, of course, impossible to separate Nicholas's religious concerns from his secular ones,

---

Certe nisi hic mundus serviret quaerenti, in vanum missus esset homo ad mundum ob finem quaerendi eundem. Oportet igitur hunc mundum praestare adminiculum quaerenti et oportet scire quaerentum quod nec in mundo nec in omni eo, quod homo concipit, est quid simile ei.

57. The connection with nominalism is difficult to document since the faculty at Cologne was anti-nominalist. On the other hand, some scholars have interpreted Cusanus as a proto-nominalist. At the very least, one can say that there are parallels between certain aspects of Cusanus's thought and nominalist thought. Therefore, this book is not attempting to argue that Cusanus was a nominalist or that his ideas were identical with those of nominalism, but merely that there are similarities.

58. *DC* I h 1, Hopkins, 163.

Scio enim hanc novam indatgandarum atrium forulam in ruditate sua occumbere non posse, si vir omnium clarissimus eam acceptatione dignam correctionis lima facere dignabitur.

his stated intentions at least focus the text as a philosophical inquiry into human understanding. We are, then, justified in using this work as a starting point for an examination of his view of the functioning of the human mind in regard to all knowledge, not merely knowledge of God.

This is not to say, however, that *De coniecturis* is written without reference to *De docta ignorantia*. Indeed, the process of conjecturing is predicated on the mind's ignorance of exactitude. But the mind is not relegated to darkness, nor does it merely guess at truth. Neither does it come to a weak, shadowy approximation of it. Instead, the mind approaches things through conjectures, mimicking not the truth, but God's creative activity.[59]

Conjectures originate in the human mind in the same way that creation is born of the divine mind. Nicholas explains:

> It must be the case that surmises originate from our minds, even as the real world originates from Infinite Divine Reason. For when as best it can, the human mind (which is a lofty likeness of God) partakes of the fruitfulness of the Creating Nature, it produces from itself, qua image of the omnipotent Form, rational entities, which are made in the likeness of real entities.[60]

There is a parallel between human and divine reason in the way that the unity of both, that is, their self-identities, informs human knowledge on the one hand, and the world on the other. The Neoplatonic unity formula that grants self-identity according to the unity of a thing, moving from the One to multiplicity, is given a nominalist extension that moves from the human mind to the notional world.

The indivisible One that imparts itself (a Neoplatonic formula) is

---

59. See also *Idiota de mente*.

60. *DC* 1.1 h 5, Hopkins, 165.

Coniecturalis itaque mundi humana mens forma exstitit uti realis divina. Quapropter ut absoluta illa divina entitas est omne id quod est in quolibet quod est, ita et mentis humanae unitas est coniecturarum suarum entitas.

seen as the model for the process of knowing in which the human mind unfolds itself conceptually in the world (a nominalist formula).[61] Though Nicholas has avoided analogical language up to this point, a kind of second-order analogy occurs in this context. The knowing subject is granted an agency that imitates the creative agency of God, and here Nicholas reverts, characteristically, to measurement terminology.

Nicholas sees the *imago dei* in the workings of the mind: "Therefore, the mind's *oneness* enfolds within itself all multitude, and its *equality* enfolds all magnitude, even as its *union* enfolds all composition."[62] The Trinity as Oneness, Equality, and Union has its counterpart in the mind's unfolding of multitude, inequality, and magnitude in the world. Contrary to the scholastic position, however, ordinary rationality is not primarily a divine trait, but a human one.[63] The *imago dei* is not rooted in the way that human rationality images divine rationality, but in the way that human rationality images divine creativity. Just as God would not be God without the Trinity unfolding him as Oneness (Father), Equality (Son), and Union (Spirit), so the world is given a unique character by the mind's unfolding of multitude, inequality, and magnitude in it.

This parallel, along with an awareness of the essential nature of the Trinity for the Christian concept of God in general, and for Cusanus's thought in particular, emphasizes the powerful role that human rationality plays for Cusanus. This is not merely a convenient parallel he is

61. Nicholas is unclear on the ontological status of conceptual entities or universals, however, due to the mixture of Neoplatonist and nominalist tendencies in his thought. In some places he sounds like a realist, allowing that universals are not merely "rational entities" (*DDI* 2.6 h 125, Bond, 143–44). Meanwhile, in the same context he restricts the reality of universals to the realm of mental abstraction. For a full discussion see Pauline Moffitt Watts, *Nicolaus Cusanus: A Fifteenth-Century Vision of Man* (Leiden: Brill, 1982), 69–72.

62. *DC* 1.1 h 6, Hopkins, 165.

Quapropter unitas mentis in se omnem complicat multitudinem eiusque aequalitas omnem magnitudinem, sicut et conexio compositionem.

63. Nicholas does, however, refer to God as "Infinite Reason" in *DC* 1.1, but he does not mean the kind of reason that adheres to the Aristotelian laws of logic.

drawing, but a locution that gets to the heart of his philosophical anthropology. "For only reason is the measure of multitude, of magnitude,
and of composition. Thus, if reason is removed, none of these three,
viz., multitude, magnitude, and composition, as conceptually measured,
will remain—even as, if Infinite Being is denied, it is evident that, likewise, the finite being of all things is denied."[64] Just as the actual world
lacks independence from God, so is the conceptual world contingent
upon the rational human mind. The mind is the "triune origin" of the
mental world in which it operates, imitating the Trinitarian origin of
the real world in which the Triune God manifests.

Cusanus's frequent use of numerical examples in this text, some of
them quite obscure, is not arbitrary.[65] In number he finds the means
to express in terms of human cognition the same *unitas-alteritas* schema that was also explored in terms of theophany.[66] While reminding us
that creatures without rational capacity also cannot count, Nicholas explains the derivation of conjectures from the human mind in the same
way that he explained the derivation of the multiplicity from the divine
unity: "Moreover, reason's unfolding of number and its using number
to make surmises is nothing other than reason's using itself and mentally fashioning all surmised things in a natural, supreme likeness of itself—just as in and through His Co-eternal Word, God (who is Infinite
Mind) communicates being to things."[67] Number is itself contracted in

64. *DC* 1.1 h 6, Hopkins, 165.
*Sola enim ratio multitudinis, magnitudinis ac compositionis mensura est, ita ut ipsa sublata
nihil horum subsistat, sicut entitate infinita negata omnium rerum entitates pariter constat esse negates.*
65. Clyde Lee Miller's chapter on *De coniecturis* provides detailed and helpful expla-
nations and diagrams. Miller, *Reading Cusanus,* 68–109.
66. Although Cusanus writes in *DP* 44 that numbers are the only concepts that are
real rather than conjectural, they are for him the primary vehicles for the rest of human
(conjectural) knowledge. Nicholas is not alone in his preference for mathematical and
numerical metaphors to illuminate both metaphysical and epistemological problems.
This approach can originally be traced to Pythagorus and was later used by Plato and
Boethius. See chapter 2, "The Implications of Theophany for Creation," and the discussion of participation for more on *unitas-alteritas.*
67. *DC* 1.2 h 7, Hopkins, 166.

otherness, just as the being of the world is God's being contracted in otherness. Numbers are opposed to one another and yet made up out of each other: the even number four, for instance, is opposed to odd numbers but reducible to the odd numbers of one and three. As a further example, each number after the number one possesses the unity of the number one, although in its own multiplicity. The number six has a unity, borrowed from the original unity of the number one, or it would not be a discrete number. Yet its unity, as the number six, is not identical to the number one but is possessed in otherness.

This legislative character of human rationality, a nominalist influence, is recast by Cusanus. By viewing concepts as human products rather than as insights into the divine intellect, nominalism had eliminated the possibility of union with God through the mental process. Contemplation of the conceptual world was no longer a direct path to the eternal truths of God, but a detour into human constructions. While agreeing to some degree with the nominalist position, Cusanus perceives that in its creative, constructive aspect, human rationality *is* the *imago dei*. Cusanus uses his view of numbering, deriving largely from Neoplatonic sources such as Thierry de Chartres, to elucidate the creative aspect of rationality. In numbering, the mind draws comparisons, synthesizes, and breaks things down. Yet one must be careful to recognize the novelty of this activity. If numbering were merely organizing, reason would be the image of the Demiurge rather than of the Creator-God. Instead, the mind *unfolds* (*explicatio,* a term we have already seen in reference to theophany) *itself* in numbering, seeing its own unity in the first term and then adding equal terms to further the multiplicity. For this reason, Nicholas calls number the prime exemplar of the mind. In numbering, measuring, and composition, the mind's conjectures mirror divine activity and evince divine presence.

Nec est aliud rationem numerum explicare et illo in constituendis coniecturis uti, quam rationem se ipsa uti ac in sui naturali suprema similitudine cuncta fingere, uti deus, mens infinita, in verbo coaeterno rebus esse communicat.

In this text, Cusanus sketches a consistent theory of the levels of human sensory and mental processes. His theory of the four unities explains the relation among the sensible world, the conceptual world, the world of contemplation, and the divine.[68] The corporeal universe is called the fourth, or final. unity and is the realm of gross sensation. As something that is completely "unfolded," it is represented by a simple four-dimensional figure, as well as the number 1000.

Though sensation occurs in the fourth unity, it merely perceives and does not distinguish between different sensations. Awareness of the difference between one sensation and another, including the awareness of a sensation's absence (negation) is the province of the third unity, *ratio* or rationality. In this sense, the corporeal world cannot really *know* itself without this higher unity. This third unity is represented by both the number 100 and the two-dimensional figure of the square. Here in the rational soul is where numerical judgments and discursive reasoning take place. Thus, at this level, Aristotelian logic is not rejected, and one surmises that the coincidence of opposites would be unacceptable. The power and importance of this third unity for Cusanus's theological anthropology have already been explored above. The difficulties of *ratio,* leading to the necessity of negative theology, have also been mentioned. Just as the sensible world cannot comprehend itself, the rational soul needs to rise above itself in order not only to grasp itself, but to approach God, who defies rational categorization.

The second unity, or the intellect, is the level at which God is grasped as the *coincidentia oppositorum.* Represented by the figure of the line and the number ten, it is unfolded into and enfolds the lower unities. Here the oppositions of the third unity are reconciled, including the oppositions between being and not-being, and rest and motion. The principle of noncontradiction is transcended. While according to

68. Cusanus explains the four unities beginning with the first absolute Unity and moving to the fourth. But since this chapter and the next move from human *ratio* toward theosis, beginning with the fourth unity is preferable here.

ratio one must use negative theology when speaking of God, according to *intellectus* one may speak in paradox. We have already seen the significance of paradox for Cusanus's thought.[69] It remains to explore the function of paradox in the movement from *ratio* to *intellectus* and the way in which this movement bridges nominalist and medieval concerns.

The underlying dynamic of human activity found in *ratio* conflicts with the passivity one must have in knowing God. Thus, it is in the intellect, where surrender rather than creative control is the rule, that the mystical union begins. Louis Dupré points toward the crux of this issue when he writes:

> The mind's cognitive *conatus* that results in a *coincidentia oppositorum,* a collapse of its distinctions, methods, and powers, underlies from the beginning an implicit drive towards a vision of God, an obscure encounter with the One who is beyond all distinctions, methods, and human potential. Yet that intellectual vision will become a genuine vision of God only if grace transforms the mind's active striving into a passive contemplation. Not until that point can we fully claim that the mind has attained the very end of the thinking process.[70]

Seeking an object, the grasping human mind is baffled in its attempt to know God, the eternal subject. Given God's infinity and the impossibility of literal language, if knowing God were purely active, a thoroughly negative theology would prevail. The human mind would stop at the darkness at the limits of its reason. Nicholas of Cusa saw that paradox and the intellect that grasps it clear the way for the passivity that allows God to illumine the human mind.

Cusanus's position is supported by the structure of his discussion of the four unities. Because he ends with the fourth unity, corporeality, he develops the theme of the increasing distance between the higher and

---

69. See "From *Ratio* to Intellect" in this chapter for a discussion of paradox.

70. Louis Dupré, "The Mystical Theology of Cusanus's De Visione Dei," *Eros and Eris* (The Netherlands: Kluwer Academic Publishers, 1992), 107.

lower unities and the impossibility of the lower grasping the higher. In addition to reiterating the limits of rationality, he writes of the "rules of the region," laws that restrict each unity's speaking to and of its own level. Though he seems to be building up to a declaration of the ultimacy of negative theology, he immediately reverses himself, writing of a return and upward regression to the absolute Unity. His circular language (he uses the term *perfecta circulatione*)[71] calls to mind the earlier thinker Jan van Ruusbroec, though Trinity is mentioned here only in passing, and the language of unity and plurality dominates.[72] A key moment in the downward and upward dynamic occurs here between rationality and intellect. The perfect circularity of the movement that begins in theophany and ends in theosis is essentially linked to the transition from active *ratio* to passive *intellectus*. Thus, Cusanus's notion of grace is born when his medievalism reasserts itself in the higher unities over the nominalist tendencies of the third unity. The first, or highest, unity is the source of this grace and transcends all other unities.

Represented by the single point and number one, the first unity is the most simple mind, or God. This is the level in which all things, concepts, and minds are enfolded. It is ineffable, the equality of everything, and the essence of all essences, yet, still, the eternal opposition to the created order. Like Pseudo-Dionysius, Cusanus uses the language of supereminence to describe this prime unity. It is neither simple nor not-simple, neither one nor not-one; it is beyond all such designations. No questions regarding this unity can be asked, for questioning presupposes the affirmation of one proposition or another, but this prime unity cannot be bound by such choices. Though this unity does not appear to take an active role in the mental processes, its significance lies in its presence, like that of the other three unities, in the mind. God,

71. Perfection-like circularity. *DC* 2.7 h 107, Hopkins, 218. Note that a similar term, *Theologia circularis,* a Lullian phrase, is found in *DDI*.

72. In other texts, notably *De dato Patris luminum* V, 112, and *De filiatione Dei,* he uses similar language that is Trinitarian.

who draws all things back to himself and in whom deification occurs, already resides in the human mind. Here, then, is the justification for Nicholas's version of Socratic and Augustinian introspection: knowing the self is knowing God.[73]

It is in the movement from the second to the first unity that the difference between *De docta ignorantia* and *De coniecturis* comes to light. While *De docta ignorantia* described God as the coincidence of opposites, *De coniecturis* locates God beyond the coincidence of opposites, in the first absolute Unity. The development of Cusanus's thought in this direction is illustrated in a later text, *De visione Dei,* and is expressed here in Christological terms:

> I see you, good Jesus, within the wall of paradise, because your intellect is equally truth and image, and you are equally God and creature, equally infinite and finite. And it is not possible that you should be seen on this side of the wall, for you are the joining of the divine creating nature and the human created nature. . . . For you are the Way to the truth and, likewise, are Truth itself; you are the way to the life of the intellect and equally Life itself.[74]

The truth of God is Jesus, who stands on the other side of the wall of the coincidence of contradictories, the wall guarded by human reason.

It is important to note that Cusanus develops the implications of the Incarnation using epistemological categories despite his position that God dwells beyond the boundaries marked by human reason. For instance, he writes, "But your Spirit has reserved for itself alone the disposition and the governance in the intellectual nature . . . for nowhere

73. This theme is developed in *DVD*.

74. *DVD* XX, 89–90, Bond, 276.

Video, Ihesu bone, te intra murum paradisi, quoniam intellectus tuus est veritas pariter et imago; et tu es deus pariter et creatura, infinitus pariter et finites. Et non est possibile quod citra murum videaris. Es enim copulatio divinae creatricis naturae et humanae creatae naturae. . . . Tu enim es via ad veritatem pariter et ipsa veritas. Tu es via ad vitam intellectus pariter et vita ipsa.

can truth be grasped in and of itself except in the intellectual nature. . . . In [Jesus'] intellect the perfection of creatable nature is at rest."[75]

Moving beyond human logic does not imply irrationality or anti-intellectualism. Even the central theological tenet of the Incarnation can be explained only in terms that take account of the essential nature of the capacity to know. Cusanus's project of instructing the brothers of Tegernsee in knowing God in a mystical way is founded on a God whose primary act placed the intellect in the central position. Nevertheless, the human intellect does not govern, but *is governed*. Being, in the absolute sense, escapes epistemological categories. Thus emerges the central paradox in the structure of Cusanus's work: his emphasis on epistemological constructs to such a degree that his discussion of intellect leads to *theosis* as *filiatio Dei* (divine Sonship) versus his ever-present denial of the capacity of human knowledge to reach God.

The Universal Receptivity of the Mind

Before we move on to *theosis* proper, it is important to examine this dual movement of Cusanus's thought. What is it about the human mind that provides such a vehicle for theological meaning for Cusanus? Why does rationality (broadly construed as pointing toward the higher unities, not as the third unity alone) furnish humanity with a possibility for *theosis* that is not granted to the rest of the universe? Certainly one can trace his fascination with the human mind to the view of humanity as microcosm, something found early on in Aristotle and developed by the Greek fathers.[76] But Cusanus is not blindly following tradition here.

He adopts the epistemological perspective and uses the language of

---

75. Ibid. XXV, 116, 118, Bond, 287–88.

Dispositionem vera atque dispensationem in natura intellectuali non nisi sibi ipsi reservit. . . . Nullibi enim capi potest veritas per se, nisi in intellectuali natura. . . . In cuius intellectu quiescit perfectio creabilis naturae.

76. The *locus classicus* of the term "microcosm" is found in Aristotle, *De Anima* III, 8. *"Anima est quodamodo omnia."* (The soul is in some way all that is.)

the instrumentality of the mind because it articulates the theophanic/
theotic movement in a way that no other language can. No action be-
sides thought has the creative or legislative character, perceived by both
Cusanus and nominalists, as well as the ability to comprehend and return things to the self or Self. The former has been discussed above; the
latter ability can be traced to the Greek understanding of what it is to
know something. Rather than the modern view of observation from
a distance, knowing for the Greeks meant uniting with something. To
become one with something, to enclose it within the self, was thus, for
Cusanus, a mirroring of God's return of all things to himself in theosis. Recognizing the Greek understanding, Cusanus's fondness of epistemological categories can be seen as based on the parallel between the
way that the mind develops and encompasses the manifold and the divine *complicatio-explicatio* of the universe.[77] No other part of creation is
as present to the human mind as that mind itself.

In *De filiatione Dei* Nicholas specifically refers to the mind's "universal receptiveness."[78] He writes:

> It can now be sufficiently clear to you that according to my conjec-
> ture, of whatever kind it may be, the intellectual nature is a university
> of things in an intellectual mode, and, while the intellect is engaged in
> the schools of this world, it seeks to bring its potency to actuality, and
> it assimilates itself to particular forms. For from its power, by which it
> intellectually bears in its potency the university of things, it exerts un-
> derstanding of this or that thing, when it actually assimilates itself to
> the thing understood. This assimilative potency, brought in this way to
> actuality in particulars, is afterwards transferred to actuality complete-

---

77. In *The Philosophy of Symbolic Forms* Ernst Cassirer, a thinker deeply influenced
by Cusanus, develops the significance of the human mind's pursuit of unity for the sake
of the self. Through symbolic forms the mind organizes the manifold into a coherent
unity in which the self can exist as a unity in its own right. In this context, however, we
are more interested in the availability of human thought as a vehicle for the relationship
between God and the universe rather than between self and self or God and self.

78. *DFD* II h 59, Bond. Also see Sermon XXII.

Scientia namque universali sua acceptione omnia scibilia, deum scilicet/et quidquid est, ambit.

ly and to the perfect art of mastery, when in the intelligible heaven it knows itself as a likeness of all things so that the intellect is actually an intellectual university of all things when it is a discriminative notion of all things.[79]

The privilege given to rational/intellectual beings is not anthropological chauvinism, but is rooted in the availability of thought as an expression of a larger theological movement. Through the mind, humanity escapes its corporeal limits, assimilating itself to the known object. The thinking process is symbolic for the universe's theosis, for the triumph over space and time, and for the return to the infinite God. Cusanus's text *Idiota de sapientia* has the Socratic structure of a supposedly ignorant layman conversing with a conventionally wise man. This traditional form stresses the necessity of humility and shows that the mind's approach to God is merely a specialized version of the entirety of the general human relationship to God. It suggests that the mind is not the sole locus of interaction between Creator and creation, but that this interaction is predicated on the original condition of a wider theophany.

In sum, the human mind is privileged for Cusanus, not because it is the universe's most complex evolutionary development or the main characteristic that differentiates human from the rest of the creatures, but because in it we meet God. Because God is the living axis of our minds, they constitute the path to theosis or becoming like the divine mind. Our pursuit of wisdom is thus representative of our more general search for God.

79. *DFD* VI h 87, Bond.

Iam tibi satis patere potest quomodo quidem secundum meam qualemcumque coniecturam intellectualis natura est rerum universitas intellectuali modo et, dum in scholis huius mundi versatur, quaerit potentiam ipsam in actu ponere et se particularibus formis assimilat. Tunc enim de virtute sua, qua rerum universitatem intellectualiter in potentia gerit, exserit huius et huius rei intellectum, quando se actu rei intellectae assimilat. Transfertur deinde haec potentia assimilative sic in particularibus in actu posita penitus in actum et artem perfectam magisterii, quando in intelligibili caelo se scit omnium similitudinem, ut tunc sit actu ipse intellectus intellectualis rerum omnium universitas, quando est discretiva omnium notio.

Yet even more than being representative, the pursuit of wisdom is, for the intellectual spirit, the path to theosis. *Idiota de sapientia* identifies divine Wisdom as the human intellect's source and goal.[80] Wisdom "proclaims itself in the streets and dwells in the highest places."[81] The same negative and supereminent terminology used about God is used about Wisdom. It is the highest beyond all high places, ineffable, inexpressible, incomprehensible, and so on. Just as God is the soul's desire, Wisdom is the object of delight and relish for the intellect. The language of identity and difference is also echoed here: "But the following speak with relish about Wisdom: viz. those who know that Wisdom is all things in such a way that it is nothing of all things."[82]

Wisdom is the Life and Source of the intellect, a Life and Source to which the intellect seeks return.

> And for every intellectual spirit it is delightful to ascend continually unto the Beginning of its life, although this Beginning remains inaccessible. For to ascend progressively unto Life is to live progressively more happily. And when the intellect, while seeking its own life, is led to the point that it sees that its life is infinite, then the more it sees its own life to be immortal, the more it rejoices.[83]

Thus, here at the level of the intellect is the beginning of the human being's theotic return to God. Here it discovers its own infinity and immortality in the ascent to its Beginning.

In *De pace fidei* wisdom is identified with God, especially with the Word, more directly. The Truth that is sought by the mind is the Word

80. Sources for the nature of divine Wisdom include the deutero-canonical Old Testament Book of Wisdom, the idea of the Logos in the Johannine writings of the New Testament, and a range of Christian thinkers from Justin and Tertullian to Augustine and Aquinas.

81. *IDS* I h 5, Hopkins, 91.

Quoniam tibi dixi sapientiam clamara in plateis, et clamor eius est ipsam in altissimis habitare, hoc tibi ostendere sic conabor.

82. *IDS* I h 10, Hopkins, 99.

Illi autem cum gustu de sapientia loquuntur qui eam ita sciunt omni quod nihil omnium.

83. *IDS* I h 11, Hopkins, 101.

in which all things are created. Absolute wisdom is none other than the One God. It is this wisdom to which the soul approaches in a closer and closer reflection. As will be seen in the next chapter, *De filiatione Dei* approaches this notion of theosis along Christological lines that are even more clearly developed. Nicholas of Cusa's epistemology has led from the negative theology of utter transcendence through the paradoxes of the coincidence of opposites to the return to absolute Wisdom that the intellect desires. An examination of his understanding of the configuration of the reasoning process in the four unities has brought us to the border of theosis, to the brink of divine Sonship, the subject of the next chapter. Having begun with created humanity's distance from God, Cusanus has moved full circle back to the divine focus of his philosophical thought.

4

THEOSIS

THE WORD OF GOD

A Christological Theosis

Nicholas of Cusa uses the Greek term *theosis* in a few key places in his works. In one of these, the first chapter of *De filiatione Dei,* he draws the connection between rationality and deification.[1]

> But you yourself know that *theosis* is ultimacy of perfection, which is called both knowledge of God and of the Word and intuitive vision. Indeed, I believe it is the view of the theologian John that the *Logos* or Eternal Reason, which "in the beginning" was God "with God," gave rational light to the human being when the *Logos* transmitted to the human spirit according to the *Logos's* own likeness. Afterwards, by vari-

---

1. Nicholas sometimes uses the term *ratio* (rationality) to refer to a certain mode of cognition that differs from other modes. For instance, in *De coniecturis* he contrasts rationality with sensation and intellection. In this context, however, rationality is broadly construed as referring to the power of human cognition in general, and the implied contrast is between sentient and nonsentient things.

134

ous admonitions of visionary prophets and finally by the Word, which appeared in the world, the *Logos* declared that this light of reason is the life of the human spirit and that in this our rational spirit, if we have the divine Word, the power of filiation arises in believers.[2]

Because the rational spirit is in the likeness of Eternal Reason, it is the seedbed out of which the power of sonship or deification springs. Along with the link between the intellect and theosis, the above passage also suggests the program for chapter 4. As the second person of the Trinity is central to theosis, this chapter will follow the direction taken by the first two chapters and uncover a profoundly Christological theology. The first part of this fourth chapter will deal with the Word of God as divine self-expression. Thus, it will focus primarily on Cusanus's understanding of revelation and creation. The second part will examine the human intellect as it meets Wisdom and discuss his views of salvation and the human being. It will examine Nicholas of Cusa's view of theosis as an ascent of the intellect and focus on the mind's desire for knowledge, self, and perfection. The third part will investigate what it means for the individual believer to be a son of God.

From a Christological standpoint then, the first part will focus on Christ as the summit of God's self-manifestation. The second will look at the notion of Christ as the *imago Dei,* and the third will present Christ as the mediator of divine sonship.[3] The natural transformation of the former into the latter reflects the outward movement of theophany and its reverse, theosis. In this manner we will arrive at an idea of what Cusanus means by deification and its place in his theology. We will uncover the sense in which, for Cusanus, theophany is a dimension of theosis. Finally, we will set the stage for a discussion in chapter 5 of one

2. *DFD* I h 52, Bond.

3. For the distinction between Christ as viewed from the theology of creation and revelation and Christ as viewed from the doctrines of anthropology and soteriology, I am indebted to a lecture given by Dr. Walter Euler on October 20, 1996, at Gettysburg Theological Seminary in Gettysburg, Pennsylvania, entitled "The Proclamation of Christ in Selected Sermons from the Brixen Period."

of the most serious difficulties to plague Cusanus's doctrine of theosis: the problem of intellectual salvation.

In this chapter, it will be important to note the points at which Nicholas is in line with traditional thought and those at which his works develop into theological novelty. From his statement that the second person of the Trinity exists as "both God and human" (*Deus et homo*)[4] Nicholas's Chalcedonian orthodoxy is evident.[5] We have already seen the passage from *De visione Dei* where Nicholas refers to Jesus as the concrete instance of the coincidence of opposites.[6] In this same text, he calls Jesus' intellect both "truth and image," "God and, likewise, creature," "infinite and, likewise, finite." "Truth" and "infinite" refer to "God," while "image" and "finite" refer to "creature."

The apparent discrepancy with the Chalcedonian definition caused by Nicholas's introduction of the term "intellect" is significant. Its importance is rooted in both Cusanus's Trinitarian thought and his anthropology. It is precisely what makes Jesus the Christ that links him to God and to humanity. Jesus' theandric nature is centered in his intellect because both Intellect (or Wisdom) and creation find their source in God. The God who speaks in creation speaks himself in the Word who is Christ.[7] Thus, the addition of "intellect" to the Chalcedonian formu-

---

4. *DDI* 3.3 h 202, Bond, 177–78.

5. The Council of Chalcedon, which took place in the year 451, formulated the following doctrine of Christ: Jesus Christ is God's Logos made man. He is a single Person in two natures that exist without confusion, change, division, or separation. See Karl Rahner and Herbert Vorgrimler, *Dictionary of Theology* (New York: Crossroad, 1985), 63.

6. See "From Ratio to Intellect" in chapter 3 of this book. The text under discussion is *DVD* XX, 89–90, Bond, 276. "I see you, good Jesus, within the wall of paradise, because your intellect is equally truth and image, and you are equally God and creature, equally infinite and finite. And it is not possible that you should be seen on this side of the wall. . . . For you are the way to the truth and, equally, Truth itself; you are the Way to the life of the intellect and equally are Life itself."

Video, Ihesu bone, te intra murum paradisi, quoniam intellectus tuus est veritas pariter et imago; et tu es deus pariter et creatura, infinitus pariter et finites. Et non est possibile quod citra murum videaris. . . . Tu enim es via ad veritatem pariter et ipsa veritas. Tu es via ad vitam intellectus pariter et vita ipsa.

7. The use of the term "intellect" may also indicate the influence of Meister Eckhart. For a comparison of Cusanus's view of theosis with Eckhart's intellectual salvation,

lation is nothing completely new, but is merely a link between the Pauline and Augustinian view of Christ as Word and the classic Christological formulation. It is, however, an essential link because it is a refutation of the Apollinarian view that Christ possessed no specifically human intellect. But, perhaps more importantly, it opens the way for the fertile theme of the intellect as the locus of deification. No longer is Christ simply the Word of God, on the one hand, and the hypostatic union of God and man, on the other.[8] Instead, the theandric convergence occurs in the intellect of Jesus and is identified with the Word. Thus, deification is given a logic that extends from deification's origin in the divine Word, to the way of Jesus' unified person, and finally to the human intellect as the location of theosis. Nicholas's doctrine of creation and his doctrine of salvation are harmonized by his Christology.

Following this logic, we will begin with an examination of Cusanus's understanding of the Word. The above suggestion that there is an identity between divine Wisdom and the Word of God or the Son must be justified. Evidence for this position is found in a conversation between orator and layman outlined in *Idiota de sapientia*:

> *Orator:* Is Eternal Wisdom anything other than God?
> *Layman:* It is far from anything but God!
> *Orator:* Didn't God form all things by His Word?
> *Layman:* He did.
> *Orator:* Is God's Word God?
> *Layman:* It is.
> *Orator:* So God's Word is also Wisdom?
> *Layman:* To say that God made all things in Wisdom is to say nothing other than that God created all things by His Word.[9]

---

see chapter 5. The idea that Christ is "the Wisdom and power of God" can be traced to Paul's first epistle to the Corinthians (1:18–2:16). It was later developed into doctrine by Augustine in *De Trinitate.*

8. The doctrine of the divine Logos originated with Philo and was later developed by Christian Neoplatonists, including Maximus the Confessor and John Scotus Eriugena.

9. *IDS* I h 21–22; translation is from Hopkins, 115, and my own.
Orator: Estne aliud sapientia aeterna quam deus?

Slightly later in the same passage, Cusanus is even more specific, noting that "in this respect God is the Father's Word, Wisdom, or Son and can be said to be *Equality of Oneness,* or *Equality of Being.*"[10] Thus, God is equated with his Word and with Wisdom.

In a passage from *De pace fidei,* he makes an extensive connection between God and other terms for Jesus Christ, using the voice of Peter:

> First, some say that the Word of God is not God; and this part has already been suffieciently explained, for the Word of God can be only God. Now this Word is reason; for in Greek logos signifies "word," which is reason. That God, who is the creator of all rational souls and spirits, possesses reason is beyond doubt. But this reason of God is only God, as has already been explained; for in God having coincides with being. For he from whom all things are embraces all things in himself and is all in all, for he is the former of all; therefore, he is the form of forms. Now the form of forms enfolds in himself all formable forms. Therefore, the Word, or Reason, the infinite cause and measure of all that can be made, is God. So those who admit that the Word of God has become flesh or man must confess that that man whom they call the Word of God is also God.[11]

Idiota: Absit quod aliud, sed est deus.
Orator: Nonne deus verbo cuncta formavit?
Idiota Formavit.
Orator: Est verbum deus?
Idiota: Est.
Orator: Sic est et sapientia?
Idiota: Non est aliud dicere deum omnia in sapientia fecisse quam deum omnia verbo creasse.
A similar point is made in *DPF* 4–5. Note that in *De docta ignorantia* III the Son is called simply "Equality." Also see *DDI* 1.7–10 and *IDM* XI h 139.
  10. *IDS* I h 21–22; Hopkins, 115.
Et his deus est verbum, sapientia, seu filius patris et potest dici unitatis seu aequalitias.
  11. *DPF* XI h 29, Bond, 30.
Primo quibusdam dicentibus Verbum Dei non esse Deum; et haec pars est iam ante sufficienter patefacta, quoniam non potest Verbum Dei nisi Deus esse. Hoc autem Verbum est ratio; logos enim Graece verbum dicit, quod est ratio; Deum enim habere rationem, qui est creator omnium rationabilium animarum et spirituum, indubium est. Haec autem ratio Dei non est nisi Deus, uti praeexpositum est; nam habere in deo coincidit cum esse. Ille enim a quo sunt omnia in se complec-

Nicholas's Christology arises out of philosophical theology rather than biblical theology. He does not aim at discovering the historical Jesus through exegesis of the biblical texts, but at coming to a philosophical understanding of the significance of God's becoming other than himself.[12] A look at Cusanus's doctrine of the Word must consist of an exploration of his philosophical approach and include an examination of the terms that Cusanus equates in the above passage. God's first motion is his Wisdom, a move that is at once paradoxical, creative, and self-reflective. It is an outward motion and an inward motion, a motion beyond himself, and yet not beyond himself. He has begotten a principle of creation and further manifestation and has become an object for himself. Because of the key role that it plays in theosis, it is this inter-Trinitarian relationship that must be teased out of Cusanus's many texts.

To begin with, the Son or Equality of being all things is not limited by temporality but is truly identical to infinite *Unitas* (Unity or God). Indeed, Cusanus makes it clear that the Word is spoken from all eternity. Since "the Word is not apart from wisdom,"[13] one can say that it is "eternal" and "everlasting." This means that the Word is not restricted to the second moment of theophany, Incarnation, but is present in the initial moment, creation, as well. Since God the Son exists prior (not temporally, but ontologically) to the Incarnation, he is in fact the creative principle.

> But as the equality of being all things, God is the creator of the universe, since the universe has been created according to God. It is to this highest and maximum equality of being all things absolutely that the nature of humanity would be united. As a result, through the assumed

---

titur omnia, et est omnia in omnibus, quia formator omnium; ergo forma formarum. Verbum igitur seu ratio, infinita causa et mensura omnium quae fieri possunt, Deus est.

12. For further analysis, see Miller, *Reading Cusanus,* 50.

13. *DPFV* h 13, Bond, 13.

Respondit Ytalus: "Ymmo non est Verbum extra sapientiam."

humanity, God would, in the humanity, be all things contractedly, just as God is the equality of being all things absolutely.[14]

Note that in this text the second person of the Trinity is the "equality of being *all things*" rather than simply "equality of being" or "equality," language found elsewhere in the same book of *De docta ignorantia*. This shift underscores the fact that the Son is not identified with the Incarnation alone but is essential to Cusanus's notion of a creation that includes a lasting immanence as well. It also sets the stage for theosis. It is because the Son is the being of all things that he is the contracted Maximum, joining God or the "equality of being *all things absolutely*" to creation through himself. Cusanus's Christology is the link between his doctrine of creation and his soteriology.[15]

We have seen in the dialogue between the orator and the layman above that God "created all things by his Word."[16] But it is not just the bare existence of things for which the Word is responsible. He is also the source of their identity with themselves: "Moreover, God causes each existing thing to exist in such a way that it is *this*—e.g., the sky— and not something else or something more or something less. And in this respect God is the Father's Word, Wisdom, or Son and can be said to be *Equality of Oneness,* or *Equality of Being.*"[17]

The referent of "Equality" is not only God the Father, but also the created order. That is, there is a parallelism between the inter-Trinitarian

14. *DDI* 3.3 h 200, Bond, 176–77.

Deus autem, ut est aequalitas essendi omnia, creator est universi, cum ipsum sit ad ipsum creatum. Aequalitas igitur summa atque maxima essendi omnia absolute illa esset, cui ipsa humanitatis natura uniretur, ut ipse Deus per assumptam humanitatem ita esset omnia contracte in ipsa humanitate, quemadmodum est aequalitas essendi omnia absolute.

15. The term "soteriology" is used throughout this book to refer not merely to redemption from the fallen state of Adam, but in a broader sense, to the total restoration and deification of humanity and the entire created order.

16. *IDS* I h 21, Hopkins, 115.

17. *IDS* I h 22, Hopkins, 115, 117.

Deus etiam tradit sibi tale esse ut sit hoc, puta caelum, et non aliud, nequee plus neque minus. Et hic deus est verbum, sapientia, seu filius patris et potest dici unitatis seu entitatis aequalitas.

relationship and the ontology of creation. The same Word that is equal to the Father is the cause of temporal things' equality, not with the divine order, but with themselves.

For a thing to be equal to itself is for it to neither lack nor have a surplus of anything it needs for it to be itself, that is, for it to have the proper *form*.[18] Here are echoes of the same theme we encountered regarding theophany and the self-identity of the universe and its components.[19] What we met before in the language of God's *complicatio-explicatio* we now meet in the Christological guise of the Form of forms. This recasting of the same thought represents not so much a change of mind regarding the locus of the identity-bestowing process in the Trinity as a refinement of an earlier notion. The integration of Christ into creation is, as we shall see, an indispensable precursor to his role in theosis.

In typical fashion, Cusanus reverts to numerical examples to explain how it is that the Word is the Infinite form of things. He invites us to consider the number one and the "power of oneness" that is in it.[20] Even if twoness or tenness is subsequently considered, the power of oneness is seen as the "most precise exemplar" of these later numbers because of its simplicity and unity-imparting character. In a similar manner "the Form of the Divine Art" is the Exemplar of the form of the sky and of the human form and of all forms.

The creative immanence of Wisdom is the origin of its designation as Form of forms: "By comparison you see that because the singular and most simple Wisdom of God is infinite, it is the most true Exemplar of all formable forms. And this serving as an Exemplar is the reach-

18. *DDI* 1.8 h 22, Bond 96–97.
19. See "The Implications of Theophany for Creation" in chapter 2 of this book..
20. *IDS* I h 24, Hopkins, 119.
Diende si hic ad formam numerorum se converteret, dualitatem aut denaritatem considerando, et reverteretur tunc ad vim actualem unitatis, ipse videret formam illam quae ponitur esse vis actualis unitatis, praecisissimum exemplar dualitatis—sic etiam denaritaatis et alterius cuiuscumque numeri numerabilis.

ing forth whereby Wisdom extends unto all things, delimits all things, and disposes all things."[21]

The presence of the Infinite Form in all forms means that the relationship between Infinite Form and finite form parallels that between original and image.

Despite Wisdom's generous self-communication, it "cannot be grasped, as it is, by anything."[22] Here it becomes apparent that some of the same themes resurface in Nicholas's Christology that were explored in earlier chapters in reference to God. All of these themes center around the notion of Christ as Wisdom or Word. For instance, his characterization of the Absolute Concept in *Idiota de sapientia* is a reworking of the "Not-other" language that we encountered in *De li Non aliud*.

The Absolute Concept

The Absolute Concept, also "called God's Word or Reason" is a name for God that Nicholas of Cusa develops.[23] According to him, a philosopher seeking a name of God that is *correct* or *precise* can come no closer than the terms "rectitude" or "precision" themselves. Likewise, justice itself comes closer to God than any just concept. When aiming at a just concept of God, it is most productive to simply consider justice itself. In fact, "the concept of concept approaches the Inconceiv-

21. *IDS* I h 25, Hopkins, 119, 121.

Sic vides unicam et simplicissimam dei sapientiam, quia est infinita, esse omnium formarum formabilium verissimum exemplar. Et hoc est suum attingere, quo omni attingit, omni finit, omnia disponit.

22. Ibid.

Et licet se omnibus communicet liberalisseme, cum sit infinite bona, tamen a nullo capi potest uti est; identitas enim infinita non potest in alio recipi, cum in alio aliter recipiatur.

23. *IDS* II h 35, Hopkins, 137.

Orator: Hic conceptus, ut puto, dei verbum seu ratio dicitur.

Nicholas also uses the familiar "Equality of all formable things" terminology in this context. Although in the following passages he refers to "God" rather than to "the Word," we are justified in exploring them in reference to Christology because of the tone of the entire book, which deals with God as Wisdom, Word, Son, Equality, and Concept.

able" because "in every conceiving the Inconceivable is conceived."[24] While there is no correct, precise, and so on, concept of God, God encompasses rectitude, precision, and the like. Nicholas has moved the ontological *Non-aliud* to an epistemological level. We saw above that the question of what God is in comparison to some thing is answered by looking at the absolute sense of the thing and finding that God is *not other* than the thing. Here one takes the concept of one's attempted conceptualization of God as the proper characterization of him.

He elaborates, "Every question about God presupposes what is being asked about; and, in regard to every question about God, that which the question presupposes is that which is to be given as the answer. For example, in every term's signification God is signified—even though he is unsignifiable."[25]

For instance, Cusanus explains, the question of the existence of something presupposes being. Thus, when God's existence is questioned, one has one's answer in the question. Likewise, "if someone asks what God is, then since this question presupposes that there is quiddity, you will reply that God is Absolute Quiddity."[26] God as Wisdom and Word is the Absolute Presupposition of whatever knowledge one attempts to gain of him. There is, thus, a Trinitarian presupposition to Cusanus's doctrine of knowledge of God.[27]

This Trinitarian aspect is further developed by Nicholas's assertion

24. *IDS* II h 28, Hopkins, 127.

Idiota: Audisti quomodo in omni conceptu concipitur inconceptibilis. Accedit igitur conceptus de conceptu ad inconceptibiliem.

25. *IDS* II h 29, Hopkins, 129.

Idiota: Omnis quaestio de deo praesupponit quaesitum; et id est respondendum quod in omni quaestione de deo quaestio praesupponit. Nam deus in omni terminorum significatione significatur, licet sit insignificabilis.

26. *IDS* II h 30, Hopkins, 129.

Sic si quis quaesiverit quid est deus, cum haec question praesupponat quidditatem esse, respondebis deum esse ipsam quidditatem absolutam.

27. For an excellent look at the notion of "Absolute Presupposition" see R. Haubst's discussion in "Theologie in der Philosophie—Philosophie in der Theologie des Nikolaus von Kues," 53ff. Haubst is concerned with the question of reason vs. revelation, as well as Cusanus's anticipation of Descartes.

that the Word is God's knowledge of himself. A word, he writes, is a disclosure of the mind that forms it. "Now, the conception by which the mind conceives itself is a word begotten from the mind—i.e., is the mind's knowledge of itself. . . . In the foregoing manner, make a conception of the Former-of-all-things, even as you made a conception of mind; and conceive that He knows Himself from the Word begotten from Him."[28]

The Word is the vehicle of God's self-disclosure in the universe and of his disclosure to himself. The creative outward movement of God is predicated upon an inner, Trinitarian movement. In the second person of the Trinity, God becomes an object for himself and knows himself. God's Word is the Absolute Concept, God's concept of himself.

Nicholas asserts that he has here moved beyond both affirmative and negative theology to what he calls *theologia sermocinalis* or "theology of the spoken Word."[29] When the Word of God is considered the absolute presupposition of all questions and things, a "more nearly true" proposition about God is formed.[30] In contrast to negative theology, locutional theology does not exclude signification but leads to God "through the meaning of a word."[31] This way of speaking about God is actually a kind of second-order affirmative theology. Rather than affirming the applicability of a word to God, it inquires after the presuppositions of the word itself. The exemplary Word who is an ontological presupposition of the *existence* of created things is also the model for the word that figures in any statement about God.

28. Nicholas of Cusa, "Compendium sive compendiossima directio." Trans. Jasper Hopkins, "Compendium," *Nicholas of Cusa on Wisdom and Knowledge* (Minneapolis: Arthur J. Banning Press, 1996), 407.

29. Hopkins translates this as "locutional theology." For more on this, see the book by Peter Casarella entitled *Nicholas of Cusa's Theology of the Word* (New Haven: Yale University Press, 1992).

30. *IDS* II h 33, Hopkins, 135, "veriores."

31. Ibid.

Nam si tibi de deo conceptum quem habeo, pandere debeo, necesse est quod locutio mea, si tibi servire debet, talis sit cuius vocabula sint significativa, ut sicc te ducere queam in vi vocabuli quae est nobis communiter nota, ad quaesitum.

The equation of "Absolute Concept" and "Reason" with the Word opens Christology to a *complicatio* (enfolding) language similar to that examined earlier. All things preexist in the Concept in the same way that things that enter existence due to a reason are said to exist previously in that reason.[32] Nicholas relies on his customary metaphors of an infinite line and an infinite circle to clarify how the Absolute Exemplar (or Form) enfolds all components of the created order. He asks us to imagine an infinite circle, despite the fact that circles cannot be truly infinite. In such a circle, the diameter would be an infinite line, but so also would be the circumference since no two things can be infinite. The circumference would not be curved because a curved line would necessarily circle back and impose limitation on itself, including a specific relation to the diameter.[33]

Nicholas continues:

You see by yourself most clearly the fact that Infinite Rectitude is to all things as an infinite line (if there were one) would be to all figures. For if infinite rectitude (which, of necessity, is absolute) is found (when considered as contracted to a line) to be, of necessity, the enfolding, the preciseness, the rectitude, the truth, the measure, and the perfection of all befigurable figures, then Absolute Rectitude, considered in a way that is altogether absolute and that is uncontracted to a line or to anything at all, is likewise, in an absolute way, the Exemplar, the Preciseness, the Truth, the Measure, and the Perfection of all things.[34]

If infinity is imposed on any figure, whether circle, triangle, or square, it becomes an infinite line. In this way, the infinite line is said to

32. *IDS* II h 35, Hopkins, 137.
33. circumference = pi x diameter
34. *IDS* II h 43, Hopkins, 149.
Idiota: Per te ipsum hoc clarissime conspicis quod infinita rectitudo se habet ad omni sicut infinita linea, si foret, ad figures. Nam si infinita rectitudo (quae est necessario absoluta) ad lineaam contracta, reperitur necessario omnium figurabilium figurarum complicatio, praecisio, rectitudo, veritas, mensura, et perfectio: tunc absoluta rectitudo, absolute penitus et incontracte ad lineam aut aliud quodcumque considerate, est similiter absolute omnium exemplar, praecisio,. Veritas, mensura, et perfectio.

be the truth of all shapes and to enfold them in its own perfection. In the same way, Absolute Rectitude, here a cognate for the Word, is the Measure and Perfection of all created things.

Cusanus argues that if the Word is the Form of forms and the Exemplar of things, their being is a "partaking" in that exemplar. Here in the Christological context he does not develop the language of participation as extensively as he does elsewhere, but it is present nonetheless. (It is, of course, the forms, rather than particular things, that participate in the Infinite Form.) He writes, "Consequently, it happens that Wisdom, received in various forms in various ways, brings it about that each form, called to sameness with Wisdom, partakes of Wisdom in the best way it can."[35] Some things partake of Wisdom from a great distance, giving them only the most elemental being. Other things partake of Wisdom according to varying gradations of spirit, by which they are endowed with mineral, vegetable, sensible, imaginative, rational, or intellectual life.

The Absolute Contracted Maximum

Nicholas's notion of Christ as Absolute Maximum in *De docta ignorantia* develops the notion of exemplarism along Christological lines. The Maximum is defined as that "than which there cannot be anything greater," something that "*is* all that can be."[36] In his enfolding and infinite totality, God is the Absolute Maximum, *uncontractible* to anything

---

35. *IDS* I h 25, Hopkins, 121.

Ex quo evenit ut sapientia in variis formis varie recepta hoc efficiat ut quaelibet ad identitqatem vocata modo quo potest sapientiam participet, ut quaedam eandem participent in quodam spiritu valde distanti a prima forma, qui vix esse elementale tribuit, alia in magis formato, qui esse minerale tribuit, alia adhuc in nobiliori gradu, qui vitam praebet vegetabilem, adhuc alia in altiori, qui sensibilem, post hoc qui imaginabilem, deinde qui rationalem, post qui intellectualem.

36. *DDI* 1.4 h 11, Bond, 91–92.

Maximum, quo maius esse nequit, simpliciter et absolute cum maius sit, quam comprehendi per nos possit, quia est veritas infinita, non aliter quam incomprehensibiliter attingimus. . . . Excedit igitur maxima aequalitas, quae a nullo est alia aut diversa, omnem intellectum; quare maximum absolute cum sit omne id, quod esse potest, est penitus in actu; et sicut non potest esse maius, eadem ratione nec minus, cum sit omne id, quod esse potest.

and existing only in itself. Contraction is the delimitation of a universal to a particular in order for it to be a thing. In contracting, for example, the species of humanity to Socrates, generality, nonquantifiability, and indivisibility are lost, while finitude, quantifiability, and specificity are gained. Because contraction entails restriction in space and time, it is utterly ruled out in the case of the infinite God. Although Nicholas analyzes universals and particulars in this way, he is ambiguous about the existence of universals independent of particulars. However, his argument for the necessity of an Absolute *Contracted* Maximum stems from the nominalist conviction that humanity exists only in the particular human.

It is Cusanus's theory of exemplarism that clarifies the ambiguity in his thought regarding universals. While in *Idiota de mente* Cusanus seems to think that forms do not exist apart from the mind, in *De docta ignorantia* he is not so clear. He follows the statement that "since the universe actually exists only in a contracted way, the same is true of all universals" with "universals are not rational entities only."[37] Universals exist by abstraction, but have real existence in the things to which they are contracted. Moreover, the speculation about whether he has nominalist or Platonic convictions is rendered pointless when one realizes just how *limiting* Cusanus found this choice. A lengthy passage from *Idiota de mente* demonstrates that Cusanus was well aware of the difference between the two positions and that he preferred the third option of Christological exemplarism. Rather than attempting to analyze Cusanus's exemplarism into either a nominalist or realist position on universals, a better approach is to recognize that Cusanus's "ambiguous" doctrine is a direct result of his own refusal to be restricted to these alternatives.[38] It is

---

37. *DDI* 2.6 h 125, Bond, 143–44.

Universum enim quia non est actu nisi contracte, ita omnia universalia: Non sunt universalia solum entia rationis, licet non reperiantur extra singularia actu; sicut et linea et superficies, licet extra corpus non reperiantur, propterea non sunt entia rationis tantum, quoniam sunt in corpore sicut universalia in singularibus.

38. For more on this topic, see Watts, *Nicolaus Cusanus*, 68–72. Watts calls Nicholas

Christ who is the Form of forms, the Maximum Exemplar in whom all universals are united.

In his article "Cusanus and the Platonic Idea"[39] Karsten Harries analyzes Cusanus's rejection of nominalism and Platonism in terms of Plato's divided line. On the one hand, Cusanus adheres to the Platonist notion that a particular is phenomenal, merely an indicator of a transcendent reality. On the other hand, "a universal must by its very nature fail to do justice to the particular. It has its roots in the connective activity of the *mens*. . . . We have remained on the third level of the divided line instead of ascending to the fourth."[40] In other words, the particular can never fully capture reality, and its alternative, the universal, is a product of the mind. Cusanus's solution to the problem of universals is explained in terms of the Exemplar, the Absolute Maximum.

Because the privatively infinite universe and its components can always be more or less contracted (they are variable in their particularity), they exist between a maximum and a minimum. No member of a species, says Cusanus, can ever be the maximum of that species because at the point of maximality it enters another species. Though at variance with modern biology, what Cusanus is trying to convey is the impossibility for any particular thing to be the exemplar of its species. Everything bounded by time and space is finite, embodying various forms but never actually being the full concrete embodiment of those forms because of its finitude and variability. A particular human being can be admired for his or her intelligence, beauty, strength, and so on, and be taken as representative of human beings in general (in a work of art, for example). He or she is not the true equal of any other member of the species, much less of all of them. Everyone knows that this person could have been taller, slimmer, or more intelligent and that he or she is

---

of Cusa's doctrine of universals "ambiguous" because it does not consistently follow either a nominalist or a realist line.

39. Karsten Harries, "Cusanus and the Platonic Idea," *New Scholasticism* 37 (1963): 188–203.

40. Ibid., 196.

mortal. A true maximum of the species would, on the other hand, not just be *taken* as representative, but would actually *be* the exemplar, unchangeable, against which all other members of the species would be measured. The problem with finding a concrete maximum is exactly that: he or she would just be another member of the species.

Just as there is no individual that is the maximum (or minimum) of a species, there is no species that is the maximum of any genus and for the same reasons as above.[41] Any time a species reaches its highest or lowest point it is subsumed under another genus. One cannot even say that the universe itself reaches "the limit of absolute maximumness" for though it is unbounded, it is not infinite in the same way that God is.[42] It is not all there is to be, definitive of both actuality and possibility. On theological grounds it is also impossible for the universe itself to be a concrete absolute maximum. If something *other* than God were an absolute maximum it would delimit God's absolute maximality, a theological impossibility since God is infinite. The contradiction between God's infinity and the limitation imposed by a concrete absolute maximum outside of God is resolved only by God himself being the concrete absolute maximum.

In the creative Word, Nicholas reminds us, God is the equality of being all things:

> It is to this highest and maximum equality of being all things absolutely that the nature of humanity would be united. As a result, through the

---

41. "Just as the minimum coincides with the absolute maximum, so also the contractedly minimum coincides with the contracted maximum." *DDI* 3.2 h 190, Bond, 173.

Et quemadmodum minimum coincidit maximo absoluto, ita etiam ipsum contracte coincidit cum maximo contracto.

See "The Implications of Theophany for God" in chapter 2 for more on this topic.

42. *DDI* 3.1 h 185, Bond, 170–71.

Non attingit itaque universum terminum maximitatis absolutae, neque genera terminum universi attingunt neque species terminum generum neque individua terminum specierum: ut omnia sint id, quod sunt, meliori quidem modo intra maximum et minimum, et Deus principium? medium et finis universi et singulorum, ut omnia, sive ascendant sive descendant sive ad medium tendant, ad Deum accedant.

assumed humanity, God would, in the humanity, be all things contractedly, just as God is the equality of being all things absolutely. Because
this human being would, by the union, exist in the maximum equality of being, this human would be the Son of God, just as this human
would be the Word, in whom all things have been made.[43]

In the hypostatic union, the Word that is equality of being all things is
contracted. In flesh and blood, time and space, the Form of forms, the
Exemplar of all things is made concrete.

It should be noted that Cusanus's search for a contracted maximum
is not idle pseudo-scientific speculation about the structure of the universe. Rather, he is trying to establish a symmetry between what could
be called the outward and the inward divine movements. God's outward creative movement is one of theophany, a self-manifestation in
which God unfolds himself in the universe. Although this functions as a
basis for theosis and, we will see later, is realized already in some sense,
it is not itself divinization in the Christian tradition. If a strongly immanent theophany were all there were to theosis, the result would be
a pantheism in which creation would be immediately identified with
God. Cusanus sees the need to complete the expressive divine motion
with a return that allows for the genuine ontological independence of
the created order and a true differentiation between God and the universe.

The lynchpin of this dual divine movement is, of course, Christ,
and Cusanus is very careful in his formulation of the hypostatic union.
He is determined to preserve the integrity of the divine, while insisting
on the reality of the union. He clarifies his position when he writes:

43. *DDI* 3.3 h 200, Bond, 176–77.

*Aequalitas igitur summa atque maxima essendi omnia absolute illa esset, cui ipsa humani-
tatis natura uniretur, ut ipse Deus per assumptam humanitatem ita esset omnia contracte in ipsa
humanitate, quemadmodum est aequalitas essendi omnia absolute. Homo igitur iste cum in ipsa
maxima aequalitate essendi per unionem subsisteret, filius Dei foret sicut Verbum, in quo omnia
facta sunt, aut ipsa essendi aequalitas, quae Dei filius nominatur secundum ostensa in prioribus;
nec tamen desineret esse filius hominis, sicut nec desineret esse homo, prout infra dicetur.*

Therefore, since the absolute God is unable to be mingled with matter and does not inform it, who could conceive of so wonderful a union, which is unlike the union of form and matter? This union would be greater than all intelligible unions; for that which is contracted, because it is maximum, would exist in such a union only in absolute maximumness and would add nothing to maximumness, for maximumness is absolute, nor would it pass over into the nature of maximumness, for it itself is contracted.[44]

The contracted Absolute Maximum would be neither God alone, nor only a creature, nor a composite of the two. Rather, "We would have to conceive of this as God in such a way that it is also a creature and as creature in such a way that it is also God, as both creator and creature without confusion and without composition."[45]

Nicholas then finds it necessary to ask what the nature of this contracted maximum should be.[46] The answer, of course, is that it must be a nature in which all of creation can be enfolded and returned to God. The Son's union with human nature, intended from all eternity, is both revelatory and soteriological in purpose.

Nicholas adopts the Neoplatonic view that the human being encompasses both lower, sensible nature and higher, intellectual nature. It is, therefore, a microcosm and an ideal medium for the Incarnation that will return all things to God. If human nature were united with Maximality, it would be the perfection of things great and small; nothing in

---

44. *DDI* 3.2 h 194, Bond, 174–75.

Quis igitur tam admirandam conciperet unionem, quae neque est ut formae ad materiam, cum Deus absolutus sit impermiscibilis materiae non informans? Omnibus profecto unionibus intelligibilibus haec maior esset, ubi contractum non subsisteret—cum sit maximum—nisi in ipsa absoluta maximitate, nihil illi adiciens, cum sit maximitas absoluta, neque in eius naturam transiens, cum sit contractum.

45. Ibid.

Oporteret enim ipsum tale ita Deum esse mente concipere, ut sit et creatura, ita creaturam ut sit et creator, creatorem et creaturam absque confusione et compositione.

46. *DDI* 3.3 h 195, Bond, 175.

Faciliter ad ista consequenter inquiri poterit, cuius naturae contractum ipsum maximum esse deberet.

the universe would be left out of the ascendance toward union with
God that would be effected by the coincidence of the Absolute Maximum with contracted being. Nicholas trades hypothetical languages for
factual when he asserts that this is exactly what occurred in the Incarnation of the divine Word. Equality of being all things, Jesus, the First-
born of all creation are all terms that signify the Absolute Maximum
Contraction and the union of God and a human being.

Jesus is the Exemplar, not only of the *being* of rational creatures,
but also of their *theosis*. The hypostatic union is programmatic for the
ascent of the human intellect to God. In Jesus, the humanity is "subsumed in the divinity."

> Because Jesus' intellect is most perfect in existing in actuality complete-
> ly, it can be personally supposited only in the divine intellect, which
> alone is actually all things. For the intellect in all human beings is po-
> tentially all things; it grows by degrees from potentiality to actuality, so
> that the greater it exists in act, the less it exists in potentiality. However,
> because the maximum intellect is the limit of the potentiality of every
> intellectual nature and exists completely in act, maximum intellect can-
> not exist at all unless it were intellect in such way that it were also God,
> who is all in all.[47]

The intellect, which, as we will see, is the locus of divinization for
human beings, follows in its own way the divine Exemplar. Cusanus
uses the metaphor of a polygon, representing human nature, inscribed
in a circle, representing divine nature. If the polygon is to be a maximum polygon, having infinite angles, it would not exist in its own
shape but through that of the circle. Jesus, who hypostatically unites
God and man, surpasses the limit of human beings. When a person is

47. *DDI* 3.4 h 206, Bond, 180.
*Intellectus enim Iesu, cum sit perfectissimus penitus in actu existendo, non potest nisi in divi-
no intellectu, qui solum est actu omnia, suppositari personaliter. Intellectus enim in omnibus hom-
inibus possibiliter est omnia, crescens gradatim de possibilitate in actum, ut quanto sit maior, minor
sit in potentia. Maximus autem, cum sit terminus potentiae omnis intellectualis naturae in actu
existens pleniter, nequaquam existere potest, quin ita sit intellectus, quod et sit Deus, qui est omnia in omnibus.*

brought to his or her maximum, that is, divinized, he or she is brought to the limit of human being, a limit that exists in and is comprehended by Jesus Christ alone.

Cusanus explains how for rational creatures, union with God occurs through the medium of Christ, in the following passage:

> Further, if in this life every rational nature turns to Christ . . . it is united, while the personal truth of each nature remains. . . . Consequently, each of the blessed, while the truth of each's being is preserved, exists in Christ Jesus as Christ and through him in God as God, and God, remaining the absolute maximum, exists in Christ Jesus as Jesus and through him in all things as all things.[48]

Thus, the mysterious link of divine and human in Christ is the gateway for a divine-human unity that allows the human to exist in its own right while existing fully in God. The ontological determinacy bestowed by the exemplary Word is complemented by the theosis made possible by the Incarnation. Theosis does not entail a monism in which the ontological independence of the created order dissolves into God. Nor does deification mean a pantheistic elevation of all things to the status of divinity. Soteriology does not exclude the unique theology of creation that, as we saw in an earlier chapter, Cusanus was so careful to construct.

Learned Ignorance and the Mystery of Christ

This divine-human union that occurs in the Incarnation is mysterious. Though Christ is the Wisdom of God and reveals God to humanity, he too is the subject of *docta ignorantia*. Thus, another Chris-

---

48. *DDI* 3.12 h 260, Bond, 204.

Deinde omnis rationalis natura Christo Domino, remanente cuiuslibet personali veritate, si ad Christum in hac vita summa fide et spe atque caritate conversa fuerit, adeo unita existit, ut omnes, tam angeli quam homines, non nisi in Christo subsistant; per quem in Deo, veritate corporis cuiusque per spiritum absorpta et attracta; ut quilibet beatorum, servata veritate sui proprii esse, sit in Christo Iesu Christus, et per ipsum in Deo Deus, et quod Deus eo absoluto maximo remanente sit in Christo Iesu ipse Iesus, et in omnibus omnia per ipsum.

tological theme, the mystery of Christ, is a reworking of an earlier theological one. Jesus, who is the goal of all understanding, sensing, and being, indeed, the goal of every utterance, is heard *incomprehensibly* in every utterance.[49] Our reasoning is not able to grasp his birth; his death and resurrection are cloaked in mystery. In addition, the hypostatic union between the man Jesus and God transcends our understanding.[50] Therefore, Christ, no less than God, must be approached in learned ignorance.

Christ is, in fact, both the goal of learned ignorance and the way toward it. It is only through faith in Christ that God is revealed to humankind and understanding is reached. Nicholas explains: "Understanding, therefore, is directed by faith, and faith is extended by understanding. Where there is no sound faith, there is no true understanding. . . . But there is no faith more perfect than truth itself, which is Jesus."[51] There is, thus, no understanding apart from faith in Christ because Christ, himself, is the Truth that is sought.

This is not to say that faith in Christ clears up the mysteries of God or makes learned ignorance superfluous. Rather it means that only in Christ do we enter into the fullness of the mysteries of God. Cusanus writes, "The greatest and proufoundest mysteries of God, although hidden to the wise, are revealed by faith in Jesus to the little ones and the humble walking in the world. For Jesus is the one in whom all the treasures of wisdom and knowledge are hidden. . . . Therefore, we also see that because of the immensity of His excellence he cannot be comprehended."[52]

---

49. *DDI* 3.11 h 247, Bond, 198.
50. *DDI* 3.2 h 192, Bond, 173–74.
51. *DDI* 3.11 h 244, Bond, 196–97.
   Dirigitur igitur intellectus per fidem, et fides per intellectum extenditur. Ubi igitur non est sana fides, nullus est verus intellectus. Error principiorum et fundamenti debilitas qualem conclusionem subinferant, manifestum est. Nulla autem perfectior fides quam ipsamet veritas, quae Iesus est.
52. *DDI* 3.11 h 245, Bond, 197.
   Maxima enim et profundissima Dei mysteria in mundo ambulantibus, quamquam sapientibus abscondita, parvulis et humilibus in fide Iesu revelantur, quoniam Iesus est, in quo omnes the-

The unapproachable and unknowable transcendence of God, which, Cusanus emphatically declared, is not the domain of the conventionally wise, is approachable through faith in Jesus. To know God is, as we will see, to be united with God, and it is only through Christ (who is also mysterious, incomprehensible, etc.) that that union occurs.

Paradoxically, "wisdom proclaims itself openly in the streets"[53] but "dwells in the highest places."[54] Though the expert on wisdom is a "poor, utterly unschooled" layman, wisdom is a lofty topic.[55] By his use of the character of the layman, Nicholas emphasizes the need for humility in approaching true wisdom and the questionable authority of traditional texts and education. A Socratic figure, the layman is the one who instructs the wealthy orator in *Idiota de sapientia* and who is sought out by the orator and the philosopher in *Idiota de mente*.[56] Wisdom is inapproachable by conventional means but accessible through the immanent Word of God.

Nicholas does not mean that the wisdom that proclaims itself in the streets is faith severed from any use of the mental processes. It is not the sudden advent of a conviction isolated from God's theophany in creation. Rather, the latter provokes the mind to ask questions about per-

---

sauri sapientiae et scientiarum absconditi sunt, sine quo nemo quidquam facere potest. . . . Qui cum in hoc mundo non sit cognoscibilis, ubi ratione ac opinione aut doctrina ducimur in symbolis per notiora ad incognitum, ibi tantum apprehenditur, ubi cessant persuasiones et accedit fides; per quam in simplicitate rapimur, ut supra omnem rationem et intelligentiam in tertio caelo simplicissimae intellectualitatis ipsum in corpore incorporaliter, quia in spiritu, et in mundo non mundialiter, sed caelestialiter contemplemur incomprehensibiliter, ut et hoc videatur, ipsum scilicet comprehendi non posse propter excellentiae suae immensitatem.

53. Proverbs 1:20.

54. *IDS* I h 3, Hopkins, 89. From Ecclesiastes 24:7.

Ergo autem tibi dico quod sapientia foris clamat in plateis, et est clamor eius quoniam ipsa abitat in altissimis.

55. Here Nicholas uses the term "wisdom" rather than "Wisdom." However, the two are identified later in the text as it becomes clear that the highest wisdom of things, the truth of things, is divine Wisdom. Ordinary wisdom is foolishness, while Wisdom is what is actually sought by the hungering mind. See *IDS* I h 21, and *DPF* IV and V for Cusanus's specific assertion that wisdom is God.

56. Nicholas of Cusa's use of the dialogue form is effectively analyzed in Clyde Lee Miller's *Reading Cusanus*, 111–16.

fection, rectitude, and the like, and these concepts lead it to the "concept of Concept" or God. Nicholas explains, "Hence, mind is a *living* description of Eternal, Infinite Wisdom. But in our minds, at the beginning, that life resembles someone asleep, until it is aroused to activity by wonder, which arises from the influence of perceptible objects."[57] The mystery of Wisdom does not exclude the perceptible world but is present in it. The mind is wakened by this immanence to an understanding of learned ignorance.

Once again, a consideration of the divine has provoked a consideration of the human mind. The representation of Christ in sapiental terms such as "Word," "Concept," and "Wisdom" is linked to the intellect as the locus of deification. The next section of this chapter will trace the ascent of the intellect to God as it enters into divine sonship through Christ the Word and Wisdom of God.

THE ASCENT OF THE INTELLECT

Beyond the Sensible World

Interweaving epistemology and soteriology, Cusanus believes that the intellect's comprehension of particular things is motivated by its desire to comprehend God. His theory of knowledge is Platonic in origin: the mind contemplates things in the temporal order and, dissatisfied, moves on to the eternal order. Certain Neoplatonic elements are omitted, however. The movement is made not through ascending levels of similarity, but between two levels wholly disproportional to one another. Because particular things are but "enigmatic signs of the true," "we who aspire to the filiation of God are admonished not to adhere to sensible things."[58]

---

57. *IDM* V h 85, Hopkins, 207.

Unde mens est viva descriptio aeternae et infinitae sapientiae. Sed in nostris mentibus ab initio vita illa similes est dormienti, quousque admiratione, quae ex sensibilibus oritur, excitetur ut moveatur.

58. *DFD* II h 61, Bond.

Tali quadam similitudine admonemur nos, qui ad filiationem dei aspiramus, non inhaerere

This is not to say that the sensible world is surpassed altogether. There is no contradiction between the above admonishment and the gathering of all things in the intellect. Nicholas is not here suggesting that we abandon the empirical world for the world of universals. Because the lower is encompassed by the higher, there is never an absolute opposition between the world of particulars and the world of ideas. Moreover, *De coniecturis* makes it clear that even the third and second unities are surpassed by the prime unity. Cusanus does not view universals as absolute, not only because they are mental abstractions, but also because they are still plural. "Then we are rightly deified when we are exalted to the extent that in the one we are the one in which are all things and the one that is in all things."[59] Thus, theosis is not the transcending of sensible and particular things, but their union.

Cusanus invites us to imagine that sensible things are books through which God, the "Teacher-of-truth" speaks:

> And then in sensible things we shall contemplate intellectual things, and we shall ascend, by a certain unproportional comparison, from transitory and fleeting temporal things, whose being is in unstable flux, to eternal things, where all succession has been carried off into a steadfast permanence of rest.[60]

---

sensibilibus, quae sunt aenigmatica signa veri, sed ipsis ob infirmitatem nostram absque adhaesione coinquinationis ita uti, quasi per ipsa nobis loquatur magister veritatis et libri sint mentis eius expressionem continentes.

59. *DFD* III h 70, Bond.

Nam, cum deus sit unum, in quo omnia uniter, qui est et transfusio unius in omnia, ut omnia id sint quod sunt, et in intellectuali intuitione coincidit esse unum in quo omnia et esse omnia in quo unum, tunc recte deificamur, quando ad hoc exaltamur, ut in uno simus ipsum in quo omnia et in omnibus unum.

60. *DFD* II h 61, Bond.

Et tunc in sensibilibus contemplabimur intellectualia et ascendemus quadam improportionali comparatione de transitoriis et fluidis temporalibus, quorum esse est in instabili fluxu, ad aeterna, ubi rapta est omnis successio in fixam quietis permanentiam, et vacabimus circa speculationem verae, iustae et gaudiosae vitae separantes nos ab omni inquinamento deorsum se trahente, ut possimus cum ardenti desiderio studii circa ipsum eam ipsam vitam magistrali adeptione hinc absoluti introire.

In this ascent of the mind from the temporal and particular to the eternal and universal, and eventually to God, epistemological theory is translated into soteriology. Deification occurs as the knowing process leads the mind into union with the divine. The mind's coinciding with the created order differs from its coinciding with God in that the latter is the goal of the former. The sensible world, though valuable in its own right, is ultimately to be used as a vehicle for the expression of God's mind. In contrast to the symbolic sensible world, God will ultimately be seen "face to face" "without any enigmatic phantasm."[61] In the created order the truth of all things resides in God.

Here one recalls Cusanus's theory of the Not-other. In creation God has become an object for himself and exists in otherness. But God is the Not-other, and the mind pushes relentlessly on to find him. "Sonship," which we will find to be Cusanus's most important cognate for theosis, is linked to the removal of otherness: "Filiation, therefore, is the ablation of every otherness and difference and the resolution of all things into one thing, which is also the transmission of the one into all things. And this is *theosis*."[62]

Though sonship means that God is seen face to face, Nicholas explicitly cautions against imagining that he is seen "as he is": "[T]he truth is not God, as God is triumphant in Godself, but it is a mode of God, through which God is communicable to the intellect in eternal life. For as triumphant in Godself God is neither intelligible nor knowable, neither is God truth nor life, nor is God."[63] Hence, theosis as as-

---

61. *DFD* III h 62, Bond.

Sed cum illi modi theophanici sint intellectuals, tunc deus, etsi non uti ipse est attingitur, intuebitur tamen sine omni aenigmatico phantasmate in puritate spiritus intellectualis, et haec ipsi intellectui clara est atque facialis visio.

62. *DFD* III h 70, Bond.

Filiatio igitur est ablatio omnis alteritatis et diversitatis et resolutio omnium in unum, quae est et transfusio unius in omnia. Et haec theosis ipsa.

63. *DFD* III h 63, Bond.

Sed si, uti in aliis nostris libellis enodavimus, subtilissime advertis, tunc veritas ipsa non est deus, ut in se triumphat, sed est modus quidem dei, quo intellectui in aeterna vita communicabilis

cent to and union with Truth does not obviate negative theology. In sonship the mind meets God face to face as he is *participable,* not in his *supereminence.*

Wisdom's Irresistible Attraction: The Desire of Self for Self

The mind is motivated in its ascent, not merely by dissatisfaction, but by attraction. Just as the sensible world repels by its blandness, wisdom attracts by its exceeding deliciousness; it is relished and savored by the intellect. Nicholas's gustatory description of Wisdom's attraction differs significantly from the desire for knowledge in Aristotle's "All men by nature desire to know."[64] For Nicholas, "Wisdom" does not refer to cognitive information but to the Wisdom of God through whom divine sonship is attained. Wisdom is a cognate for the second person of the Trinity.

In both thinkers' formulations the intellect is active. For Nicholas, however, the intellect is not just the highest natural function of humanity, but the point where the grace of God meets the individual in theosis. The intellect "is above all those intelligible things that are rational."[65] Moreover, intellectual natures are governed by a king named "Theos or God" who is the perfection of all things. Intellectual natures are attracted to God as they are to their own perfection.

The key to the irresistible attraction of Wisdom is the dialectic of

----

exsistit. *Nam deus in se triumphans nec est intelligibilis aut scibilis, nec est veritas nec vita, nec est, sed omne intellitgibile antecedit ut unum simplicissimum principium.*

64. The first line of Aristotle's *Metaphysics.* In using such terminology, Nicholas shows the influence of mystics such as Pseudo-Dionysius and Bernard of Clairvaux. Rudolf Haubst points out that the difference between the Aristotelian and Cusan versions of the natural desire for knowledge is Cusanus's awareness that because of the *imago Dei,* nothing finite could satisfy the desire. Haubst, "Theologie in der Philosophie—Philosophie in der Theologie des Nikolaus von Kues," 65–66.

65. *DQD* I h 25, Bond, 220.
Deinde altius ad intellectum perge, qui est super omnia intelligibilia, quae sunt rationabilia.

The possible sources for Cusanus's notion of the trans-discursive character of the intellect include Augustine's *De Trinitate,* the works of Pseudo-Dionysius, and Meister Eckhart.

immanence and transcendence. Nicholas writes, "Wisdom is all things in such a way that it is nothing of all things. For all inner relishing of Wisdom is by means of Wisdom and in Wisdom and from Wisdom."[66] The familiar pattern of divine immanence balanced by divine transcendence is the basis for "relishing" Wisdom. It is the attraction of self to Self in which the search for true understanding leads not to objective knowledge but to mystical union with the divine on the one hand and realization of selfhood on the other.

Wisdom, writes Nicholas, "is the life of the intellectual spirit."[67] The sons of God have incessant joy "when the intellectual life, because of its incorruptible nature, not only is not corrupted in annihilation, but also lives on through intellectual tasting."[68] Because the intellectual spirit holds within itself a foretaste of Wisdom, the intellect is attracted to it. Theophany means that Wisdom shines forth in the intellectual spirit and provides the impetus for the intellect's return to its Source. Cusanus argues that apart from this concreated foretaste of Wisdom, the intellectual spirit would not be motivated to seek its Source nor recognize it if it did. The intellectual spirit's desire for Wisdom could not be stronger if it were seeking its own life, as indeed we will see below that it is.

Nicholas explains the intersection of the desire for Wisdom and the desire for one's own life as follows:

> Accordingly, the intellectual spirit is moved toward Wisdom as toward its own life. And for every intellectual spirit it is delightful to ascend

66. *IDS* I h 10, Hopkins, 99.

Per sapientiam enim et in ipsa et ex ipsa est omne internum sapere. Ipsa autem, quia in altissimis habitat, non est omni sapore gustabilis.

67. *IDS* I h 11, Hopkins, 101.

Cum enim ipsa sit vita spiritus intellectualis.

68. *DFD* II h 61, Bond.

Tali quadam licet remotis-sima similitudine gaudium est filiis dei absque intermissione, quando non solum intellectualis vita non corrumpitur annihilatione ob suam incorruptibilem naturam, sed et vivit intellectuali gustu, quo se vivere sentit vita vera intellectuali, quem pura veritas sempiterne reficit.

continually unto the Beginning of its life, although this Beginning remains inaccessible. For to ascend progressively unto Life is to live progressively more happily. And when the intellect, while seeking its own life, is led to the point that it sees that its life is infinite, then the more it sees its own life to be immortal, the more it rejoices.[69]

Nicholas is not here arguing that the human mind merely needs to recognize that it is divine in its own right. Certainly his soteriology has an intellectual cast, but this does not mean that divinization is revelation of the preexisting divine status of all intellectual spirits. Cusanus is no Origenist. Rather, "our mind, the image of the Eternal Mind, endeavors to search out in the Eternal Mind—as does a likeness in its true nature—the measure of itself."[70] Eternal Mind is not the same as mind; the latter is but a reflection of the former.

The intellectual spirit aims at insight into the truth of itself and at a self-conscious life. Because its life, in the absolute sense, coincides with Wisdom, it is drawn toward Wisdom and discovers there its own infinity and immortality. At the same time, the autonomy and transcendence of Wisdom is maintained since the ascent is continual and the Beginning "remains inaccessible." At least one element of theosis, therefore, is this movement toward perfection of the self.

The Search for Self: The Beginning of Modern Subjectivity?

The mind's search for the measure of itself that is included in its quest for Wisdom has invited comparisons with the modern philosoph-

69. *IDS* I h 11, Hopkins, 101.

Cum enim ipsa sit vita spiritus intellectualis, qui in se habet quondam connaturatam praegustationem, per quam tanto studio inquirit fontem vitae suae, quem sine praegustatione non quaereret nec se repperisse sciret, si reperiret: hinc ad eam ut ad propriam suam vigam movetur. Et dulce est omni spiritui ad vitae principium quamvis inaccessibile continue ascendere. Nam hoc est continue felicius vivere: ad vitam ascendere. Et quando eo ducitur vitam suam quarens, ut eam infinitam vitam videat, tunc tanto plus gaudet, quanto suam vitam immortaliorem conspicit.

70. *IDM* XI h 133, Hopkins, 275.

Unde mens nostra, imago mentis aeternae, in mente ipsa aeterna ut similitude in veritata, sui ipsius mensuram venare contendit.

ical preoccupation with the self. The extent to which Nicholas of Cusa can be read as a forerunner of modern thought is important because it will influence our interpretation of his doctrine of theosis. If Nicholas of Cusa's theories concerning the mind's measuring and knowing of itself are taken as the final word on epistemological motivation, then Cusanus is thoroughly modern. If, however, Cusanus's epistemology is driven by a search for something *other* than the self, that is, God, this statement cannot be so easily made. Moreover, if Nicholas is concerned with subjectivity in the modern sense, mystical union through deification cannot be seen as the total aim of human life. Though union with God might still be a *religious* goal for Cusanus, it is conceivable that, on a purely philosophical level, self-consciousness and the knowledge that it makes possible would suffice. We will see that, although Nicholas of Cusa may anticipate modern concerns, he is ultimately a medieval philosopher and theologian.

Some scholars have seen in Cusanus's notion of perfection not merely medieval beatitude but modern subjectivity. Ernst Cassirer, for example, traces a direct line from Nicholas of Cusa's measuring *(mensurare)* activity of the mind *(mens)* to Kant's transcendental unity of apperception.[71] Cassirer believes that Cusanus develops a "new" Neoplatonism that makes him a forerunner of modern thought. Passages such as the following from *Idiota de mente* are often cited in support of this position. According to Nicholas, "*Mens* receives its name from *mensura* . . . in order to attain the measure of itself. For mind is a living measure that attains unto its own capability by measuring other things. For it performs all its operations in order to know itself. But when seeking the measure of itself in all things, mind finds it only where all things are one."[72]

---

71. Ernst Cassirer, *Das Erkenntnisproblem in der Philosophie und Wissenschaft der neueren Zeit* (Berlin: Bruno Cassirer, 1906), I, 21–61.

72. *IDM* IX h 123, Hopkins, 261.

Ut sui ipsius mensuram attingat. Nam mens est viva mensura quae mensurando alia sui capacitatem attingit. Omnia enim agit, ut se cognoscat. Sed sui mensuram in omnibus quarens non invenit, nisi ubi sunt omnia unum.

Knowledge is reached when "all things are one," when plurality is unified by the power of the mind. Cassirer believes that a foreshadowing of the Kantian a priori can be found in medieval Neoplatonism, especially in Cusanus's understanding of the mind as beholding "in its own simplicity all things."[73]

Clearly, Cusanus states that the mind measures all things in order to measure itself. In addition, he is aware of the unifying ability of the mind, calling it "that power present in us which enfolds conceptually the exemplars of all things."[74] The combination of these two elements, however, must not be viewed apart from his larger project. Cusanus's epistemology can be understood only in light of his anthropology, that is, his doctrine of the *imago Dei*. When this doctrine is considered, it is evident that there is no "self-contained" human endeavor, no element of life that can be realized on a purely secular level. All activities of the person, including the project of developing a unified self-consciousness, aim toward the knowledge of (and union with) God that is deification.

After explaining that mind sees all things in the simplicity of its own self and that someone may thereby see how "absolute being itself" is participated, he writes:

> Assuredly, such a man would see (beyond all determinate necessary connection) all the things that he previously saw in a variety—would see them most simply, without variety, in terms of absolute necessity, without number and magnitude, and without otherness. Now, in this most lofty manner mind uses itself insofar as it is the image of God. And God, who is all things, shines forth in mind when mind, as a living image of God, turns to its own Exemplar and assimilates itself thereto with all its effort. . . . In the one thing which is all things it very tran-

73. *IDM* VII h 105, Hopkins, 237.
Et hoc modo in simplicitate sua omnia intuetur.
74. *IDM* II h 58, Hopkins, 173.
Si de vi vocabuli diligentius scrutandum est arbitror vim/illam quae in nobis est, omnium rerum exemplaria notionaliter complicantem, quam mentem appello, nequaquam proprie nominari.

quilly finds rest as in the goal of all its concepts and as in the most delightful true being of its life.[75]

The assimilative activity of the mind is not motivated by a restless search
for self as it is confronted and threatened by a host of perceived objects.
Rather, the mind exercises its given self in the knowing process and in
doing so discovers itself in God. Although the mind does not *constitute*
itself through the knowing process, it does *find* itself. However, it finds
only that which it already is, the image of God.[76]

The mastery of truth through the intellect's unifying power satis-
fies the intellect's desire for its own life and brings beatitude. Cusanus
explains how the mystical union and its corresponding beatitude rest
upon the premises of the Word and the *imago Dei:*

> And this is the highest intellectual joy, when knowing that its begin-
> ning, middle, and end surpass all its height of apprehension, the intellect
> contemplates in its proper object, namely in pure truth. And this means
> it apprehends itself in truth in such excellence of glory that it under-
> stands that nothing can be outside itself but in it all things are it.[77]

This passage locates beatitude in the *imago Dei.*

75. *IDM* VII h 106, Hopkins, 237.
*Talis profecto, supra determinatam complexionis necessitatem, videret omni quae vidit in vari-
etate, absque illa in absoluta necessitate simplicissime, sine numero et magnitudine et omni alteritate. Utitur autem, hoc altissimo modo, mens se ipsa ut ipsa est dei imago; et deus, qui est omnia,
in ea relucet, scilicet quando ut viva imago dei ad exemplar suum se omni conatu assimilando convertit. Et hoc modo intuetur omni unum et se illius unius assimilationem, per quam notions facit
de uno quod omnia . . . ubi tamquam in fine omnium notionum quam suaviter ut in delectabilis-
sima veritate vita suae quiescit.*
76. Karsten Harries in his article "Cusanus and the Platonic Idea," 199–200, points
out that every appearance has two antithetical deficiencies: "it falls short of the unity of
the *mens* and it falls short of the being at which it aims." Rather than opposing these
two, "the element of universality which has its origin in the *mens* to an element of im-
mediacy which has its roots in the *non aliud,*" Cusanus aims toward a reconciliation via
the image of God. Although man can find himself as unity in the realm of mathematics,
this is inadequate to what he essentially is.
77. *DFD* III h 64, Bond.
Et in hoc est gaudium altissimum intellectuale, quando suum principium, medium et finem

To further explain his doctrine of theosis and the *imago Dei,* Nicholas suggests that we envision a perfect mirror that is the reflection of God himself. This most lofty reflection is the "mirror of truth," which reflects without blemish not only God but all lesser contracted mirrors. Moreover, the mirror of truth reflects both God and all things into the *living* mirrors, that is, human intellects with their powers of assimilation. Of course, due to their various curvatures, living mirrors receive this reflection in different ways. "Therefore," Cusanus writes, "in that first mirror of truth, which can also be called the Word, Logos, or Son of God, the intellectual mirror attains filiation so that it is all things in all things and all things are in it, and its kingdom is the possession of God and of all things in a life of glory."[78]

Thus, it is the *imago Dei,* rather than the modern, autonomous "self," that is the focus of the mind's search for itself. Moreover, no metaphor so clearly elucidates the role of the Son, the fulfillment of the image of God, as does the metaphor of the mirror. Because the procession of creation from God occurs through the creative activity of the Son, its return depends on his power of reconciliation. Theophany, self-identity or sustenance-in-being, and theosis are fundamentally Christological.

For Nicholas's theory of deification this means that the human mind finds the basis and possibility for mystical union in its own ability. One must be careful here, however, because while this ability is "natural" to the mind, it is not something that occurs apart from the grace of God. Because of the *imago Dei,* that which is one's "own" never ceases being that which is God's. The *imago Dei,* bestowed on humanity in creation and sustained by divine immanence, is something to which the

---

omnem altitudinem apprehensionis excellere cognoscens in priprio obiecto, scilicet in pura veritate, intuetur. Et hoc quidem est epsum in veritate apprehendere in tali quidem excellentia gloriae, ut nihil extra se esse posse intelligtat sed omnia in ipso ipse.

78. *DFD* III h 67, Bond.

In speculo igitur illo primo veritatis, quod et verbum, logos seu filius dei dici potest, adipiscitur intellectuale speculu00m filiationem, ut sit omnia in omnibus et omnibus et omnia in ipso, et regnum eius sit possessio dei et omnium in vita gloriosa.

mind is called. It is here that the differences with modern notions of subjectivity become clear. Nicholas asks, "And how will you give yourself to me if you do not at the same time give me heaven and earth and all that are in them? And, even more, how will you give me yourself if you do not also give me myself?"[79] The primary object of the epistemological project is God, and the mind finds its true being only as it finds itself in God.

Even Nicholas's apophaticism illustrates his essential medievalism. People can never adequately speak of God because they are able only to speak of themselves. Cusanus is not critical of the ability to know and name *as such* (he is not a skeptic), but critical of the ability to know and name *God*. When he does express doubts about our capacity for knowing things in the created order, it is because they are God's self-manifestation, because they are "created gods."

When Nicholas's theories on the activity of the mind are viewed in isolation, one may well observe modern elements. When, however, the larger body of his thought is taken into account, one cannot escape his essential medievalism. Cusanus's world was seamless; there was no gap between seeking self and seeking God. At every level, philosophical as well as theological, theosis was the goal. God is still the origin, center, and goal of all things. No thing and no activity exists for its own sake, and even this new subjectivity is a result of reflection on the divine.

One might argue that Nicholas of Cusa *was* a modern, though ignorant of possible developments of his thought and blind to his own novelty. But to foresee the future is too much to ask of anyone, and Cusanus was much too learned a man to be unaware of his own uniqueness. Instead, it is more correct to say that, while standing squarely in the medieval tradition, Nicholas reworks certain Platonic concepts that would later be developed by modern thinkers such as Kant.

79. *DVD* VII, h 25, Bond, 246.
   Et quomodo dabis tu te mihi, si non pariter dederis mihi caelum et terram et omnia quae in eis sunt? Immo quomodo dabis tu te mihi, si etiam me ipsum non dederis mihi?

SONSHIP

The desire for one's own perfect self, later echoed by the modern notion of the subject, is the motivation behind the individual move toward theosis. Cusanus's text *De filiatione Dei (On Divine Filiation)* defines theosis as perfection. Linking deification with the image of the Logos, he writes:

> Moreover, in summary, I consider filiation of God to be reckoned as nothing else than deification, which, in Greek is also called *theosis*. But you yourself know that *theosis* is ultimacy of perfection, which is called both knowledge of God and of the Word and also intuitive vision. Indeed it is the view of the theologian John that the *Logos* or Eternal Reason, which "in the beginning" was "God with God," gave rational light to the human being when the *Logos* transmitted to the human a spirit according to the *Logos'* own likeness.[80]

Of all Nicholas's works, *De filiatione Dei* most directly addresses deification or theosis. Here the definitions of theosis include "filiation," "ultimacy-of-perfection," "knowledge of God and His Word," and "intuitive vision." Later in the same passage Nicholas clarifies the connection between the definitions. He explains that the light of reason is "the life of our spirit," and that an acceptance of the Divine Word causes the power of sonship to arise in the rational spirit. Bearing in mind that the true life of the spirit is its finding of its own infinity in Wisdom, (see above and *IDS* I, 11) the former can be identified with perfection. Thus, when the intellectual spirit, created by the Word in the *imago Dei,* proceeds to knowledge of God and the Word, it too becomes

---

80. *DFD* I h 52, Bond.

Ego autem, ut in summa dicam, non aliud filiationem dei quam deificationem, quae et theosis graece dicitur, aestimandum iudico. Theosim vero tu ipse nosti ultimitatem perfectionis exsistere, quae et notitia dei et verbi seu visio intuitive vocitatur. Hanc enim ego theology Iohannis sententiam esse arbitror quomodo logos seu ratio aeterna, quae fuit "in principio" deus "apud deum," lumen homini dedit rationale, cum ei spiritum tradidit ad sui similitudinem.

a son of God. The cognate "intuitive vision" is a reminder that knowledge of God is not discursive but arises out of learned ignorance.

On the basis of the analysis of Nicholas's Christology in the earlier part of this chapter, his understanding of deification as sonship can now be explored. This section will include a look at sonship as perfection, "the sonship of many sons," and union and the removal of otherness. With this, the groundwork for addressing certain controversial topics in the next chapter, especially the problem of intellectual salvation, will be laid. We will conclude by observing the aptness of Cusanus's admonition in the dedication of *De filiatione Dei*:

> Take, Right Reverend Confrere, what occurs here with this agreement that you do not suppose that I am adding anything new to what you have read in my past conceptions. For nothing has remained, even in the inmost heart, that I have not committed to these writings, which express my general conjectures of whatever sort.[81]

We will indeed "sufficiently understand" in his work on divine sonship. Though Nicholas has not articulated it until now, he has been talking about theosis all along.

Sonship as Sustenance and Perfection

We saw above that the intellect's desire for knowledge, especially knowledge of God, is driven by its quest to measure itself by measuring all things. "In this world we study by means of the senses, which attain only to particulars. We are brought from the sensible world of particulars over to the universal art, which exists in the intellectual world. For the universal exists in the intellect and belongs to the intellectual realm."[82]

---

81. *DFD* I h 51, Bond.

Confrater merito colende, recipe eo pacto id quod occurrit, ut non putes me quidquam his adicere, quae in praeteritis meis legisti conceptibus. Nihil enim in intimis etiam remansit praecordiis, quod non illis ipsis mandaverim litteris meas generales qualescumque exprimentibus coniecturas.

82. *DFD* II h 57, Bond.

Nam nihil in variis obiectis particularibus quaesivit medio sensuum intellectus in hoc mundo nisi vitam suam et cibum vitae scilicet veritatem, quae est vita intellectus.

For something to be perfect is for it to exist in its fullness, in its maximum condition. But from *De visione Dei* we know that it is the second person of the Trinity who is the Absolute Maximum, both of the human intellect and of all things. It is "Jesus, in whom the humanity is supposited in the divinity; for, otherwise, his humanity could not be maximum in its own fullness."[83] It is in the Christ, then, that true perfection is found because it is only there that humanity reaches its limit, divinity.

This means that perfection is not reached autonomously or independently, but only when the intellect is confronted by and united with the infinite perfection of God. It is significant that Cusanus was not troubled by an existential view of the divine Infinite as a threat to the potentially infinite human self. We recall Werner Beierwaltes's comments on *De visione Dei* that "Analogous to thought and self-recognition, in the sight of God, the countenance of the human being is not rendered contourless or denied; its individuality is not extinguished. Instead, it is in God as *God himself,* just as the intellect . . . is only then able to then recognize itself 'when it sees itself in God just as it is.'"[84] Here in the language of *De visione Dei* is the idea of theosis as sustenance in being. Unblinded by God's overwhelming infinity, human sight recognizes itself in its vision of God. Not only is the human face not eclipsed by God, it comes to know its own self in God.

Seeking its own perfection, the intellect is both sustained by the presence of the divine and oriented toward the destined theosis of uni-

---

83. *DDI* 3.4 h 206, Bond, 180.

Quare quadam licet remota similitudine ita in Iesu considerandum, ubi humanitas in divinitate suppositatur, quoniam aliter in sua plenitudine maxima esse non posset.

84. Werner Beierwaltes, *Visio Facialis: Sehen in Angesicht,* Bayerische Akademie der Wissenschaften Philosophische-Historische Klasse Sitzungsberichte 1988, Heft 1 (Munchen: Verlag der Bayerischen Akademie der Wissenschaften, 1988), 27. "So ist—analog zum Denken und zur Selbsterkenntnis des Intellects—das Angesicht des Menschen im Sehen Gottes nicht negierend konturlos gemacht, nicht als individuelles ausgeloescht, sondern es ist *in* Gott als *es selbst Gott,* so wie der Intellekt (die Vernunft als "intellectualis viva dei similitude") sich nur dann *selbst* zu erkennen imstande ist 'wenn er sich in Gott selbst schaut so wie er ist.'"

ty with God. The proximity of sustenance in being to Equality, the second person of the Trinity, is evident. For a thing to be equal to itself is for it to have its proper self-identity. Equality of being, says Cusanus, "is that which is in a thing as neither more nor less, as nothing too much and as nothing too little."[85] It is for a thing to have exactly what it is to be itself. Situating equality in the Trinitarian rubric of Oneness, Equality, and Union, Cusanus calls this quality "itness."

> Although the equality of unity is begotten from unity and the connection proceeds from them both, nevertheless, unity, equality of unity, and the connection proceeding from both are one and the same: It is as if we used the words "this" [*hoc*], "it" [*id*], and "the same" [*idem*] to refer to the same thing. What we name "it" is related to a first thing, but what we call "the same" connects and joins the related object to the first thing. If, therefore, from the pronoun "it" we should form the word "itness" [*iditas*], we could speak of "unity," "itness," and "sameness" [*unitas, iditas, identitas*], which would closely enough apply to the Trinity.[86]

Divine Equality or Itness is the exemplar for the self-identity of all things. The Son is the Form of forms through whom all things have their self-identity, their own proper form. It is my position that deification is not only sanctification but also participation or, if viewed from the side of God, that divine immanence that makes a thing what it is.

---

85. *DDI* 1.8 h 22, Bond, 96–97.
Aequalitas vero essendi est, quod in re neque plus neque minus est; nihil ultra, nihil infra.
86. *DDI* 1.9 h 25, Bond, 97–98.
Quamvis ab unitate gignatur unitatis aequalitas et ab utroque connexio procedat, unum tamen et idem est unitas et unitatis aequalitas et connexio procedens ab utroque,—velut si de eodem dicatur: "hoc, id, idem." Hoc ipsum quidem, quod dicitur id, ad primum refertur; quod vero dicitur idem, relatum connectit et coniuingit ad primum. Si igitur ab hoc pronomine, quod est id, formatum esset hoc vocabulum, quod est iditas, ut sic dicere possemus "unitas, iditas, identitas," relationem quidem faceret iditas ad unitatem, identias vero iditatis et unitatis designaret connexionem, satis propinque Trinitati convenirent.

Theophany as a Dimension of an Infinite Theosis

As was suggested above, the closely related notions of sustenance in being and perfection are the lenses through which theophany can be viewed as a dimension of theosis. Cusanus himself does not always clearly separate the self-identity possessed by things in this present age and the ultimate perfection of things in the world to come. He does, as we will see, distinguish in a few significant passages between the present temporal and future eternal lives and argue for the fullness of deification in the latter. These passages serve to maintain his orthodoxy against any threat of replacing the Christian notion of history with Neoplatonist timelessness. His tendency in the vast majority of his works to collapse the distinction between the two is evidence that he saw theosis in the next world as an extension of a process that had already begun in this one.

Beierwaltes makes the connection between the *sein-gebend* (being-giving) vision of God and *filiatio* (sonship) or theosis. Nicholas, however, fully develops the term "sonship" in *De filiatione Dei*, rather than in *De visione Dei*. The aspiration unto sonship is an intellectual power that is capable of reaching the heights of divinity. So great is the power that participates in divine power, it is "as if the intellect were a divine seed."[87] Because for Cusanus the divine is the infinite, the divinizing intellectual power is infinite as well.

Sonship is not fully realizable in this life, however, as he explains:

And since this filiation is the ultimate of all power, our intellectual faculty is not exhaustible this side of *theosis,* nor does it attain that which

---

87. *DFD* I h 53, Bond.

Haec est superadmiranda divinae virtutis participatio, ut rationalis noster spiritus in sua vi intellectuali hanc habeat potestatem, quasi semen divinum sit intellectus ipse, cuius virtus in credente in tanum ascendere posit, ut pertingat ad theosim ipsam, ad ultimam scilicet intellectus perfectionem, hoc est ad ipsam apprehensionem vertatis, non uti ipsa vertas est obumbrata in figura et aenignmate et varia alteritate in hoc sensibili mundo sed ut in se ipsa intellectualiter visbilis.

is ultimate perfection at any level this side of that stillness of filiation's perpetual light and life of eternal joy.[88]

The power of sonship is the ultimate power, and Cusanus always associates the ultimate with the infinite. Though the intellectual power is inexhaustible, it does not reach its ultimacy or infinity in this life but only "when we will have been loosed from this world."[89]

Deification remains a promise fulfilled only in the life to come because of the restrictions on knowledge resulting from the "contracted mode" of all things. By the unenlightened "contracted mode," Cusanus means the embodied, particular, and multiple character of knowable things. Objects and even concepts are limited by the conditions of existence in this world and can be apprehended by the mind only as such.

Though Nicholas is influenced by Platonism here, he is not espousing the unreality of the contracted universe. On the contrary, the contracted world has its own truth, a truth that is not comprehended in itself by the limited and imperfect intellect. The problem is that the intellect and knowable things are both contracted, and one contracted thing cannot encompass another. The intellectual power to see the truth itself, apart from all figuration, symbolism, and contraction, is the perfection and deification of the intellect, something that will occur in the next life.

Nicholas's Neoplatonism is, of course, evidenced in the reciproc-

---

88. *DFD* I h 54, Bond.

Et cum filiatio ipsa sit ultimum omnis potentiae, non est vis nostra intellectualis citra ipsam theosim exhauribilis neque id ullo gradu attingit, quod est ultima perfectio eius, citra quietem illam filiationis lucis perpetuae ac vitae gaudii sempiterni.

89. *DFD* I h 54, Bond.

Nam cum nihil in hoc mundo in cor hominis, mentem aut intellectum quantumcumque altum et elevatum intrare queat, quin intra modum contractum maneat, ut nec conceptus quisquam gaudii, laetitiae, veritatis, essentiae, virtutis, sui ipsius intuitionis aut alius quicumque modo restrictivo career posit—qui quidem modus in unoquoque varius secundum huius mundi condicionem ad phantasmata retractus erit—, dum de hoc mundo absoluti fuerimus, ab his etiam obumbrantibus modis relevatus, sic scilicedt ut felicitatem suam intellectus noster, ab his modis subtrahentibus liberatus, sua intellectuali luce divinam vitam nanciscatur, in qua, licet absque sensibilis mundi contractis aenigmatibus, ad intuitionem veritatis elevetur.

ity between present self-identity and future deification. Sonship is both sustenance in being and future perfection. The former is given meaning by the latter's promise, and the latter finds its seeds in the former. Nevertheless, Nicholas's tendency to obscure the boundaries between the present life and the life to come and his suggestion of an infinite theosis should not be read as a Neoplatonic timelessness. Though there is an eternal element to Jesus' Sonship, there is no evidence that Nicholas has lost sight of the Incarnation as a decisive historical event that grounds theosis. Moreover, while sonship is an eternal movement, it is not circular but progressive.

Our condition in this world and the next can be compared to boyhood and manhood. Nicholas writes, "However, manhood does not belong to the world of childhood where a person is still growing, but to the world of completion. The boy and the man are the same. But the filiation is not apparent in the boy, who is numbered among the servants, but rather in an adult state, when he reigns together with the father."[90] Now we are deified in the way that we manifest God's self, but "we will then be in another mode that which we are now in this mode."[91]

The idea that the fullness of deification occurs in the next life is both a defense against monism and a justification of the third aspect of theosis, theosis as return. The idea that both theophany and the existence of the created order as itself are elements of theosis may inspire charges of monism. If, in the language of Neoplatonism, procession, remaining, and reversion are identified, no actual differentiation has taken place. Or, in the language of causality, the effect would not really return

90. *DFD* II h 56, Bond.
Virilitas autem non est de mundo pueritiae, ubi adhuc homo crescit, sed de mundo perfectionis. Idem est puer qui et vir. Sed non apparet in puero, qui servis conumeratur, ipsa filiatio, sed in adulta aetate, ubi conregnat patri.
91. *DFD* II h 56, Bond.
Non arbitror nos fieri sic filios dei, quod aliquid aliud tunc simus quam modo. Sed modo alio id tunc erimus, quod nunc suo modo sumus.

to the cause because it was never different from the cause in the first place. Theosis nullifies itself because there is no separate existence to *be deified* if all things are already divine.

The problem, which has plagued Neoplatonists since Proclus, is an extension of the problem of identity and difference in procession and return.[92] Something that exists as a result of procession is both identical to and different from that from which it proceeds.[93] In both its procession and its return, identity and difference are present. But if there is no point at which the participant is completely ontologically independent of the participated, no point when it is free of both its origin and its goal, its actual existence must be questioned. If reversion is the exact reversal of procession, the real significance, and thus the real existence, of that which proceeds is in doubt. If nothing new and separate occurs in procession, if that which proceeds is no different from what was there all along, theosis is only a veil over an ultimately monist system.

Cusanus, however, consistently refers to theosis as a "path" by which we are "to go on with the pursuit of filiation."[94] It is a process and a journey that is completed in the next life. The Word with whom the intellect is mystically united in deification is nourishment that is only partially received at this time.[95] Though "God is not knowable in this world,"[96] still the intellect has a foretaste of his Wis-

---

92. See E. R. Dodds, *Proclus: The Elements of Theology,* 2nd ed. (Oxford: Oxford University Press, 1963), and Gersh, *From Iamblichus to Eriugena.*

93. It is important to note here that the word is "proceeds" rather than "proceeded," since it is the ontological order that is at issue rather than the temporal.

94. *DFD* IV h 72, Bond.

Quoniam autem te maxime optare non haesito, ut tibi conceptum viae pandam, qua in huius temporis fluxu ad studium ipsum filiationis pergendum esse conicio, hinc adhuc prout occurrit, id ipsum explicare conabor.

This concept is also reinforced by the language of *manuductio* ("being led by the hand") in *De visione Dei.*

95. Compare the New Testament notion of "Kingdom."

96. *DDI* 3.11 h 245, Bond, 197.

Qui cum in hoc mundo non sit cognoscibilis, ubi ratione ac opinione aut doctrina ducimur in symbolis per notiora ad incognitum, ibi tantum apprehenditur, ubi cessant persuasiones et accedit fides; per quam in simplicitate rapimur, ut supra omnem rationem et intelligentiam in tertio caelo simplicissimae intellectualitatis ipsum in corpore incorporaliter, quia in spiritu, et in mundo non

dom.[97] Theophany and sustenance in self-identity may be elements of theosis, but they are incomplete. The return to God is not the reversal of theophany but its fulfillment.

Furthermore, deification is an *infinite* movement of the intellectual spirit toward God. According to Cusanus, "Since that vital movement cannot rest except in Infinite Life, which is Eternal Wisdom, then that spiritual movement (which never infinitely attains unto Infinite Life) cannot cease. For the intellectual spirit is always moved by most joyous desire, so that it will attain unto never becoming satiated with the delightfulness of its contact with Wisdom."[98] In no sense, then, is theosis the simple negation of theophany or a movement back to a simple static point. Rather, the intellectual spirit has an infinite distance to travel as it pursues likeness to the Infinite God. Nor is the spirit's appetite sated by its union with God; it is simply provoked to greater desire. The Son, God's Eternal Wisdom, is indeed "the beginning, the middle, and the end of all things," but the End is not identical to the Beginning.[99]

The Sonship of Many Sons

Charges of monism are also parried by Cusanus's denial that theosis resolves the modes of this world into homogeneous unity. Rather, deification reflects the creative variety of theophany. The epistemological doctrine that the vision of God bestows self-recognition rather than wiping out individuality is here given ontological significance. Nicholas's notion of the "sonship of many sons" implies that theosis does not

---

mundialiter, sed caelestialiter contemplemur incomprehensibiliter, ut et hoc videatur, ipsum scilicet comprehendi non posse propter excellentiae suae immensitatem.

97. *IDS* I h 15, Hopkins, 107.

98. *IDS* I h 18, Hopkins, 111.

Si igitur exemplar est aeternum et imago habet vitam in qua praegustat suum exemplar et sic desideriose ad ipsum movetur, et cum motus ille vitalis non posit quiescere nisi in infinita vita, quae est aeterna sapientia, hinc non potest cessare spiritualis ille motus, qui numquam infinitam vitam infinite attingit. Semper enim gaudiosissimo desiderio movetur, ut attingat quod numquam de delectabilitate attactus fastiditur.

99. *DFD* IV h 72, Bond. *quod est omnium principium, medium et finis, immo in omnibus omnia, in nihilo nihil.* Also *IDS* I h 15, Hopkins, 107.

obviate differentiation, but that it too has "modes."[100] Because it is as varied as creation, the mode of theosis is called "participation in adoption." Only the sonship of the Son is without mode because only the Son is absolutely identical to God. Here, again, is confirmation that Nicholas's doctrine of theosis cannot be separated from his doctrine of theophany. In the same way that all things participate in God due to God's self-manifestation, their deification can also be called "participation."

The doctrine of the sonship of many sons has important repercussions for Nicholas's soteriology. Above all, it distinguishes his thought from Neoplatonism, on the one hand, and scholasticism, on the other. For Cusanus, freeing the intellect from the mode of contraction does not entail returning to an undifferentiated One. In the mystical union the intellect is intimately joined with God but not eclipsed. The intellect coincides with God but is not identical to him. "Therefore, the filiation will be in many children by whom it will be participated in various modes."[101] Participation is a condition not only of sustenance in being, an element of theophany, but of deification as well.

Furthermore, unlike the Thomistic analogical model in which theosis is predicated upon an original similarity, for Cusanus theosis is similitude based on the tension between an original *dis*junction and identification between God and creation. Nicholas of Cusa avoids attributing similar perfections between God and man. Instead of becoming more and more *like* God, deification is the coinciding of God and creation. As we have seen, this identity is not solely a terminal soteriological event, but is a present condition.

---

100. The term "mode" has a long history in philosophy. Descartes used it to describe an accident or quality of a thing; Spinoza used "mode" to mean an affection of the substance or something that inheres in something else through which it can be understood (*Ethics* Book I, definition 5); and Locke used "mode" to refer to a complex idea (*Essay Concerning Human Understanding* 2,12 4–5 and 2, 13 ff.). Thomas Mautner, *A Dictionary of Philosophy* (Cambridge, Mass.: Blackwell Publishers, 1996). Nicholas himself uses it three times in *DFD* I h 54, Hopkins, 161.

101. *DFD* I h 54, Bond.
Igitur filiatio ipsa in multis filiis erit, a quibus variis participabitur modisl.

Universal Knowledge

Cusanus further explains the concept of sonship as union by developing the idea of universal knowledge: "For the filiation of God is then in the intellect when the art is in it; nay more, when the intellect is itself that divine art in which and through which all things are; nay more, when it is itself God and all things in accord with that mode in which it has it has attained the mastery."[102] We mentioned above the assimilative activity of the mind that makes it a living measure of all things, able to encompass and unify them in itself. In *De filiatione Dei*, Nicholas articulates his theory of divine sonship in terms of this activity. The intellect's natural desire to master the truth, to have universal knowledge, drives it to look beyond the world of particulars. Divine sonship is the possession of universal knowledge, "when the intellect finds itself to be in that realm where the Master of all workable works is, namely the Son of God, that Word through which the heavens and every creature were formed."[103]

Sonship is the reflection in the image, or intellect, of theosis in its three forms: its origin in the creative act of the Word, its sustenance-in-being, and its return to God. In sonship, divine universal knowledge and human mastery of truth coincide as "the intellect is both God and all things." The original union of all things in God is transposed into the union of all things *and* God in the intellect. The idea that in the intellect "all things are the intellect"[104] echoes the notion that "[I]n you

102. *DFD* II h 58, Bond.
Est enim tunc in ipso ipsa dei filiatio, quando in eo est ars illa; immo ipse est ars illa divina, in qua et per quam sunt omnia; immo ipse est deus et omnia modo illo, quo magisterium adeptus est.
103. *DFD* II h 58, Bond.
Quietatur igitur studium vitae et perfectionis atque omnis motus intellectus, quando se comperit in ea regione esse, ubi est magister omnium operum operabilium, scilicet filius dei, verbum illud, per quod caeli formati sunt et omnis creatura, et se similem illi.
104. *DFD* II h 59, Bond.
Intellectus igitur illius secundum modum magisterii ambit deum et omnia ita, ut nihil eum aufugiat aut extra ipsum sitg, ut in ipso omnia sint ipse intellectus.

my God the tree is you yourself."[105] It is this "universal receptivity" of the mind that makes it the perfect *imago Dei*. Deification is the process whereby the mind takes on the divine unitive power, coinciding with both God and created things.

In conclusion, it is evident that Nicholas of Cusa viewed theosis as more than a simple, one-directional movement of the human being to God. His treatise *De filiatione Dei* makes it clear that his doctrine of divine sonship is not an isolated theme, tacked on to the main body of his work. Instead, he advises "that you do not suppose me to be adding anything new to what you have read in my past conceptions."[106] Theosis is multidimensional, encompassing theophany and divine immanence, as well as the ultimate return to God.

105. *DVD* VII h 24, Bond, 246.
Et ita arbor est in te deo meo tu ipse deus meus.
106. *DFD* h 51, Bond.
Confrater merito colende, recipe eo pacto id quod occurrit, ut non putes me quidquam his adicere, quae in praeteritis meis legisti conceptibus.

5

THE PROBLEM OF

INTELLECTUAL SALVATION

CUSANUS AND NEOPLATONISM

An analysis of Nicholas of Cusa's doctrine of theosis would not be complete without addressing a controversy that concerns the systematic importance of the intellect to his thought. The essence of the problem consists of the strong influence of Neoplatonist philosophy on Nicholas's theology. Although it was Pseudo-Dionysius whom Martin Luther accused of being *plus platonisans quam christianisans,* Nicholas of Cusa faced the same problems of intellectual salvation and the consequent privileging of the mind over the body.[1] Nicholas of Cusa's mystical orientation and Neoplatonic background are strongly influenced by the conversation that his predecessors had with the Greek philosophy of their day. All of these thinkers have been accused to one degree or an-

1. Martin Luther, *Heidelberg Theses,* vol. 31 of Luther's *Works* (Philadelphia: Muhlenberg Press, 1957).

other of allowing their Neoplatonic terminology to take over the essential Christian content of their thought. Charges of philosophical schizophrenia have been leveled against Gregory of Nyssa by Harold Cherniss, for instance, who cites Gregory's simultaneous censure and wholehearted acceptance of Greek metaphysics.[2] Other Greek Christians were accused of Origenism. We saw in the first chapter's historical introduction of the term "theosis," however, that such charges are unsubstantiated for Gregory of Nyssa, Maximus the Confessor, and Pseudo-Dionysius.

Since this issue touches upon central Christian doctrines, it is important with respect to Nicholas's orthodoxy. Along with undermining the goodness of creation and the place of repentance from sin in salvation, an intellectual salvation threatens to make Christ into merely a Christian dressing of an otherwise pagan philosophical system.[3] Despite the fact that his approach occasioned such a controversy, a look at this topic will show that he maintains an orthodox position both objectively and in his own mind.

Nicholas of Cusa's troublesome emphasis on the human intellect is evident in many of his works. It is precisely the rubric that Cusanus finds so fertile, the capacity of the mind to encompass a multitude of things and to thus imitate God, that lies at the heart of the debate. It has been suggested that perhaps his Neoplatonic epistemology has replaced his Christian soteriology. The claim that Nicholas advocates an intellectual salvation and neglects a doctrine of sin is not without basis. Evidence that the influence of Platonism led him to view salvation as illumination and theosis as enlightenment can be found in his works. In addition to the emphasis on knowledge of God and the intellect as the locus of deification, Nicholas tends to view sin as an ontological divide rather than in terms of moral wrongdoing and evil.

2. Harold F. Cherniss, *The Platonism of Gregory of Nyssa*, (New York: B. Franklin, 1971).

3. Pseudo-Dionysius faced similar accusations. For instance, Paul Rorem in his article "The Uplifting Spirituality of Pseudo-Dionysius," *Christian Spirituality: Origins to the Twelfth Century*, ed. B. McGinn, J. Meyendorff, and J. LeClercq (New York: Crossroad, 1988), 132–44, calls Pseudo-Dionysius' Christ a "cosmetic figure."

The light metaphor is favored by Cusanus since "the intellectual spirit is that which, in reason, understands, and the Divine Spirit is the one who illuminates the understanding intellect."[4] The very idea that sonship is "taught" through contemplation of the sensible world suggests that a Platonic ascent has replaced Christian grace. The created order exists "to the end that by means of sensible signs the teaching of the highest mastery would transmit itself into human minds and effectively transform them into a similar mastery."[5] It is not the soul that is restored after the fall, but the intellect that transcends its own limitations. Sin is not a matter of human disobedience but of finite existence and viewpoint. Salvation tends to be intellectually based, a matter of education, rather than transformative.

In several passages he suggests that there *is* a moral element to the wisdom that deifies, though that element tends to be purgative. Wisdom is received in "a temple purged of all moral failing"[6] and is clung to with "fervent love."[7] Certainly, Wisdom is not purely cognitive, not found in books and rhetoric, but experiential. Cusanus explains:

> For just as all knowledge of the taste of a thing-never-tasted is empty and sterile until the sense-of-taste attains unto that taste, so too a simi-

4. *DQD* II h 35, Bond, 224–25.

Sicut igitur ratio discretiva est, quae in oculo discernit visibilia, ita intellectualis spiritus est, qui in ratione intelligit, et divinus spiritus est, qui in ratione intelligit, et divinus spiritus est, qui illuminat intellectum.

5. *DFD* IV h 76, Bond.

Tali quadam similitudine principium nostrum unitrinum bonitate sua creavit sensibilem istum mundum ad finem intellectualium spirituum, materiam eius quasi vocem, in qua mentale verbum varie fecit resplendere, ut omnia sensibilia sint elocutionum variarum orationes a deo patre per filium verbum in spiritu universorum explicatae in finem, ut per sensibilia signa doctrina summi magisterii in humanas mentes se transfundat et ad simile magisterium perficienter transofrmet, ut sit totus iste sensibilis mundus sic ob intellectuaem et homo finis sensibilium creaturarum et deus gloriosus principium, medium et finis omnis operationis suae.

6. *IDS* I h 27, Hopkins, 123.

Sic nunc pro hoc brevi temmpore haec sic dicta sufficient, ut scias sapientiam esse non in arte oratoria aut voluminibus magnis, sed in separatione ab istis sensibilibus ac in conversione ad simplicissimam et infinitam formam et illam recipere in templo purgato ab omni vitio et fervido amore ei inhaerere, quousque gustare eam queas et videre quam suavis sit illa quae est omnis suavitas.

7. Ibid. *fervido amore*

lar thing holds true of that Wisdom, which no one tastes through hearing but which he alone tastes who receives it in terms of an inner tasting. He gives testimony not about things which he has heard but about what he has tasted experientially within himself. (To know the many descriptions of love that the saints have left us is, without a tasting of love, a certain emptiness.)[8]

This love, however, that grows out of experience does not seem to have a social element. Instead, it appears to be merely an intensification of the total desire of the mind for illumination.

Nicholas of Cusa presents a theological anthropology in which human failing is equated with finitude. He complements this with a Christology that neglects a portrayal of Jesus as savior. Christ is the bridge of the ontological divide between God and man. Cusanus calls Christ the supreme Exemplar according to which all things are formed, the Word spoken by God, the Absolute Concept, Reason, and divine Wisdom. In the Incarnation ignorance is banished but sin is not expiated. Along with abandoning the traditional doctrine of sin, Nicholas's soteriology would appear to deal inadequately with the problem of evil. He fails to emphasize that Christ has grappled with evil and triumphed over death. His humanity appears to be essential, not for sacrifice, but for revelation. Because the perfection of Christ's humanity is emphasized over the death of his humanity, his human nature seems too spiritual to be real.

That Nicholas's soteriology has an intellectual character is undeniable. Whether or not he has replaced an essential Christian doctrine with Neoplatonic philosophy is not so clear. This question can be fully answered only with reference to the historical precedent of

8. *IDS* I h 19, Hopkins, 113.

Sicut enim omnis scientia de gustu rei numquam gustatae vacua et sterilis est, quousque sensus gustus attingat, ita de hac sapientia, quam nemo gustat per auditum, sed solum ille qui eam accipit in interno gustu. Ille perhibit testimonium non de his quae audivit, sed in se ipso experimentaliter gustavit. Scire multas amoris descriptiones quas sancti nobis reliquerunt, sine ammoris gustu vacuitas quaedam est.

the doctrine of theosis in the Greek fathers. Along with a reflection on the precedent set by Gregory of Nyssa, Maximus the Confessor, and Pseudo-Dionysius, a comparison with a thinker who is generally recognized as accepting the theory of intellectual salvation, Meister Eckhart, will be helpful. In addition, a look at Nicholas of Cusa's theology of the cross as found in his sermons and an exploration of Cusanus's doctrine of grace will help us answer the thorny question of Cusanus's Neoplatonist soteriology.

In his emphasis on the divinization of the intellect rather than the salvation of the soul, Nicholas departs from the Western theological tradition. How extensively Cusanus actually read thinkers like Gregory of Nyssa and Maximus the Confessor who successfully incorporated a Platonic concept of theosis into their Christian systems was discussed in chapter 1. He certainly did read both Meister Eckhart and John Scotus Eriugena, both of whom refer to the Greek fathers. Even if Cusanus only received these ideas filtered through Eckhart and Eriugena, the mere existence of this precedent is significant.

If an intellectual approach to deification is accepted in the Eastern tradition, the same latitude should be allowed for a Western thinker like Nicholas of Cusa. His focus on the intellect should not be viewed as an importation of non-Christian elements into a purportedly Christian system, but as an attempt to bridge the gulf between Eastern and Western Christian traditions. Nicholas's Eastern tendencies should not cause him to be suspect in Western eyes, but, given his involvement in attempts at reconciliation between the two branches of the church, should alert the reader to the depth of Nicholas's convictions on "the peace of faith." Given his beliefs about the unity of the church, Nicholas felt free to borrow from the Eastern tradition and did not at all see himself as surrendering central Christian tenets.

The issue of intellectual salvation poses two interrelated questions: Does salvation occur only *by means of* the mind? And, does salvation or deification occur only *to* the mind? The first concerns whether deification occurs only through the intellect, and the second whether it is the intellect alone that is deified. The two questions are closely intertwined, of course. If, for instance, the created order, including the body, is viewed in negative terms, theosis would tend to consist of an intellectual detachment from it. If, however, the created, material world is good and destined for salvation in its own right, the human mind is not alone in its deification.

Many of the defining elements of theosis that help answer such questions are deeply embedded in Greek Christian thought. These include such notions as God's self-manifestation in creation, redemption as infinite theosis, and the possibility of cosmic redemption and universal salvation. It may be, therefore, unnecessary to extend the debate concerning the paganism or orthodoxy of Pseudo-Dionysius to Nicholas of Cusa since the accepted place of Neoplatonist philosophy in Patristic thought may render the debate moot on both accounts.

While he did bring a new focus to the role of human thought in the divine-human relationship, he neither anticipated modern subjectivity and cosmology nor capitulated to Neoplatonic philosophy. Rather, he was engaged in the development and reintroduction of an ancient Christian theme. Just as Aquinas was indebted to John of Damascus and Bonaventure to Dionysius, Nicholas of Cusa was influenced by Byzantine and possibly Patristic thought. Therefore, the same acceptance that is granted to the intellectual approach to salvation in Eastern Christian theology should be extended to Nicholas of Cusa's thought.

We have seen the strong tradition of theosis that preceded Cusanus's own development of the term. While Gregory of Nyssa, Maximus the Confessor, and Pseudo-Dionysius tended to emphasize the intellect in deification, a close reading showed that they are clearly distinguishable from Neoplatonism. Although only Pseudo-Dionysius's direct influence on Cusanus is known for certain, the similarities between Cusan thought and Patristic thought are remarkable.

Gregory of Nyssa's positive view of the body and the material world and his suggestion of a universal and cosmic salvation are both not far from Cusanus's own ideas. For instance, Cusanus tells us that

> [d]oubtlessly, our mind was put into this body by God for its own development. . . . Similarly, the power of the mind—a power that grasps things and is conceptual—cannot succeed in its operations unless it is stimulated by perceptible objects; and it cannot be stimulated except by the intermediacy of perceptual images. Therefore, the mind needs an instrumental body.[9]

And it is not the case that the mind needed a body and a perceptual world so that after the creation of minds, God created the latter. Instead, mind is prior "by nature, not temporally."[10]

Maximus's preoccupation with the paradox of divine immanence and transcendence, as well as their unity in Christ, is one of Nicholas of Cusa's chief concerns also. And Cusanus's debt to Pseudo-Dionysius, particularly in the area of negative theology, has never been a case for debate.

While these thinkers evince important differences from pagan thought, none of them has a clearly developed theology of the cross. Cusanus too has deficiencies in this area and, like them, has been accused of substituting a theology of enlightenment. The question of Cusanus's lack of a theology of the cross has been directly addressed in a study done by Walter Andreas Euler and presented to the American Cusanus Society.[11] Based on his extensive review of Cusanus's writings, and especially his sermons, Euler concludes that Cusanus does indeed have a general and unique, although not traditional, theology of the cross.

---

9. *IDM* 4 h 77, Hopkins, 197.

Indubie mens nostra in hoc corpus a deo posita est ad sui profectum . . . sic vis mentis, quae est vis comprehensiva rerum et notionalis, non potest in suas operations, nisi excitetur a sensibilibus; et non potest excitari nisi mediantibus phantasmatibus sensibilus Opus ero habet corpore organico, tali scilicet sisne quo excitatio fieri nonn posset.

10. *IDM* 5 h 81, Hopkins, 203. *natura, non tempore*

11. Walter Andreas Euler, "Does Nicholas of Cusa Have a Theology of the Cross?" *Journal of Religion* 80 (2000): 405–20.

Euler finds that along with a view of Christ's death in Anselmian satisfaction terms[12] and as a victory over the devil,[13] two other interpretations appear most often in Cusanus's sermons. Most commonly, Nicholas interprets Jesus' death on the cross according to the Johannine notion of revelation.[14] God's self-revelation culminates in the death suffered by Jesus as a result of his witness to the truth. Moreover, Jesus' sacrifice justifies and judges all of humanity because the person of Christ enfolds all people, and Christ is the Maximum of human being.[15] The final interpretation of Christ's death found in the sermons complements and completes the first three. Because of Christ's knowledge of his own death *(scientia mortis)* he, and he alone, experienced the total estrangement from God that comprises the penalty of damnation. Our justification, then, depends on a combination of Christ's awareness in his suffering of punishment, his enfolding of all humankind in himself, and his witness to divine truth.

Euler's conclusion that Nicholas of Cusa did not, even in his sermons, present a Lutheran theology of the cross, but rather a more general theory, is well founded.[16] If "theology of the cross" is broadly understood as ascribing to the cross of Christ a substantial meaning providing insight into divine revelation and the event of salvation, then Cusanus does indeed have such a theology.[17]

It is evident that Cusanus recognizes two conditions that separate humankind from God: the subjective condition of sin and the objec-

---

12. Sermo I, n. 17–25 (Christmas 1430), Opera omnia XVI, 14–19; Sermo XXXV, n. 3 (Good Friday 1444), Opera omnia XVII/1, 63–68.

13. Sermo LIII (Good Friday 1445), Opera omnia XVII/3, 240–48. Christ's death is also seen as a victory over death in *De docta ignorantia* and *De pace fidei.*

14. Sermo CXXII (Good Friday 1452), Opera omnia XVIII/1, p.1–10; Sermo XXVII, n. 4 (Good Friday 1443), Opera omnia XVII/1, 1–10; Sermo CLIV (Palm Sunday 1454), unedited; and *DDI* III, 6.

15. See discussion of Christ as Maximum in "The Epistemology of Cusanus" in chapter 3.

16. In Luther's Heidelberg theses, 1518, he defines *theologia crucis* as focusing on the visible things of God seen through suffering and the cross, as opposed to speculation about God through reason and metaphysics. Luther's *Works,* vol. 31, 40.

17. Euler, "Does Nicholas of Cusa Have a Theology of the Cross?"

tive condition of human finitude. The finite human mind cannot reach divine truth unless it is virtuous.[18] Cusanus is not silent on the issue of virtue. He writes, "Now, moral failings are what we have of our own, whereas from Eternal Wisdom we have only things that are good. Therefore, the Spirit of Wisdom does not dwell in a body subjected to sins or in a malevolent soul but dwells, rather, in its own morally pure field—its morally pure image—as its own holy temple."[19]

Moreover, Cusanus identifies the virtues with divine illuminations:

Whoever turns to the virtues walks in the ways of Christ, which are the ways of purity and immortality. Virtues are divine illuminations. Therefore, whoever in this life turns by faith to Christ, who is virtue, will then be found in purity of spirit when this person is set free from this temporal life, so that one is able to enter into the joy of eternal possession. When according to all its intellectual powers our spirit turns by faith to the purest and eternal truth, to which it subordinates all else, and when it chooses and loves this truth as alone worthy of being loved, then, indeed, there is a turning of our spirit.[20]

The intellect is not divided from the moral center of a person; no gap exists between intellectual illumination and purity of action. Truth and morality go hand in hand.

18. Abelard has a similar view.
19. *IDS* I h 20, Hopkins, 113, 115.

Id autem quod de nostro habemus, vitia sunt, de aeterna vero sapientia non nisi bona. Quapropter spiritus sapientiae non habitat in copore subdito peccatis neque in malivola anima, sed in agro sujo puro et sapientiali, munda imagine quasi in templo sancto suo.

From I Corinthians 3:8. Cf. *IDS* I h 27, Hopkins, 123, 125.

Id autem quod de nostro habemus, vitia sunt, de aeterna vero sapientia non nisi bona. Quapropter spiritus sapientiae non habitat in copore subdito peccatis neque in malivola anima, sed in fyings.

20. *DDI* 3.9 h 237, Bond, 193–94.

Qui se ad virtutes convertit, ambulat in viis Christi, quae sunt viae puritatis et immortalitatis. Virtutes vero divinae illuminations sunt. Quare qui se in hac vita per fidem ad Christum convertit, qui est virtus, dum de hac temporali vita absolvetur, in puritate spiritus reperietur, ut intrare possit ad gaudium aeternae apprehensionis. Conversio vero spiritus nostri est, quando secundum omnes suas potentias intellectuales ad ipsam purissimam aeternam veritatem se convertit per fidem, cui omnia postponit, et ipsam talem veritatem solam amandam eligit atque amat.

Wisdom is not bare knowledge, but experiential and moral. More-over, Cusanus sounds a Lutheran theme when he writes that virtue accompanies, but does not accomplish justification:

> You see now, Brother, that no virtue of any kind justifies us so that we deserve to receive this most excellent gift, nor does any worship or law or instruction. But a virtuous life, observance of the commandments, outward devotion, mortification of the flesh, contempt for the world, and the other things of this kind accompany those who rightly seek the divine life and eternal wisdom.[21]

While Cusanus discusses the issues of sin and moral purity, his work does concentrate on the ontological separation between God and humanity. Perhaps he recognizes that the subjective problem of human sin arises out of the more basic and objective problem of the ontological divide. Perhaps he is simply remaining true to a tradition long established in the Eastern Church. Regardless, Cusanus clearly views the Incarnation as transformative, not merely sapiential and persuasive. Theosis is transformation, not education.

The cosmic Christ, the Christ that is the Maximum of creation, offers transformation into the fullness of the *imago Dei,* not the Christ whose story is told by the gospel narrative of suffering and death on a cross. It is not that Cusanus sees these two Christ figures as opposed; his approach is not preferable to the traditional theology of the cross. Rather, given his understanding of deification as ordained by God from the moment of creation and of creation itself as a kind of deification, it

---

21. *DQD* III h 42, Bond, 227.

Vides nuinc, frater, quamcumque virtutem non iustificare nos, ut merito hoc excellentissimum donum assequamur, neque cultum neque legem neque disciplinam. Sed virtuositas vitae, observantia mandatorum, devotio sensibilis, mortifcatio carnis, contemptus mundi et cetera huiusmodi concomitantur recte quaerentem divinam vitam et aeternam sapientiam.

Cf. *DC* 2.17 h 183, Hopkins, 257. "But you see that all moral virtue is enfolded in the just-mentioned equality and that there cannot be any virtue unless it exists through partaking of this equality." And in *DDI* 3.6 h 218–20 (Bond, 184–86) he writes that justification is received only through faith in Christ Jesus.

makes sense to him to find the truth and grace of Christ in creation it-self. The surmounting of the ontological separation between God and humanity requires not merely divine forgiveness of human moral fail-ing, but a Christ who enfolds all humanity, who embodies divine rev-elation, and whose total life returns creation to God.

Nicholas's emphasis on the incarnate Christ, the Christ as the Max-imum of creation, is an important balance to his doctrine of the second person of the Trinity as the eternal Logos. Here he differs significantly from another medieval mystic, Meister Eckhart, whose version of the mind's ascent includes transcending, rather than enfolding, determinate existence.[22] The contrast between Nicholas and Eckhart is instructive because the latter is generally recognized as emphasizing intellectual salvation.

Unlike Cusanus, Eckhart does not set up a polarity between Cre-ator and creation, but rather between God and that which is "in the principle" in God.[23] For Eckhart, the essence of creation is eternal,

22. A significant contrast between Meister Eckhart's 48th sermon, where he speaks of going to the source of the three Persons of the Trinity, beyond all distinctions, and Cusanus's emphasis in Book III of *DDI* on the endurance of individual differences even in union with Christ. *Meister Eckhart: The Essential Sermons, Commentaries, Treatises, and Defense,* trans. Edmund Colledge, O.S.A., and Bernard McGinn, The Classics of Western Spirituality (New York: Paulist Press, 1981), 198. *DDI* 3.12 h 255, Bond, 201–2.

23. *Eckhart: The Essential Sermons,* 198. A further understanding of Eckhart's phrase "in the principle" is found in his other works. *The Commentary on John* (*Essential Sermons,* 122ff.) asserts the preexistence of things that proceed from other things *in* those other things. Here, as in his sermons, the fluidity of his movement between the concept of the Son and the notion of creation is significant for the process of his thought. In the first chapter he says that this preexistence applies to both the Godhead and natural and artificial things and then goes on to analyze it primarily in terms of the Godhead. The Word, which proceeds from God, is distinguished from God only in terms of that pro-cession. It is with God, receiving the total nature of God. He continues by remarking that the Son is the same as the Father or Principle and uses the example of a chest and its maker to illustrate his point. In principle, the chest is in the maker insofar as it exists in the maker's mind. It has existence "before it exists" and after it is destroyed in the un-derstanding of the maker. His abrupt move from the Word to the idea or logos of things is an extension of his understanding of "in the principle." His remark that in created things "only their ideas shine" and survive change indicates his Platonic understanding of created being. It is the essence, the what-it-is, of things that remains and their exis-

though only borrowed, while its existence as autonomous is something to be overcome in theosis. Because created being tends to be viewed by Eckhart merely as divine being borrowed by a fallen world, the ideal preexistence of things in the Word constitutes their true existence. Creation is divided from God insofar as it is creature, united only insofar as it reclaims its existence in God's mind.

Since the "becoming" aspect of creation is exposed as total nothingness, Eckhart's vision of theosis is a kind of decreation.[24] Creation's existence gives way to its abstract essence, and its createdness is robbed of reality and meaning. Not merely its temporal and physical aspects, but its identity *as creation* is undermined. Thus arise the sharply contradictory claims of unity and separation between God and man, as well as the two pulls, one divine and one of nothingness, on human being. Created being is not authenticated by its orientation toward fulfillment in deification, but is suspended, at least before its final return to God, between the extremes of the absolute and nothingness.

The distinction between the two thinkers is instructive. Cusanus's opposition between Creator and creation gives way in Eckhart to a more Platonic opposition represented in the *Parables of Genesis* as heaven and earth.[25] This is not to say that Eckhart is a thorough Platonist, but merely to assert that his Platonizing tendencies have caused him implicitly, if not explicitly, to adhere to an intellectual salvation. While

---

tence or that-by-which-a-thing-is by which they are distinguished from God. The negative theology that applies to God is also applicable to the ground of the soul, not merely because of the unity of God and soul, but because of the soul's inherent emptiness.

24. This interpretation of Eckhart is reinforced by a look at his notion of theosis as detachment. Detachment is not an ascetic withdrawal from the ordinary life, but an inward poverty that wipes out the soul as even an empty place for God to work. The most intimate poverty is explained in Sermon 52 as being free, not only of created things, but of one's created place. (*Eckhart: The Essential Sermons,* 177.) This freedom is a freedom even of "God" and thus a reclamation of one's real being above the God of created things. Through this kind of poverty the soul achieves a breaking-through to its eternal self above creaturehood. This involves a total abandonment of the created will so that a person is "as he was when he was not."

25. *Eckhart: The Essential Sermons,* 82.

for Eckhart, the mind comes to rest in divine stillness, for Cusanus, deification is bound up in the life of Christ. The entire created order participates in theosis both in this life and in the life to come. Theosis, for Nicholas, is modeled on the incarnate Christ, rather than on the Godhead, where none of the names of the Trinity, nor even the name "God," apply and where the mind seeks a final stage of rest.

Like Eckhart, Cusanus owes a philosophical and theological debt to Pseudo-Dionysius. However, the nature of Cusanus's debt supports the argument that Cusanus's emphasis on the mind in deification does not amount to a Neoplatonic intellectual salvation. While he borrows the negative and supereminent theology of Pseudo-Dionysius, he does not press the latter as one-sidedly as Eckhart.[26]

Moreover, Cusanus's thoughts on the grace of God in Christ are an important corrective to the Neoplatonic understanding of the intellect's capacity for reaching salvation. Like the Areopagite, Nicholas of Cusa views the intellect as able to prepare us for deification, but not as able to achieve it. We saw above that although the mystical union is "natural," it does not occur apart from the grace of God.[27] Louis Dupré points out that "[i]n the high Middle Ages *nature,* taken in the sense of creation as a whole or in the sense of human nature, cannot be thought

26. Pseudo-Dionysius's puzzling formulation "The being of all things is the divinity beyond being" (*Pseudo-Dionysius: The Complete Works*) is developed by Eckhart into the extreme notion that not only is creation not God's self, but not even the Trinity is God's self. In effect, this makes theosis into decreation, poverty, detachment. On the other hand, Eckhart also uses stronger language than Cusanus in identifying creation *with* God. This axis of his thought has opened him to charges of pantheism. Not only does the same negative theology with its lack of names and forms that applies to God apply to the soul, but, in a celebrated passage, he argues that "The Father . . . gives me birth, me, his Son and the same Son. . . . He gives birth not only to me, his Son, but he gives birth to me as himself, and himself as me, and to me as his being and nature" (*Eckhart,* Sermon 6). The human soul is identified especially with the second person of the Trinity since God "gives me, his Son, birth without any distinction." The poles of Eckhart's theology are not as well integrated as Nicholas of Cusa's, and in contrasting the two thinkers we are, admittedly, only looking at one direction of his thought.

27. "From *Ratio* to Intellect" in chapter 3, especially "The Universal Receptivity of the Mind."

independently of a transcendent dimension. A relation to God conveyed ultimate intelligibility to the entire cosmos as well as final meaning to human activity."[28]

And according to Cusanus, "Therefore, the intellect (whose potency encompasses everything except its Creator) needs the Creator's gift of grace to activate to apprehension."[29]

The *imago Dei* is already a gift of divine grace, which we are called to fulfill through Christ. It is never a question of intellectual achievement or the mastery of secret knowledge. Cusanus calls even the highest kind of knowledge "learned *ignorance*." Moreover, both *Idiota de mente* and *De coniecturis* make it clear that it is not the mind alone that is the image of God, but humanity's creative will that organizes the world.[30] Human *activity* and the potential for that activity also comprise the *imago Dei*. While the intellect may be the highest natural function of humanity, it is, more importantly, the point where the grace of God meets the individual in theosis.

In *De quaerendo Deum* he writes:

> And just as sight does not discern, but rather a discriminating spirit discerns in it, so it is with our intellect, which is illuminated by the divine light of its principle in accord with its aptitude for the light to be able to enter. We will not understand or live the intellectual life in and of ourselves, but rather God, who is infinite life, will live in us.[31]

---

28. Louis Dupré, "Nature and Grace in Nicholas of Cusa's Mystical Philosophy," *American Catholic Philosophical Quarterly* 44 (Winter 1990): 153–70. See also his article "The Mystical Theology of Cusanus's De Visione Dei," and the discussion in Chapter 2, under "The Universe: Infinite, Eternal, Unified."

29. *DPL* I h 94; translation mine.

Quoniam autem non omnis autem non omnis natura data gradum possibilis perfectionis speciei suae actu attingit, sed quaelibet indivualis contractio speciei ab ultima perfectione activitatis poteniae—praeterquam in uno domino nostro Iesu Christo—abesse dinoscitur, tunc opus habet intellectus, cuius potentia ambit omne, quod non est creator eius, ad/hoc, ut ad apprehensionem actuetur, dono gratiae creantis.

30. *IDM* argues that the will makes physical objects as well.

31. *DQD* III h 38, Bond, 226.

Et sicut visus non discernit, sed in eo discernit spiritus discretivus, ita in nostro intellectu il-

Moreover, in his primary text on deification, *De filiatione Dei,* Cusanus distinguishes between "the filiation of the Only-Begotten," "which is without mode in the identity of nature with the father," and the filiation of humanity, which is adoption. Though the latter arises in the rational spirit, it does so in those "who receive the Word and believe."[32] It would seem here that Cusanus's view is similar to that of the Greek fathers. The human spirit is created with an openness to the divine, an openness that is only fulfilled by the grace of God in Christ. And, although the locus of the power of sonship is the human rational spirit, sonship is not something reached by the intellect in isolation from grace.

Nicholas of Cusa presents an intellectual faith that is infused by grace, not a faith that is a product of philosophy or natural theology. Rudolf Haubst's masterful attempt to separate the strands of Cusanus's theology and philosophy concludes that while various texts may be primarily or exclusively philosophical, he never drew a strict line between faith and knowledge.[33] Although Cusanus was convinced of the value of philosophy as a basis for his theology, his formal philosophical questions were seen in the light of faith. While he did distinguish between the simple faith of the uneducated believer and the intellectual

---

luminato divino lumine principii sui pro aptitudine, ut intrare posit, non nos intelligemus aut vita intellectuali vivemus per nos, sed in nobis vivet deus vita infinita.

32. *DFD* I h 54, Bond.

Nam ait theologus/quomodo ratio—nis lumen potestatem ipsem habet in omnibus recipientibus verbum et credentibus ad filiationem dei pertigendi . . . Non igitur erit filiatio multorum sine modo, qui quidem modus optionis participatio forte dici poterit. Sed ipsa unigeniti filiatio sine modo in identitate naturae patris exsistens est ipsa superabsoluta filiatio, in qua et per quam omjnes adoptionis filii filiationem adipiscentur. Here Cusanus is quoting John 1:2. Augustine makes a similar distinction between sonship by generation and by adoption in his *Commentary on the Psalms* 49, 2.

33. "Theologie in der Philosophie—Philosophie in der Theologie des Nikolaus von Kues." Haubst classifies *De venatione sapientiae, De coniecturis,* and *Idiota de sapientia* as largely philosophical, *De visione Dei* as a theological text, and *De docta ignorantia* as integrating philosophy and theology in a varied manner. Haubst's concern is defending Cusanus not just against charges of intellectual salvation, but also against charges of fideism. He compares the natural spiritual hunger for truth, a truth sought in both revelation and metaphysics, with what Augustine called "wisdom" (48ff.).

unfolding of the understanding of faith, he never practiced philosophy independently of theology or vice versa.

Cusanus recognizes that the power of cognition *is* a unique human ability. It may be the portal to union with God. It may prepare us to meet God by bringing us to our own limits. But it cannot achieve salvation on its own. Wisdom is paradoxical: since it is identified with the Son of God, it is utterly beyond us; yet, at the same time, the natural openness of our minds makes it a real possibility. Whatever privileged place the mind holds in deification, it is only by virtue of "God, who is Infinite Life," living in us, that it is realized.

Cusanus says that he follows "all our forefathers" in his view of the relationship between faith and understanding, quoting Isaiah 7:9:

> Indeed, all disciplines presuppose certain things as first principles, which are grasped by faith alone and from which is obtained an understanding of the things to be treated. For everyone willing to rise to learning must believe those things without which no ascent is possible. As Isaiah says, "Unless you believe, you will not understand." Faith, therefore, enfolds in itself everything understandable, but understanding is the unfolding of faith. Understanding, therefore, is directed by faith, and faith is extended by understanding. Where there is no sound faith, there is no true understanding. . . . Who does not understand that the most excellent gift of God is a right faith?[34]

If Nicholas of Cusa is understood within a purely Western context, he certainly does seem to suffer from a number of serious deficiencies.

---

34. *DDI* 3.11 h 244, Bond, 196–97. Here Cusanus agrees with Augustine and Anselm in seeing the relation of faith and reason as "faith seeking understanding" *(credo ut intelligam)*.

In omni enim facultate quaedam praesupponuntur ut principia prima, quae sola fide apprehenduntur, ex quibus intelligentia tractandorum elicitur. Omnem enim ascendere volentem ad doctrinam credere necesse est hiis, sine quibus ascendere nequit. Ait enim Jsaias: "Nisi credideritis, non intelligetis." Fides igitur est in se complicans omne intelligibile. Intellectus autem est fidei explicatio. Dirigitur igitur intellectus per fidem, et fides per intellectum extenditur. Ubi igitur non est sana fides, nullus est verus intellectus. Error principiorum et fundamenti debilitas qualem conclusionem subinferant, manifestum est. Nulla autem perfectior fides quam ipsamet veritas, quae Iesus est. Quis non intelligit excellentissimum Dei donum esse rectam fidem?

Not only does he appear to be a transitional figure between old and new concerns, but, more importantly, he seems to have surrendered the core of his Christianity to pagan philosophy. His doctrine of sin *is* muted; he *does* stress finitude over the fall, ignorance over disobedience. Except for a few sermons, redemption as an existential breaking of death's grip on the soul doesn't enter into his theology. Revelation and purgation are emphasized over propitiation and expiation. But if one bears in mind the significant similarities between Cusanus's theology and Eastern thought, it is questionable whether the question of intellectual salvation is adequate to the historical locus of his thought.

At the very least, it is one-sided to pose such a question without also exploring his relationship to the theological tradition of the East. As mentioned in chapter 1, a complete study of this topic is still needed in Cusanus scholarship. He almost certainly saw his emphasis on the intellect in deification not as an adaptation of Christianity to Neoplatonism, but as a continuation of an earlier tradition. In using the philosophy of his day, he was doing no more than centuries of scholars had done before him.

The Eastern Church's approach to theology concerns primarily the transhistorical relationship between Creator and creation and is at once more audacious and more humble than the West's focus on the story of God in history. The ability of Eastern theologians to use both the language of deification and the language of negation depends on the attempt to perceive God beyond manifestation and the recognition of the futility of that attempt. The East has self-consciously, and not uncritically, adopted much of the Platonic and Neoplatonic terminology in its effort to understand the ontological tension between God and creation and has made itself vulnerable to charges of Hellenism and Origenism. While Eastern theology does not ignore the divine economy, it sees it as a means for realizing and knowing eternal realities. *Every* point in history is oriented toward the divine infinity.

Ultimately one must choose between widening one's definition of the heart of the gospel message and dismissing a broad sweep of historical theology. Perhaps the choice between a *theologica Platonica* and a theology of the cross is too limited. Not only were the pre-Reformation questions still open at the time of Nicholas of Cusa, but an emphasis on the intellect has a strong tradition in the Eastern Church. Perhaps the message of the gospel is Christ himself, a theme that Western theology tends to develop in terms of a theology of the cross and Eastern theology tends to develop in terms of the cosmic Christ. Christian thought has always used the philosophical language of its time, borrowing its terminology and concepts. While protecting the gospel from a surrender to any philosophy is a worthy cause, accepting the variety of its flowering throughout a history of reflection by thinkers from an equally varied background is also.

And, finally, if I am correct in arguing that for Nicholas of Cusa theophany and sustenance in being or self-identity are also dimensions of theosis, then the mind's ascent to God is but one aspect of a rich understanding of theosis. In light of the total picture of theosis as divine self-manifestation, divine immanence in creation, and the return to God through the grace of Jesus Christ, Nicholas of Cusa cannot be said to adhere to a pagan intellectual salvation.

A look at the notion of "theosis" in Cusanus's philosophical and theological treatises shows that even those texts that deal primarily epistemological issues (*De docta ignorantia,* for instance) give clues to his metaphysics. The movement from cataphatic to negative and supereminent theology is driven by a certain understanding of human beings and God. It is only because we can theorize about the infinity of God that we can make statements about learned ignorance and the limitations of human rationality.

Nicholas of Cusa stands at the very beginning of Renaissance thought, and thus the modern world. He makes claims of both radical union with and complete separation between God and creation similar to those of the earlier thinkers. His suggestion that created things may be just as unknowable as God derives from the interplay of both claims. Nicholas's concern with subjectivity in knowledge and his cosmological speculation have been the focus of intensive study because of their implications for his location within either medieval or early modern thought. The issue of whether he is a medieval or a modern is a peculiarly Western question that leads to doubts about his orthodoxy. He is clearly a medieval thinker but is much closer to the Eastern Church fathers than to other medievals.

While Gregory was significant for his contributions to a doctrine of creation that is foundational for a theory of deification, Maximus is important for his Christology. Moreover the crucial influence of Pseudo-Dionysius is indisputable. Theophany in Nicholas of Cusa is both a basis for theosis and as an aspect of theosis in its own right.

Cusanus's unique name for God, "the Not-other" eclipses ordinary categories of definition. It emphasizes divine self-referentiality, highlights God's immanence, and describes the foundational ontological role that God plays for creation. God defines all things, but is himself indefinable. Moreover, for God, "to define" means to be the cause both of things and of their possibility.

Since theophany is the primary disclosure of God, Cusanus does not favor an analogical approach to God (although in *De coniecturis* he admits a second-order analogy). Instead, he sees God as enfolding both being and not-being, that is, absolute possibility or nothingness. Moreover, instead of a traditional doctrine of creation ex nihilo, Nicholas offers his theory that the infinity of God encompasses even the opposites of possibility and actuality.

The Absolute that manifests in plurality leads to an affirmation of the individuality and (limited) perfection of all things. Not only does Cusanus avoid traditional medieval hierarchical views of creation, but he also locates the source of things' variety in contingency. Because it reflects the absolutely Infinite and Eternal, the universe itself is seen as (privatively) infinite and eternal in its own right. Its unity is a result of the divine manifestation of Unity into difference. Moreover, in the third book of *De docta ignorantia*, Cusanus defines the *maximum contractum* (contracted maximum) as something that would be both absolute and contracted, existing as both God and creature. Because humanity is a microcosm, including both the lower and higher natures, the contracted maximum would be a human being. Thus, Cusanus sketches the logic behind God's self-manifestation in Christ, whom he calls "the Equality of being all things."

Although human reason is negatively portrayed in *De docta ignorantia,* it has a positive, constructive aspect as well. Not only is the frustration encountered by the mind in its attempts to know God something that moves the mind beyond itself, but *De coniecturis* points to its locus as the *imago Dei*. Human creativity is the imaging of divine fecundity as the conjecturing mind creates the conceptual world.

Cusanus had good reasons for adopting an epistemological perspective and an emphasis on the instrumentality of the mind. Rather than simply following the tradition of Greek philosophy, he is aware of the availability of thought as an expression of a larger theological movement. The "universal receptivity" of the mind is symbolic for the deification of the created order, the triumph over space and time, and the return to the infinite God.

Although Cusanus compares things of the sensible world to books through which God speaks, he argues that the mind ascends from the temporal and particular to the eternal and universal, and then to God. The attraction of divine Wisdom is rooted in the fact of the *imago Dei*. Due to the latter, the intellectual spirit holds a foretaste of wisdom that sparks its desire for its own true self. Although there is a foreshadowing of modern subjectivity, the mind's search for the measure of itself, described in *Idiote de mente,* must be viewed in terms of the mirror metaphor of *De filiatione Dei*. The doctrine of the *imago Dei* reminds us that Cusanus's were essentially medieval concerns and that the self is truly found only in God. The cardinal inhabited a seamless world in which there was no rupture between seeking the self and seeking God.

The immanence and perfection of Christ not only makes things what they are, but also orients them toward a destined theosis. While Cusanus does not always distinguish between the self-identity of things in this world and their future perfection, he does indicate that theosis is fulfilled in the life to come. Both the infinity of theosis and the fact that deification does not eclipse differentiation contrast the Cusan doctrine with Neoplatonism. Deification in the thought of Nicholas of Cusa is clearly not a simple return to God, but a multidimensional and Christological construct.

The extent of Neoplatonic influence on Cusanus's soteriology—

specifically, whether he has replaced the latter with pagan philosophy—
is an important question in this context. Admittedly, Cusanus does neglect portraying sin as a matter of moral wrongdoing, favoring instead a
view of it as human finitude. Similarly, Christ tends to be portrayed as
a bridge of the ontological divide between God and man, rather than
as the suffering savior who takes on the sins of the world. Chapter 5 argued for the importance of considering the orthodoxy of the Patristic
and Byzantine tradition of theosis when answering the question of intellectual salvation in Nicholas of Cusa.

Nicholas of Cusa's place in the history of Christian thought depends
on how he is read. If he is viewed through the narrow lens of a Western definition of the gospel message, deficiencies in his theology do appear. He does emphasize revelation and illumination over propitiation
and expiation, and the intellect does play a central role in deification. If,
however, the emphasis in the Eastern Church on the transhistorical relationship between God and creation is recognized, the Cusan perspective
does not seem so unorthodox. The fact that the cosmic Christ is stressed
over the Christ of the cross reflects an understanding of history in which
every point is oriented toward God. And the focus on the intellect as the
point at which the cosmic Christ meets and enfolds the human being is
not a sign of surrender to a pagan doctrine of intellectual salvation, but a
reflection of a long-established Christian tradition.

My purpose in this book is not to offer a general survey of Nicholas of Cusa's theology and philosophy; many other excellent articles
and books are available to that end. My aim is simply to trace Cusanus's
intriguing doctrine of theosis in as comprehensive a way as possible, a
project that had not yet been done in Cusanus scholarship. While there
are other important questions that could be asked regarding the notion
of deification, including the open issue of the direct access that Nicholas had to the texts of early Greek Christian theologians, this book is
restricted to the question of intellectual salvation.[1]

1. Other interesting analyses of Cusanus's thought that could be made include

Cusanus does use the mind to approach what is beyond the mind. But the mind has its limits; it does not accomplish salvation but only brings itself to where salvation is possible. The theosis that permeates human existence, and indeed all of creation, is wrapped up in the concept of a boundless God to which his very ineffability leads. Moreover, Nicholas of Cusa's emphasis on grace, his discussion of virtue, and his "general" theology of the cross cannot be ignored.

Because he consciously follows Pseudo-Dionysius in refusing to allow the paradox of immanence and transcendence to ever be overcome, his understanding of theosis is unique. He is, for example, radically different from another medieval, Meister Eckhart. According to one trend in Eckhart's thought, the language of immanence is only justified by the fact that created being is loaned from God, who is identical to being. The self can be identified with God only because in itself it is absolute nothingness, and whatever it *is* is God. There is a tendency, then, to see theosis as the disincarnate return of the intellect to the Godhead. For Cusanus, however, the tension of immanence and transcendence allows for the participation that gives creation a genuine ontological status and the Incarnation a central importance.

Nicholas is commonly viewed as having been a bridge between the medieval, human-centered universe and the modern, infinite universe and between medieval thought and modern subjectivity. But, as noted in chapter 4, if he was heavily influenced by the Greek fathers, he probably did not see himself as inaugurating a new era, but merely as reemphasizing concerns that had been there all along. It is Cusanus's mystical metaphysics that gives him his understanding of the person and the cosmos, and it is precisely here that the question of his roots in the Eastern Church arises. Because of the way that it focuses the relationship between the Creator and creation, the doctrine of theosis is an excellent path to follow in pursuit of this theme.

---

further comparisons with Pseudo-Dionysius and the church fathers, especially regarding the doctrine of endless salvation, negative anthropology, and the role of hierarchy.

Nicholas of Cusa's dedication of *De filiatione Dei* reminds us that this, his text dealing specifically with deification, should not be taken as "adding anything new to what you have read in my past conceptions."[2] What he here presents is merely an explication of what he has covered in a more general way in other texts. Our analysis of his understanding of divine theophany or immanence, God's transcendence and unknowability, and his Christological view of deification as divine sonship reveals that his doctrine of theosis is fully consonant with the body of his other thought. Indeed, theophany, self-identity, and the return to God in Christ are all aspects of his rich and multilayered understanding of theosis.

2. *DFD* h 51, Bond.
Confrater merito colende, recipe eo pacto id quod occurrit, ut non putes me quidquam his adicere, quae in praeteritis meis legisti conceptibus.

BIBLIOGRAPHY

Texts and Translations

Gregorii Nysseni Opera. Edited by Werner Jaeger, H. Langerbeck, et al. 11 vols. Leiden: E. J. Brill, 1952–.

From Glory to Glory: Texts from Gregory of Nyssa's Mystical Writings. Translated by Herbert Musurillo, S.J. New York: Charles Scribner's Sons, 1961; London: J. Murray, 1962. Reprint; Crestwood, N.Y.: St. Vladimir's Seminary Press, 1979.

Gregory of Nyssa: The Life of Moses. Translated by Abraham J. Malherbe and Everett Ferguson. Classics of Western Spirituality. New York: Paulist Press, 1978.

Selected Writings and Letters of Gregory, Bishop of Nyssa. Translated by William Moore, M.A., and Henry Austin Wilson, M.A. The Nicene and Post-Nicene Fathers of the Christian Church: Series 2, vol. 5. Grand Rapids: Eerdmans, 1994.

Maximus the Confessor. *The Ascetic Life: The Four Centuries on Charity.* Translated by Polycarp Sherwood, O.S.B., S.T.D. Westminster, Md.: Newman Press, 1955.

————. *The Mystagogia.* Translated by Julian Stead. Still River, Mass.: St. Bede's Publications, 1982.

Maximus Confessor: Selected Writings. Translated by George C. Berthold. Classics of Western Spirituality. New York: Paulist Press, 1985.

Meister Eckhart: The Essential Sermons, Commentaries, Treatises, and Defense. Translated and introduction by Edmund Colledge, O.S.A., and Bernard McGinn. Classics of Western Spirituality. New York: Paulist Press, 1981.

Meister Eckhart: Teacher and Preacher. Edited by Bernard McGinn. Classics of Western Spirituality. New York: Paulist Press, 1986.

Nicholas of Cusa. *Apologia doctae ignorantiae discipuli ad discipulum.* Translated by Jasper Hopkins. "A Defense of Learned Ignorance from One Disciple to Another," in *Nicholas of Cusa's Debate with John Wenck.* Minneapolis: Arthur J. Banning Press, 1981.

————. *Complete Philosophical and Theological Treatises.* Translated by Jasper Hopkins. 2 vols. Minneapolis: Arthur J. Banning Press, 2001.

————. *De aequalitate.* Translated by Jasper Hopkins. "On Equality," in *Nicholas of Cusa: Metaphysical Speculations.* Minneapolis: Arthur J. Banning Press, 1998.

————. *De apice theoriae.* Translated by H. Lawrence Bond. "On the Summit of Contemplation," in *Nicholas of Cusa: Selected Spiritual Writings.* Classics of Western Spirituality. New York: Paulist Press, 1997.

————. *De Beryllo.* Translated by Jasper Hopkins. "On Intellectual Eyeglasses," in *Nicholas of Cusa: Metaphysical Speculations.* Minneapolis: Arthur J. Banning Press, 1998.

————. *De coniecturis.* Translated by Jasper Hopkins. In *Complete Philosophical and Theological Treatises.* Vol. 1. Minneapolis: Arthur J. Banning Press, 2001.

————. *De coniecturis.* Translated by William F. Wertz. "On Conjectures," in *Toward a New Council of Florence: "On the Peace of Faith" and Other Works by Nicholas of Cusa.* Washington, D.C.: Schiller Institute, 1993.

————. *De coniecturis.* Translated by Dietlind and Wilhelm Dupre. *Nikolaus von Kues: Philosophisch-Theologische Schriften.* Vol. 2. Wien: Herder, 1966.

————. *De dato Patris luminum.* Translated by Jasper Hopkins. "The Gift of the Father of Lights," in *Nicholas of Cusa's Metaphysic of Contraction.* Minneapolis: Arthur J. Banning Press, 1983.

————. *De Deo abscondito.* Translated by H. Lawrence Bond. "Dialogue on the Hidden God," in *Nicholas of Cusa: Selected Spiritual Writings.* New York: Paulist Press, 1997.

————. *De Deo abscondito.* Translated by Jasper Hopkins. "On the Hidden God," in *A Miscellany on Nicholas of Cusa.* Minneapolis: Arthur J. Banning Press, 1994.

————. *De docta ignorantia.* Translated by H. Lawrence Bond. "On Learned Ignorance," in *Nicholas of Cusa: Selected Spiritual Writings.* New York: Paulist Press, 1997.

————. *De docta ignorantia.* Translated by Jasper Hopkins. "On Learned Ignorance," in *Nicholas of Cusa on Learned Ignorance: A Translation and Appraisal of De Docta Ignorantia.* 2nd ed. Minneapolis: Arthur J. Banning Press, 1985.

————. *De filiatione Dei.* Translated by H. Lawrence Bond. *On Divine Filiation.* (2000). Online. Available from www.appstate.edu/~bondhl/defil.htm [accessed 12 December 2005].

————. *De filiatione Dei*. Translated by Jasper Hopkins. "On Divine Sonship," in *A Miscellany on Nicholas of Cusa*. Minneapolis: Arthur J. Banning Press, 1994.

————. *De genesi*. Translated by Jasper Hopkins. "On Genesis," in *A Miscellany on Nicholas of Cusa*. Minneapolis: Arthur J. Banning Press, 1994.

————. *De pace fidei*. Translated by H. Lawrence Bond. *Nicholas of Cusa on Interreligious Harmony: Text, Concordance, and Translation of* De Pace Fidei. Texts and Studies in Religion 55. Lewiston, N.Y.: Edwin Mellen Press, 2000.

————. *De pace fidei*. Translated by Jasper Hopkins. "The Peace of Faith," in *Nicholas of Cusa's De Pace Fidei and Cribratio Alkorani*. Minneapolis: Arthur J. Banning Press, 1990.

————. *De principio*. Translated by Jasper Hopkins. "On the Beginning," in *Nicholas of Cusa: Metaphysical Speculations*. Minneapolis: Arthur J. Banning Press, 1998.

————. *De quaerendo Deum* . Translated by H. Lawrence Bond. "On Seeking God," in *Nicholas of Cusa: Selected Spiritual Writings*. New York: Paulist Press, 1997.

————. *De quaerendo Deum*. Translated by Jasper Hopkins. "On Seeking God," in *A Miscellany on Nicholas of Cusa*. Minneapolis: Arthur J. Banning Press, 1994.

————. *De theologicis complementis*. Translated by Jasper Hopkins. "Complementary Theological Considerations," in *Nicholas of Cusa: Metaphysical Speculations*. Minneapolis: Arthur J. Banning Press, 1998.

————. *De venatione sapientiae*. Translated by Jasper Hopkins. "On the Pursuit of Wisdom," in *Nicholas of Cusa: Metaphysical Speculations*. Minneapolis: Arthur J. Banning Press, 1998.

————. *De visione Dei*. Translated by H. Lawrence Bond. "On the Vision of God," in *Nicholas of Cusa: Selected Spiritual Writings*. New York: Paulist Press, 1997.

————. *De visione Dei*. Translated by Jasper Hopkins. "The Vision of God," in *Nicholas of Cusa's Dialectical Mysticism: Text, Translation, and Interpretative Study of De Visione Dei*. Minneapolis: Arthur J. Banning Press, 1985.

————. *Directio speculantis seu de Non Aliud*. Translated by Jasper Hopkins. "On God as Not-Other," in *Nicholas of Cusa on God as Not-Other: A Translation and an Appraisal of De Li Non Aliud*. Minneapolis: University of Minnesota Press, 1979.

————. *Idiota de mente*. Translated by Jasper Hopkins. "The Layman on Mind," in *Nicholas of Cusa on Wisdom and Knowledge*. Minneapolis: Arthur J. Banning Press, 1996.

————. *Idiota de mente*. Translation and introduction by Clyde Lee Miller. *The Layman: About Mind*. New York: Abaris Books, 1979. Because this book uses the Paris manuscript instead of the critical edition Heidelberg edition, it was not used in this study.

———. *Idiota de sapientia.* Translated by Jasper Hopkins. "The Layman on Wisdom," in *Nicholas of Cusa on Wisdom and Knowledge.* Minneapolis: Arthur J. Banning Press, 1996.

———. *Trialogus de possest.* Translated by Jasper Hopkins. "On Actualized-Possibility," in *A Concise Introduction to the Philosophy of Nicholas of Cusa.* 3rd ed. Minneapolis: University of Minnesota Press, 1980.

Plotinus. *Enneads.* Translated by S. MacKenna. London: Penguin Books, 1969.

Pseudo-Dionysius. *Pseudo-Dionysius: The Complete Works.* Translated by Colm Luibheid. New York: Paulist Press, 1987.

Wenck, John. *De ignota Litteratura.* Translated by Jasper Hopkins. "On Unknown Learning," in *Nicholas of Cusa's Debate with John Wenck.* Minneapolis: Arthur J. Banning Press, 1981.

Studies

Balás, David L. *METOUSIA THEOU. Man's Participation in God's Perfections according to Saint Gregory of Nyssa.* Studia Anselmiana 55. Rome: Herder, 1966.

Balthasar, Hans Urs von. *Cosmic Liturgy: The Universe according to Maximus the Confessor.* Translated by Brian Daley. San Francisco: Ignatius Press, 2003.

———. *Herrlichkeit: eine theologische Äesthetik II, Facher der Stile.* Einsiedeln: Johannes Verlag, 1962. ———. *Presence and Thought: Essay on the Religious Philosophy of Gregory of Nyssa.* Translated by Mark Sebanc. San Francisco: Ignatius Press, 1995.

Baeumker, Clemens. "Das pseudo-hermetische 'Buch der 24 Meister' (Liber XXIV Philosophorum) Studien und Charakteristiken zur Geschichte der Philosophie des Mittlealters." *Beitraege zur Geschichte der Philosophie und Theologie des Mittlealters* 25 (1927): 194–214.

Bebis, George S. "Gregory of Nyssa's 'De Vita Moysis': A Philosophical and Theological Analysis." *Greek Orthodox Theological Review* 12 (1967): 369–93.

Beierwaltes, Werner. *Visio Facialis: Sehen in Angesicht.* Bayerische Akademie der Wissenschaften Philosophische-Historische Klasse Sitzungsberichte 1988. Heft 1. Munchen: Verlag der Bayerischen Akademie der Wissenschaften, 1988.

Blumenberg, Hans. *The Legitimacy of the Modern Age.* Translated by R. Wallace. Cambridge, Mass.: MIT Press, 1983.

Bolberitz, Paul. *Philosophscher Gottesbegriff bei Nikolaus Cusanus in seinem Werk: "De non aliud."* Leipzig: St. Benno Verlag, 1989.

Bond, H. Lawrence. "Nicholas of Cusa and the Reconstruction of Christology: The Centrality of Christology in the Coincidence of Opposites." In

Contemporary Reflections on the Medieval Christian Tradition, edited by G. H. Shriver. Durham, N.C.: Duke University Press, 1974, 81–94.

Boyle, Marjorie O'Rourke. "Cusanus at Sea: The Topicality of Illuminative Discourse." *Journal of Religion* 71 (April 1991).

Brient, Elizabeth. *The Immanence of the Infinite: Hans Blumenberg and the Threshold to Modernity.* Washington, D.C.: Catholic University of America Press, 2002.

Brons, B. *Gott und die Seienden: Untersuchungen zum Verhaeltnis von neuplatonischer Metaphysik und christliche Tradition bei Dionysius Areopagita.* Goettingen: Vandenhoeck and Ruprecht, 1976.

Casarella, Peter. "Nicholas of Cusa and the Power of the Possible." *American Catholic Philosophical Quarterly* 64 (1990): 7–34.

————. "Wer Schrieb Die Ex Greco-Notizen im Codex Cusanus 44?" *Mitteilungen und Forschungsbeitraege der Cusanus Gesellschaft* 22 (1995): 123–32.

Cassirer, Ernst. *Das Erkenntnisproblem in der Philosophie und Wissenschaft der neueren Zeit.* Berlin: Bruno Cassirer, 1906.

————. *The Individual and the Cosmos in Renaissance Philosophy.* Translated by Mario Domandi. Oxford: Blackwell, 1963.

Cherniss, Harold F. *The Platonism of Gregory of Nyssa.* New York: B. Franklin, 1971.

Cranz, F. Edward. *Nicholas of Cusa and the Renaissance.* Varorium Collected Studies. Aldershot: Ashgate Publishing, 2000.

————. "The Transmutation of Platonism in the Development of Nicolaus Cusanus and of Martin Luther." In *Nicolo Cusano agli Inizi del Mondo Moderno,* 73–102. Glorence: Sansoni, 1970.

Dangelmayr, S. *Das Sehen Gottes nach Nikolaus von Kues.* Trier: Paulinus Verlag, 1989.

Danielou, Jean. *Platonisme et theologie mystique: Essai sur la doctrine spirituelle de saint Gregoire de Nysse.* 2nd ed. Paris: Aubier, 1954.

————. "La Qeuria chez Gregoire de Nyssa." *Studia Patristica* 11 (1967): 130–45.

————. "Mystique de la tenebre chez Gregoire de Nyssa." In *Dictionaire de Spiritualite.* Paris: Beauchesne, 1932–.

de Certeau, Michel. "The Gaze of Nicholas of Cusa." *Diacritics* 17 (1987): 2–38.

de Gandillac, Michel. *Nikolaus von Cues.* Duesseldorf: Schwann, 1953.

————. "Nikolaus von Kues zwischen Platon und Hegel." *Mitteilungen und Forschungsbeitraege der Cusanus Gesellschaft* 11 (1975): 21–38.

Dodds, E. R. *Proclus: The Elements of Theology.* 2nd ed. Oxford: Oxford University Press, 1963.

Duclow, Donald. "Nicholas of Cusa." In *Dictionary of Literary Biography.* Vol. 115: *Medieval Philosophers,* edited by Jeremiah Hackett, 289–305. Detroit: Bruccoli Clark Layman, 1992.

————. "Mystical Theology and Intellect in Nicholas of Cusa." *American Catholic Philosophical Quarterly* 44 (Winter 1990): 111–29.

Dupré, Louis. *The Deeper Life: An Introduction to Christian Mysticism.* New York: Crossroad, 1981.

———. *Metaphysics and Culture.* Milwaukee: Marquette University Press, 1994.

———. "The Mystical Theology of Cusanus's De Visione Dei." In *Eros and Eris.* The Netherlands: Kluwer Academic Publishers, 1992.

———. "Nature and Grace in Nicholas of Cusa's Mystical Philosophy." *American Catholic Philosophical Quarterly* 44 (Winter 1990): 153–70.

———. *Passage to Modernity: An Essay in the Hermeneutics of Nature and Culture.* New Haven: Yale University Press, 1993.

———. *Religious Mystery and Rational Reflection.* Grand Rapids: W. B. Eerdmans, 1997.

Dupré, Wilhelm. "Der Mensch als Mikrokosmos im Denken des Nikoaus von Kues." *Mitteilungen und Forschungsbeitraege der Cusanus Gesellschaft 13 (1978).* Trier: Paulinus Verlag, 68–87.

Euler, Walter Andreas. "Does Nicholas of Cusa Have a Theology of the Cross?" *Journal of Religion* 80 (2000): 405–20.

Flasch, Kurt. *Die Metaphysik des Einen bei Nikolaus von Kues.* Leiden: Brill, 1973.

Gaith, Jerome. *La Conception de la Liberte chez Gregoire de Nysse.* Paris: Libraire Philosophique J. Vrin, 1953.

Gay, John. "Four Medieval Views of Creation." *Harvard Theological Review* 56, no. 4 (1963): 243–73.

Gersh, Stephen. *From Iamblichus to Eriugena: An Investigation of the Prehistory and Evolution of the Pseudo-Dionysian Tradition.* Leiden: E. J. Brill, 1978.

Gilson, Etienne. *Being and Some Philosophers.* 2nd ed. Toronto: Pontifical Institute of Medieval Studies, 1952.

Golitzin, Alexander. "The Mysticism of Dionysius Areopagita: Platonist or Christian?" *Mystics Quarterly* 19, no. 3 (1993): 98–114.

———. *Et Introibo Ad Altare Dei: The Mystagogy of Dionysius Areopagita, with Special Reference to its Predecessors in the Eastern Christian Tradition.* Thessaloniki: George Dedousis, 1994.

Haas, A. M. *Deum mistice videre in caligine coincidencie: Zum Verhaeltnis Nikolaus von Kues zur Mystik.* Basel: Helbing und Lichtenhahn, 1989.

Harries, Karsten. "Cusanus and the Platonic Idea." *New Scholasticism* 37 (1963): 188–203.

———. "The Infinite Sphere: Comments on the History of a Metaphor." *Journal of the History of Philosophy* 13 (Jan. 1975): 5–15.

Hathaway, R. F. *Hierarchy and the Definition of Order in the Letters of Pseudo-Dionysius.* The Hague: Nijhoff, 1969.

Haubst, Rudolf. *Das Bild des Einen und Dreieinen Gottes in der Welt nach Nikolaus von Kues.* Trierer Theologische Studien 4. Trier: Paulinus, 1952.

—————. *Die Christologie des Nikolaus von Kues.* Freiburg: Herder, 1956.

—————. "Die erkenntnistheoretische und mystische Bedeutung der 'Mauer der Koinzidenz.'" *Mitteilungen und Forschungsbeitraege der Cusanus Gesellschaft 18* (1989). Trier: Paulinus Verlag, 167–195.

—————. "Nikolaus von Kues als Interpret und Verteidiger Meister Eckharts." In *Freiheit und Gelassenheit: Meister Eckhart heute.* Muenchen: Kaiser; Mainz: Gruenewald, 1980.

—————. "Nikolaus von Kues und die analogia entis." In *Streifzuege in die Cusanische Theologie,* 232–242. Muenster: Aschendorff 1991.

—————. "Nicolaus von Kues und die heutige Christologie." In *Universitas. Dienst an Wahrheit und Leben,* vol. 1, edited by L. Lenhart, 165–75. Mainz: Matthias-Gruenewald, 1960.

—————. "Theologie in der Philosophie—Philosophie in der Theologie des Nikolaus von Kues." In *Streifzuege in die Cusanische Theologie.* Muenster: Aschendorff, 1991.

Haug, Walter. "Die Mauer des Paradieses: Zur mystica theologia des Nicolaus Cusanus in *De visione Dei.*" *Theologische Zeitschrift* 45 (1989): 216–30.

Helander, Birgit H. *Die visio intellectualis als Erkenntnisweg und -ziel bei Nikolaus Cusanus.* Stockholm: Almqvist and Wiksell, 1988.

Herold, Norbert. "Bild der Wahrheit—Wahrheit des Bildes: Zur Deutung des Blicks aus dem Bild in der Cusanische Schrift *De visione Dei.*" In *Wahrheit und Begruendung,* edited by V. Gerhardt and N. Herold, 71–98. Wuerzburg: Konigshausen und Neumann, 1985.

Hojsisch, B. "Die Andersheit Gottes als Koinzidenz, Negation und Nicht-Andersheit bei Nikolaus von Kues: Explikation und Kritik." *Documenti e studi sulla tradizione filosofica medievale* 7 (1996): 437–54.

Hopkins, Jasper. *Nicholas of Cusa's Dialectical Mysticism: Text, Translation, and Interpretive Study of De visione Dei.* Minneapolis: Arthur J. Banning Press, 1985.

Izbicki, Thomas. "The Church in the Light of Learned Ignorance." *Medieval Philosophy and Theology* 3 (1993): 186–214.

Jacobi, Klaus. *Die Methode der Cusanischen Philosophie.* Symposion 31. Freiburg-Muenchen: Alber, 1969.

Kelly, C. F. *Meister Eckhart on Divine Knowledge.* New Haven: Yale University Press, 1977.

Koch, Josef. *Die ars coniecturalis des Nikolaus von Kues.* Cologne: Westdeutscher Verlag, 1956.

Koenigsberger, Dorothy. "Universality, the Universe and Nicholas of Cusa's Untastable Foretaste of Wisdom." *European History Quarterly* 17 (Jan. 1987): 3–33.

Kremer, Klaus. "Gott: in allem alles, in nichts nichts." *Mitteilungen und Forschungsbeitraege der Cusanus Gesellschaft 17* (1986). Trier: Paulinus Verlag, 188–219.

———. "Philosophische Ueberlegungen des Cusanus zur Unsterblichkeit der menschlichen Geistseele." *Mitteilungen und Forschungsbeitraege der Cusanus Gesellschaft 23 (1996).* Trier: Paulinus Verlag, 21–70.

Leinkauf, Thomas. "Die Bestimmung des Einzelseienden durch die Begriffe Contractio, Singularitas, und Aequalitas bei Nicolaus Cusanus." *Archiv fuer Begriffsgeschichte* 37 (1994): 180–211.

Longeway, John L. "Nicholas of Cusa and Man's Knowledge of God." *Philosophy Research Archives* 13 (1967–68): 289–313.

Lossky, Vladimir. *In the Image and Likeness of God.* London and Oxford: Mowbrays, 1975.

———. "La Notion des 'Analogies' chez Denys le Pseudo-Areopagite." *Archives d'histoire doctrinale et litteraire du Moyen Age* 5 (1931): 279–309.

———. *The Mystical Theology of the Eastern Church.* Crestwood, N.Y.: St. Vladimir's Seminary Press, 1976.

———. *The Vision of God.* Translated by Ashleigh Moorhouse. London: Faith Press, 1963.

Louth, Andrew. *Maximus the Confessor.* London: Routledge, 1996.

———. *The Origins of the Christian Mystical Tradition from Plato to Denys.* Oxford: Oxford University Press, 1981.

Luther, Martin. *Heidelberg Theses.* Vol. 31 of *Works.* Philadelphia: Muhlenberg Press, 1957.

Mahnke, Dietrich. *Unenliche Sphaere und Allmittelpunkt.* Halle: Max Niemeyer Verlag, 1937.

Mautner, Thomas. *A Dictionary of Philosophy.* Cambridge, Mass.: Blackwell Publishers, 1996.

McGinn, Bernard. "Meister Eckhart on God as Absolute Unity." In *Neoplatonism and Christian Thought,* 129–39. Norfolk, Va.: International Society for Neoplatonic Studies.

McTighe, Thomas. "*Contingentia* and *Alteritas* in Cusa's Metaphysics." *American Catholic Philosophical Quarterly* 44 (Winter 1990): 55–71.

Meinhardt, Helmut. "Das Geheimnis des Todes und der Auferstehung Jesu Christi nach Cusanus, ineins damit sein Verstaendnis der Auferstehung der Toten." *Mitteilungen und Forschungsbeitraege der Cusanus Gesellschaft 23 (1996).* Trier: Paulinus Verlag, 71–82.

———. "Exaktheit und Mutmassungscharakter der Erkenntnis." In *Nikolaus von Kues: Einfuehrung in sein philosophisches Denken,* edited by Klaus Jacobi, 101–20. Munich: Alber, 1979.

Meuthen, Erich. *Nikolaus von Kues, 1401–1464. Skizze einer Biographie.* 7th ed.
    Muenster: Aschendorff, 1992.
Meyendorff, John. *Byzantine Theology.* New York: Fordham University Press,
    1974.
———. *Christ in Eastern Christian Thought.* Washington, D.C.: Corpus Books,
    1969.
Miller, Clyde Lee. "Metaphor and Simile in Nicholas of Cusa's *Idiota de mente.*"
    Acta 8 (1981): 47–59.
———. "Nicholas of Cusa and Philosophic Knowledge." *Proceedings of the
    American Catholic Philosophical Association* 54 (1980): 155–63.
———. "Nicholas of Cusa's *On Conjectures (De coniecturis).*" In *Nicholas of Cusa:
    In Search of God and Wisdom,* edited by Gerald Christianson and Thomas
    Izbicki. New York: Brill, 1991.
———. *Reading Cusanus: Metaphor and Dialectic in a Conjectural Universe.*
    Washington, D.C.: Catholic University of America Press, 2003.
———. "A Road Not Taken: Nicholas of Cusa and Today's Intellectual World."
    Proceedings of the American Catholic Philosophical Association 57 (1983): 135–48.
Moran, Dermot. *The Philosophy of John Scotus Eriugena: A Study of Idealism in the
    Middle Ages.* New York: Cambridge, 1989.
Nellas, Panayiotis. *Deification in Christ.* Translated by Norman Russell.
    Crestwood, N.Y.: St. Vladimir's Seminary Press, 1987.
Niarchos, C. "The Concept of Participation according to Proclus, with
    Reference to the Criticism of Nicolaus of Methone." *Diotima* 13 (1985):
    78–94.
Paetzold, Detler. *Einheit und Andersheit: Die Bedeutung kategorialer Neubildungen in
    der Philosophie des Nicolaus Cusanus.* Cologne: Pahl-Rugenstein, 1981.
Rahner, Karl, and Herbert Vorgrimler. *Dictionary of Theology.* New York:
    Crossroad, 1985.
Rist, John M. *Eros and Psyche: Studies in Plato, Plotinus, and Origen.* Toronto:
    University of Toronto Press, 1964.
———. "Mysticism and Transcendence in Later Neoplatonism." *Hermes* 92
    (1964): 213–25.
———. *Plotinus: The Road to Reality.* Cambridge: Cambridge University Press,
    1967.
Rondet, Henri. *The Grace of Christ.* Translated by Tad W. Guzie, S.J. New York:
    Newman Press, 1967.
Roques, Rene. "Y propos des sources du Pseudo-Denys." *Revue d'histoire
    ecclesiastique* 56 (1961): 449–64.
———. "Contemplation, extase, et tenebre chez le Pseudo-Denys." In
    Dictionaire de Spiritualite. Paris: Beauchesne, 1932–.

————. "De l'implication de meehodes theologiques chez le Pseudo-Denys." *Revue d'ascetique et de mystique* 30 (1954): 268–74.

————. "Introduction." *La Hierarchie Celeste, Sources Chretiennes* 58, 2nd ed., v–xcvi. Paris: Janvier, 1970.

————. "Symbolisme et theologie negative chez le Ps.-Denys." *Bulletin de l'association Guillaume Bude* (1957): 97–112.

Rorem, Paul. *Biblical and Liturgical Symbols within the Pseudo-Dionysian Synthesis.* Toronto: Pontifical Institute of Mediaeval Studies, 1984.

————. "The Uplifting Spirituality of Pseudo-Dionysius." In *Christian Spirituality: Origins to the Twelfth Century,* edited by B. McGinn, J. Meyendorff, and J. LeClercq. New York: Crossroad, 1988.

Santinello, G. "Einleitung" to Nikolaus von Kues, *Idiota de mente,* edited by R. Steiger, 9–28. Hamburg: Meiner, 1995.

Scharlemann, R. *Naming God.* New York: Paragon House, 1985.

Schmidt, M. "Nikolaus von Kues im Gespraech mit den Tegernseer Moenchen ueber Wesen und Sinn der Mystik." *Mitteilungen und Forschungsbeitraege der Cusanus Gesellschaft 18* (1989). Trier: Paulinus Verlag, 25–49.

Schoenborn, Christoph. "Ueber die richtige Fassung des dogmatischen Begriffs der Vergoettlichung des Menschen." *Freiburger Zeitschrift fuer Philosophie und Theologie* 34 (1987): 3–47.

Senger, Hans Gerhard. "Die Sprache der Metaphysik." In *Nikolaus von Kues: Einfuehrung in sein philosophisches Denken,* edited by Klaus Jacobi, 74–100. Munich: Alber, 1979.

Sherwood, Polycarp, O.S.B. *The Earlier Ambigua of Saint Maximus the Confessor and His Refutation of Origenism.* Rome: Orbis Catholicus, Herder, 1955.

Stallmach, Josef. "Der 'Zusammenfall der Gegensaetze' und der unendliche Gott." In *Nikolaus von Kues: Einfuehrung in sein philosophisches Denken,* edited by Klaus Jacobi, 56–73. Munich: Alber, 1979.

Stock, A. "Die Rolle der 'icona Dei' in der Spekulation *De visione Dei.*" *Mitteilungen und Forschungsbeitraege der Cusanus Gesellschaft 18* (1989). Trier: Paulinus Verlag, 50–62.

Thomas, M. *Die Teilhabegedanke in den Schriften und Predigten des Nikolaus von Kues (1430–1450).* Muenster: Aschendorff, 1996.

Thunberg, Lars. *Man and the Cosmos: The Vision of Maximus the Confessor.* Crestwood, N.Y.: St. Vladimir's Seminary Press, 1985.

————. *Microcosm and Mediator.* Lund, Sweden: Hakan Ohlssons Boktryckeri, 1965.

Voelker, Walther. *Gregor von Nyssa als Mystiker.* Wiesbaden: F. Steiner, 1955.

Von Bredow, Gerda. *Im Gespraech mit Nikolaus von Kues: Gesammelte Aufsaetze (1948–1993).* Edited by H. Schnarr. Muenster: Aschendorff, 1995.

Watts, Pauline Moffitt. *Nicolaus Cusanus: A Fifteenth-Century Vision of Man*. Leiden: Brill, 1982.

Wyller, Egil. "Nicolaus Cusanus' *De non aliud* und Platons Dialog *Parmenides*. Ein Beitrag zur Beleuchtung des Renaissanceplatonismus." In *Studia Platonica: Festschrift fuer Hermann Gundert,* edited by K. Koering and W. Kullmann, 239–51. Amsterdam: Gruener, 1974.

Zimmermann, A. "'Belehrte Unwissenheit' als Ziel der Naturforschung." In *Nikolaus von Kues: Einfuehrung in sein philosophisches Denken,* edited by Klaus Jacobi, 129–34. Munich: Alber, 1979.

INDEX